Enquiries at the Interface:
Philosophical Problems
of Online Education

Enquiries at the Interface: Philosophical Problems of Online Education

Edited by
Nigel Blake and
Paul Standish

BLACKWELL
Publishers

Blackwell Publishers Ltd
108 Cowley Road
Oxford OX4 1JF, UK

Blackwell Publishers Inc
350 Main Street
Malden, MA 02148, USA

British Library Cataloguing in Publication Data has been applied for

Library of Congress Cataloging-in-Publication Data has been applied for

Typeset by Dobbie Typesetting
Printed and bound in Great Britain by
MPG Books, Bodmin, Cornwall

This book is printed on acid-free paper

Contents

Preface

Information and Communication Technology (ICT) is changing the face of education, as of so much in our world. The examples are familiar enough. All knowledge, it may appear, is now located somewhere in cyberspace, accessible at the touch of a few keys, and so the authority of the school, college or teacher – the traditional fonts of knowledge – is undermined. At the same time the new technology foregrounds *interpretation* rather than the search for propositional truth. The World Wide Web presents infinite possibilities of re-presenting and recontextualising material through the medium of hypertext. Knowledge then is less linear and hierarchical than (appropriately enough) web-like in structure. Its ramifications proliferate endlessly, so that anything, it sometimes seems, can be related to anything else. Our received ideas of order are put in question.

Nothing here is straightforward. Does ICT raise information above all other aspects of knowledge, or does the capacity of computers to handle information for us rather release us to develop the richer kinds of understanding that computers cannot possibly display? Do email, online chat-groups and so on diminish the status of face-to-face communication, or paradoxically, increase it as we become aware of what speaking face-to-face does uniquely well? And, above all, are we living through a paradigm shift from the printed word, or is the (albeit electronically) written word acquiring new significance as email comes to replace the telephone and the Web site offers, above all, *text* in multifarious and fascinating forms?

There is much at stake, then, both educationally and philosophically, in our understanding of ICT. We are surrounded by lazy and facile assumptions about our brave new electronic world, which risk hardening into orthodoxy and even policy if they are not challenged and analysed. Perhaps the most common of those assumptions is that the printed word is now dead. So it is worth pointing out that this book originally appeared as the first Special Issue of the *Journal of Philosophy of Education* for the new millennium (and in that form it is readable on the Web by those with authorised access). Text, it seems, flourishes as never before. In contributing to and problematising its electronic and printed flourishing, and in engaging with other issues too that ICT raises, the writers in this book, and especially its editors Nigel Blake and Paul Standish, have shown the continuing ability of philosophy of education to engage critically and creatively with the changing world of education.

Richard Smith

Introduction

NIGEL BLAKE AND PAUL STANDISH

Last year, my eldest son was doing a project on the poetry of Robert
Frost. His task was to make a film about 'The Road Not Taken' and he
dropped in to ask if I knew where he could get his hands on a recording
of Frost reading the poem. My first reaction was to telephone the BBC.
But then I suggested—with nothing more than a mild sense of
optimism—that he try hunting for it on the Web. In a few minutes, he
had found a scholarly archive somewhere in the United States with
recordings of Frost, and shortly after that we both sat stunned,
listening to the poet's gravelly voice, distorted by compression and
data corruption, but still speaking directly to our hearts.
(John Naughton, *A Brief History of the Future: The Origins of the
Internet*, 1999, p. 12.)

The Internet has recently enjoyed its thirtieth birthday. In 1969, a
computer at the University of California sent a message down a wire
to another in a research centre at Stanford. The message was just two
letters, 'LO'.[1] Since then the development of the Internet—of the
physical infrastructure of computers and the material or broadcast
links between them, along with the digital protocols that enable it to
function—has been largely an academic achievement. Up until six
years ago, the world's richest entrepreneur, Bill Gates himself, was still
unconvinced of its immense importance and economic potential.[2] For
the World Wide Web (WWW), the most popular and elaborate
application on the Net, is itself only about six years old. It is its
stunning exponential growth that makes it seem to some of us as if it
has been with us forever.

Those who are instantly sceptical of the educational value of the
Internet would do well to remember its academic origins. The early
usage Internet was largely used by academics passing files between
each other, in furtherance of academic research. So the idea that such
a practice might be modified and developed as an adjunct to
university teaching was surely inevitable. Besides, academic progress

1

has always been entwined with technological development since the invention of papyrus, never mind printing.

But scepticism about the educational worthiness of the Net is not quickly to be dismissed. This academic development has always been compromised by non-academic influences, initially and importantly by links between academia and the military (though these have been much less tight than is often alleged).[3] Its entanglement with business began only with the explosion of the WWW, but perhaps is particularly worrying for educationalists. Those who take a radical or a seriously conservative view of society and its needs have plenty of grounds for their critique.

Perhaps the most developed critique of the role of information technology in general—and a remarkably prescient one for its date (1979)—was Jean-François Lyotard's *The Postmodern Condition* (1984), a radical critique with much to say to conservatives.[4] Lyotard insists over and again on the role of information technologies and information sciences in the social and political ascendance of the economic goal of 'performativity' and analyses the impact of this goal on education, particularly for the universities. Lyotard introduces 'performativity' to mean 'the optimisation of the global relationship between input and output' (Lyotard, 1984, p. 11), where input and output are economic measures. He attributes to various forms of sociological functionalism the view that the 'true goal' of the social system is indeed performativity; and such a view is patently echoed in a myriad of contemporary official pronouncements on the Internet and its future role in our lives, not least in education. Talk about Information and Communications Technology (ICT) in education is rarely far distant from talk about vocational education and training, globalisation, new forms of economic activity including e-commerce and the 'massification' and digitisation of higher education. Here, for example, is Lord Bell, Baroness Thatcher's media advisor in government, praising 'Tools for Schools', a scheme (sponsored by the *Guardian* newspaper in the UK) to recycle unwanted computers from industry to schools for free:

> Tools for Schools is an imaginative and innovative way of giving our children access to electronic technology at low entry cost and thus speeds up the process of equipping tomorrow's consumers with the necessary skills and understanding to prosper in the next phase of the market. (*Guardian, Media Supplement*, 25 October, 1999, p. 10).

More cautious and better-informed speakers are less blatantly materialistic than this, yet it is commonplace for exhortations to online education to take a coarsely economistic and crudely utilitarian turn. But as Lyotard warns:

One can decide that the principal role of knowledge is as an indispensable element in the functioning of society, and act in accordance with that decision, only if one has already decided that society is a giant machine . . . Conversely, one can count on [knowledge's] critical function, and orient its development and distribution in that direction, only after it has been decided that society does not form an integrated whole, but remains haunted by a principle of opposition. The alternative seems clear: it is a choice between the homogeneity and the intrinsic duality of the social, between functional and critical knowledge. (Lyotard, 1984, p. 13)

If these words are in turn too haunted by Marxism for some tastes, they at least indicate where grounds still lie for a critical reception of the role of information technology in society and education—a reception based in any view that emphasises at least the relative autonomy of the individual in society and the power of ideas profoundly to change how we live, and that seems as antithetical to globalising capitalism as to the more mechanistic forms of Marxism.

However, no serious critique should permit any facile Luddite rejection of ICT in education. Indeed, the critics themselves have their own uses for information technology. This very collection of essays was put together almost entirely by use of email. Lyotard's words do not imply that there is no such thing as useful knowledge, or indeed useful technologies, or that they are of lowly value. The point is rather that judgements of usefulness presuppose broader moral, ethical, political and even aesthetic judgements. Judgements of utility are deeply contestable. The problem is that the startling novelty of the Internet currently occupies the foreground of our attention, rather than the diversity not only of the material available, but also of the possibilities for using it. This seems to create an illusion of homogeneity in the content and form of the Net and what we do with it. This in turn combines with the prevailing, uncritical economism to obscure the fundamental point that the question of the Internet's *usefulness* is an essentially political one.

There is, happily, no lack of radical or libertarian optimism as well. After all, the social impact of the Internet is arguably different in respect of its different applications—email, the WWW, file transfer and their myriad hybrids, modes and sub-genres. To be sceptical about certain aspects of the Internet is not to be indiscriminately dismissive. One might coherently like or dislike different applications and their uses. So it does remain possible to discuss with critical enthusiasm a radical variety of potentials of the Internet, not least in education. Nonetheless, critical scepticism about the Internet retains its serious purpose, and we anticipate that this will be an ever-present and important strand in educational writing on online education.

But one reason scepticism cannot be the whole story is precisely the academic provenance of the Net. For Lyotard himself underlined the properly academic nature of the disciplines informing the development of ICT:

> It is fair to say that for the last forty years [as of 1979], the 'leading' sciences and technologies have had to do with language: phonology and theories of linguistics, problems of communication and cybernetics, modern theories of algebra and informatics, computers and their languages, problems of translation and the search for areas of compatibility among computer languages, telematics [the long-distance transmission of computerised information] and the perfection of intelligent terminals, problems of information storage and data banks, paradoxology. The facts speak for themselves (and this list is not exhaustive). (Lyotard, 1984, pp. 3–4)

He opens his main text (Ibid., pp. 3–5) by pointing not only to the new role of knowledge in 'the postmodern age' as 'an informational commodity indispensable to productive power'—the aspect that enthuses Lord Bell—but also to the way that technological transformations are changing our very conception of knowledge:

> [Knowledge] can fit into the new channels, and become operational, only if learning is translated into quantities of information [i.e. computerised bits and bytes]. We can predict that anything in the constituted body of knowledge that is not translatable in this way will be abandoned . . . along with the hegemony of computers comes a certain logic, and therefore a certain set of prescriptions determining which statements are accepted as 'knowledge' statements. (*ibid.*, p. 4)

These words seem less worrying now than when he wrote them. Why? Because it becomes increasingly difficult to imagine just what kinds of public knowledge *cannot* be digitised and so stand to be ruled out. Personal tacit knowledge, as theorised by Polanyi, seems perhaps the most resistant to any form of mediation, including text and speech. Yet news comes through of digitised simulations of medical surgery with hi-tech mannequins that enable doctors to acquire their essential physical and intuitive tacit knowledge without practising—in the worrying sense—on live patients. Obviously this provides potential for recording and analysis not normally associated with this kind of knowledge. The digital bodysuits associated with virtual reality seem set potentially to digitise even skin and muscular sensations—those of weightlessness or sexual pleasure, for instance. It might even turn out that the digitisation of knowledge will actually *expand* what can count as knowledge rather than diminish it. What remains valid in Lyotard's prediction, however, is the importance of considering always just what the relation might be between the digitising processes of ICT and any given register of knowledge. The possibility of digitisation is fast becoming the socially pre-eminent test of whether experience can be encoded and shared; and thus, by extension, of what may count as knowledge. What matters is perhaps less likely to be 'what is ruled out', but just *how* it is ruled *in*. If the relation between experience and digital information is sometimes worrying (think of surveillance of individual computer users), it is often intellectually intriguing in its own right (think again of virtual-reality simulations).

With this point in mind, our concern in this particular collection is less with the danger of the transformation of knowledge to a commodity (a danger we also fear, nonetheless), but more with the impact of computer technologies, and Internet technologies in particular, on both our conceptions of knowledge and, correlatively, our conceptions of teaching and study across the spectrum of education. For in the long run no critique will be taken seriously unless it is informed, thoughtful and undogmatic. And as soon as one attempts to think about online education in this way, one cannot possibly see it in black and white terms, but as richly textured, as full of high spots as of low. John Naughton's anecdote, which we quoted at the beginning of this Introduction, can hardly fail to enchant or excite any educator. It speaks to us straight past the dreary preoccupations of Lord Bell. Naughton includes it in the first part of his book, which he calls 'Wonderment', where he skilfully evokes a sense of sheer astonishment at what the Internet already offers in terms of human interaction. One author of this Introduction shares this delight when teaching, from the London suburbs, distant students in Mongolia or British Colombia.

Nothing is predictable as one explores education on the Net. Huge and exciting potentials open up, alongside aspects that occasion alarm or even horror. Minor innovations take on major significance (word-processing perhaps, or the listserv) whilst elaborate technological developments begin to look educationally marginal or trivial (is multimedia as important as email or file transfer? how useful is videoconferencing really?). Some intellectual possibilities seem to close down whilst others open up, as Lyotard above suggests; and the more one thinks about the Internet, the less one seems technologically at its mercy, yet the more locked in conflict with the forces in society who seek to control or promote it.

So the essays gathered here do not repudiate the educational use of the Internet. On the contrary, consistently they betray a fascination with it. But what they do not do is take too much for granted or echo fashionable assumptions or, worse, state-sanctioned prescriptions or commercial ambitions for the use of ICT in education. Engagement with the Internet here is both enthusiastic and critical. By the same token, we avoid futuristic fantasy and the wilder shores of cyber-radicalism. These essays stay close to the actual contemporary uses, practices and products of online education.

Our purpose in this volume then is twofold: first, to introduce the topic into philosophy of education in a sustained and coherent way. A number of philosophers and philosophers of education have begun to address these issues, but only a few have yet built significant portfolios in the field. It is the Editors' view that it is time to concentrate and develop this work. We offer this collection not as the definitive 'first word' (much less last word) on the subject, but in the spirit of a catalyst. We are prepared to discover that many issues that seem salient now will not do so in even five years' time. But such concentration of attention improves the chances that philosophers of education will be contributing significantly to the subject as it develops. Second, of course, we hope to contribute critically and constructively to more general educational discussion on the use of ICT and of the Internet in particular. To absent ourselves from these debates is effectively to bow out of the future development of education on almost every front.

HOW MIGHT THE INTERNET CHANGE EDUCATION?

Of course, there is room for a less politically committed form of scepticism about the potential importance of the Internet than the kind acknowledged above. In particular, there are those who see in it no more than a collection of electronic devices and practices for doing the same things we were doing, say, ten years ago, but with added electronic glamour and glitz—and, of course, with added possibilities of failures, breakdowns and abuses. There are those who remain to be convinced that anything significant is being offered for education, or indeed that what is offered is more than a mixed blessing, if not a snare and delusion, but who all agree that nothing essential is likely to be changed in education. Clearly we would not be editing this volume if we agreed.

There are perhaps four principal possibilities of change that seem worth considering at this moment. Of these, two might be loosely termed conservative and two radical. The first 'conservative' possibility is that the Internet will have no real impact other than to help us do the same things we currently do in education, but more efficiently, more cheaply or more effectively. The second conservative possibility is that, whether or not the first is true, the educational importance of the Internet will rest mainly with a few new practices that it might add to our educational repertoire, like video-conferencing or electronic searches of texts—welcome certainly but minor. As to those more familiar activities that might become more cheap, efficient or effective, such as the use of the Web and email for administrative purposes, a change in their medium or mode of delivery will not alter their essential character.

By contrast, the radical possibilities are, first that the medium makes a difference, even a profound one, as we have hinted, both to the character of old practices translated to the Net and to any new ones that might evolve in the new medium. It is often suggested, for instance, that the Net introduces new concepts of text (and textual authority) that must impact on our epistemologies, new forms of interpersonal interaction that must modify our views of identity and community, new ways of manipulating imagery, both visual and auditory, that must modify our notions of representation. If any of this is so, it can hardly be irrelevant to education.

The second radical possibility is less often articulated, but perhaps no less important. Critical implications sometimes arise from mismatches and differences between conventional institutions and practices and their nearest equivalents in 'cyberspace'. We are perhaps more familiar with the idea that traditional practices are paradigms to which their online equivalents fail adequately to 'measure up'—classroom teaching, face-to-face interaction, a sense of place and belonging in educational institutions, for instance. But the burden of invidious comparison can also fall the other way. Sometimes, online practices seem to constitute standing condemnations of conventional practice. So far, unhappily, the managerial technicists have made the most of such comparisons. For instance, the apparent cheapness and efficiency of the Internet as a medium for delivering educational materials are frequently cited as indices of populist, even democratic value and opposed to the putative élitism of face-to-face teaching, the relatively expensive small-scale interactions found in the leading conventional educational institutions. But there is no obvious reason why all critical arguments arising from such comparisons must favour a populist managerialism. Proponents of the Internet as a democratic (as opposed to populist) forum conducive to critical debate may compare detrimentally the limitations (in time and space) of conventional education as well.

Set out like this, it seems obvious that philosophers of education will tend to be more interested in the radical possibilities. And we believe most or all of the contributions in this volume actually do fit one of the radical paradigms. But we would also like to argue here that even if the radical possibilities are dismissed, the advent of the Internet to education is still virtually certain to alter the agenda of philosophy of education, at least by adding to it, probably by shifting emphases and focuses of attention and eventually by recasting the way familiar philosophical problems in education are described, because the social reality of education will itself change. Even if the impact of the Internet has to do only with efficiency, effectiveness and cost, the economies and socio-technical innovations here are potentially so great that they will inevitably effect major institutional, social, economic and ultimately political transformations.

For instance, we are obviously looking at the possibilities of greatly extended participation in education, in terms both of numbers and of levels and frequency of participation through the lifespan. And this need not just refer to the grim electronic realisation of the treadmill—for such it threatens to be—of Lifelong Learning. (Lifelong Learning, tied to the uncertain economic strategies of capital and State, is seen by many as the very death-knell of Adult Education, an essentially emancipatory project.) Large-scale expansion is likely to alter the form and function of educational institutions and the educational values they embrace. It will change the shape and potential purpose of individual educational careers. It will alter the funding relationship of government to education. Changes like these will push to the fore and alter our conceptions of student independence and of the nature of teachers and teaching, will raise questions about authority, issues in the distribution of educational opportunities and their accreditation, questions about the content and structure of curricula under changed patterns of participation. And the changes that raise these questions are not just future possibilities, of course, but transformations already under way.

It seems to us that a philosophy of education that just disregarded these changes would soon become terminally irrelevant. And it takes no radical view about the nature of the Internet to anticipate such a change of agenda. The 'conservative' view of the educational impact of the Internet can at most be only *relatively* conservative. Radical change at some level or other seems inevitable. In view of this, a major task for educators must be the cultivation of the kind of literacy appropriate to education in the age of the Internet. What might that literacy look like?

LITERACY ON THE LINE

Governments today are understandably impressed by the idea that the limits of literacy are the limits of education, and it is plain that their commitment extends to literacy online. In his Foreword to *Connecting the Learning Society*, Tony Blair writes: 'By 2002, all schools will be connected to the superhighway, free of charge; half a million teachers will be trained; and our children will be leaving school IT-literate, having been able to exploit the best that technology can offer.'[5] There is a real danger, however, that the way this literacy is understood will remain within bounds of such modesty that resources will be wasted and the real potential of online education lost.

It is something of a truism that children outstrip their parents (and teachers) in their facility with computers. When information is only a few keystrokes away, children can show a mastery that leaves their elders watching like admiring and bewildered novices. Children have their hands on the tools of learning, so it seems, in a way that can make their parents' knowledge and know-how seem obsolescent and out of touch. As has been remarked, this is the motivation for many of the adults currently seeking to become computer literate. What is it that they (and many educators) imagine that they need? Alan Clarke is helpfully explicit: the first confidence-building steps must involve familiarity with the keyboard, dexterity with the mouse and the ability to print out documents; this progresses to the location and accessing of a website, and presumably includes a growing facility with word-processing programs and the like (Clarke, 1998, pp. 18–19). He argues plausibly enough that such a grasp of information technology should be within the capabilities of most people, regardless of age, gender or previous educational experience. In these terms Tony Blair's expressed aim of creating a computer literate work-force for the twenty-first century seems a happily realistic one. Moreover, there is a visibility about the skills listed here that makes the project particularly attractive politically—visions of learning centres filled with people tapping competently and contentedly at keyboards. (It is scarcely necessary to mention the political attractiveness of establishing a British market in educational software to meet this need.)

One thing this shows is the political desirability of maintaining a conception of computer literacy that is modest, even though this may be extolled with a heady evangelism. Realisable, affordable, visible and attractive, computer literacy might figure as a convenient metonym for social inclusion in the twenty-first century. The computer is cast as merely technical, manageable, simple, even 'friendly', with the skills of access readily identified, learned, assessed and recorded. Yet insofar as it is skills acquisition of this order that is thought the key to social inclusion, the chances of sustaining any richer vision of civic life are slim indeed. Does this not reveal the dangers of a token inclusion that is politically neutralising in its effects even as it ostensibly enskills?

The modest conception of computer literacy is then scarcely enough, and it may surreptitiously undermine the democratic aspirations in the name of which it is in part espoused. What can be said to achieve greater clarity here? The computer is not, we can agree, a glorified typewriter. Whatever our concept of initial computer literacy might amount to, we need also a richer notion, just as we have one for literacy. The kind of literacy associated with advancement through 'reading ages' contrasts with that richer sense of literacy where what is at stake has more to do with critical sensitivity and cultural breadth, and where the former kind is largely taken for granted. Two points should be made about computer literacy in the modest sense. First, to think of it in terms of the literacy of learning to read is surely to dignify it unduly. To a large extent, computer literacy in this sense is a matter of competence with easy-to-use tools, some familiarity with what is perhaps a useful but relatively small range of programs and applications and the minimal ability normally required to access websites. It is true that for many people this will only be achieved once considerable fear has been overcome. But this problem is not to do with any intrinsic difficulty in the use of the tools themselves. And, immensely useful though these skills are, it is obvious that they do not represent anything like the kind of advancement in learning that learning to read must be. There is good reason to wonder whether this acquisition of skills is appropriately called literacy at all. Second, the visible nature of the competencies associated with this modest computer literacy can make all the more opaque the problems and challenges in terms of literacy that information technology poses at the deeper level (just as a gulf opens between the congenial and craft-like ease of the instruments themselves, with the attractive results that are so easily produced, and the electronics hidden within). At this deeper level, at least, the question of computer literacy blends into the richer sense of literacy in terms of critical sensitivity and cultural breadth. It is arguable that a person's literacy in this sense is in some degree deficient if the world of information technology remains for her a closed book. Educators need to address the structures and the semiotics of the Web in a critical way, the better to assess the kind of pedagogy it might sustain.

It is in this vein that Nicholas Burbules asks whether reading on the Internet is something new or the same reading, involving the usual skills and strategies but exercised in a new medium (Burbules, 1997). Any strict division here may be unhelpful, but there are salient points that are worth noting. The speed of reading, the movement between sections of text, the methods of skipping and repeating are factors that distinguish this from reading a book. Where printed texts are by nature selective and exclusive, hypertexts on the Web are by nature inclusive, linking more or less unlimited numbers of texts online. We need then perhaps to turn our attention from the information points of the texts to the 'links' of hypertexts, and these Burbules fruitfully examines in the terms of rhetorical analysis. Prior to this, however, he makes three key points. First, while links vary in kind in terms of their significance, the action of clicking on a highlighted word or icon to activate them is more or less the same in each case. Second, the links we encounter are ready-made and so are the products of the author or designer of the hypertext: they reflect then in some degree that person's pre-occupations and biases. The naturalness that the links so quickly come to have covers over the more or less idiosyncratic nature of the connections they supply. (The problem is deepened, it might be added, by the ways that the operations of search engines are determined and by the user's common oblivious-ness to this.) Third, a link does not simply associate two givens but changes the way (and the order) in which material will be read and understood; links are generally one-way (although one can return to a page already visited). Of course, with the printed text also it is juxtapositions that partly determine significance, but there the significance might be construed as an element within the author's conception of the whole (the unified text). The absence of anything quite like a unity in hypertext and, again, the seeming ease with which one can move around it can remove the anchor of one's reading even as it lulls one into an acceptance of apparently natural flow.

There are important lessons here for teachers, but especially for the designers of learning materials. We need to remind ourselves that so much remains still to be decided about how learning materials on the Internet are to be designed and used. The fact that links are generally encountered in a particular direction means that there is the opportunity to impose hierarchical tree-like structures even though the encompassing structure remains a network. This tendency is exacerbated by factors concerning the nature of pages themselves. The standard category of 'page' on the Web encourages a conception of texts as units within a system in a way that corresponds with an atomisation of knowledge and with the unitisation of learning. Unitisation may come to seem an internal property of what is to be learned (a kind of logical atomism). This makes it all the more probable that learning will be conceived in terms of systematic progression along the lines of programmed learning. It makes it easier to think in terms of units of learning bolted together than in terms of less clearly defined flows of meaning. In some contexts this may be appropriate, but in others it is not. Designers of learning materials need to understand the significance of the different possibilities here. We need painstaking and sensitive attention to the substance of the curriculum; what we do *not* need, as the diversity of these contexts and practices should make plain, is a new generalised learning theory.

The Internet is much more than the WWW alone and it is not only the potential of hypertext that modifies the nature of writing and reading on the Internet. To take here one subset of these other characteristics, consider in particular email and its derivative genres, such as chat-rooms, Bulletin Boards and listservs—uses of language that are not face-to-face, yet that in many ways resemble conversation in written form. Linguisticians have been quick to realise that language is used in email in some quite special and distinctive ways and that these have a particular value for education. Skills in using these new genres should be conceived as an extension of this richer literacy.

As a form of rapid message delivery, email shares some of the attractions of telephone conversation. It can be casual and chatty and also quick. It is good to use for fixing up arrangements, for instance. But unlike the telephone or even the posted letter, email is remarkably flexible as to the length of any individual utterance. It is cheap and easy to email a message of just a few words, in contrast to the telephone, and of course this does not depend on the recipient's synchronous presence at the other end. On the other hand, emails may support long and complex messages, in a way that a telephone call cannot. Unlike use of the telephone, one's use of language in an email message can be very carefully crafted and revised. It shares with the letter the potential to be saved and archived, whilst it is also much easier to 'post' the same email to a large group of people all at once. Thus email has a potential that the teacher can exploit for communication that is searching and reflective in character.

The association of email with quick and informal communication, and the fact that it is not destined for publication, fosters in email a use of language that is intermediate between the casualness of conversation and the formalities of dominant forms of writing. Email is not encumbered by the rhetorical conventions that letter-writing has acquired down the centuries. The intermediate forms of language that it encourages answer perhaps to a real educational need. Email, where academic precision can be mixed comfortably with social informality, fits readily into an open niche. Quick, informal contact between academics is also something we have long been waiting for and only recently achieved. Quick informal teaching at a demanding level becomes possible in new ways through its use.

THE POWERS THAT BE—LANGUAGE, COMMERCE, GLOBALISATION

Obviously the spread of online education, with its virtues of overcoming distances of space and time between learners and educators or resources, is tightly intertwined with the dynamics of globalisation. Certainly there is an optimistic, even utopian tendency in globalisation to emphasise the peaceful potentials of communication across cultural, geographical and time divides and to celebrate the supposedly inevitable spread of the political freedom—so it appears—of cyberspace. But state education policy is driven everywhere by terrors of economic globalisation and pressures of commercialism. The watchwords here are massification of higher education and 'flexibility', and it may be that these militate against the development of the kind of literacy that is most needed. Both are forces favouring learning that is tidily programmed or packaged. The personal element in tuition becomes harder to provide in conditions of mass education. The demand for flexibility discourages members of the labour force from concentrating on any particular knowledge specialism, because, we are told, the future economy is technologically too unpredictable for this to be a safe strategy. But if this is the name of the game, who will care very much anyway for that depth of learning that requires more dialogical teaching and learning? If designed instruction proves to be the future of online education, it will be globalisation (and a narrow interpretation of it)[6] that we have to thank, not the nature of the technology itself.

There are deeper pedagogical dangers here too. As part of this globalising process, talk of 'delivery of the curriculum', itself an oxymoron, is rapidly ousting the language of teaching. But one cannot 'deliver' knowledge. As any philosopher knows, knowledge is not knowledge until it is understood and arguments or evidence have been corroborated in some public conversation or dialogue. In fact, arguably one cannot even 'deliver' information, but only the texts and files that carry it. Globalisation is leading our concern with media to blind us all to serious questions of curriculum and pedagogy. And where teaching is still mentioned, it is increasingly in the phrase 'teaching and learning'. Mere learning is increasingly taken to be self-sufficient. These problems of globalisation have a life independent of the Internet. But the Internet compounds them in a way we have not mentioned. All these richer and deeper potentials require an intellectual and cultural context and background to a degree that mere learning may not.

But culture, of course, is not merely mediated by language but constituted within it. Access to one's own culture depends heavily on the use and grasp of one's own language. For English-speaking users of the Net, there is no obvious problem here. But for everyone else, it is salient and worrying that the language of the Net is English. And this is not simply a function of the dominance of the USA in the early development of the Net, crucial as that has been. Of course, the vast preponderance of Internet resources are still American. In principle that could change, but we need to be realistic here. Not all possibilities for change are in fact readily available, for technological reasons. Personal computers work by constructing a hierarchy of relationships between the digitised 'machine code' that operates the microchips and the natural language spoken by the user. The design of software translates between the one and the other at a series of levels. And it is not widely appreciated at what a deep level of the hierarchy the natural language dictates the design. Even simply changing software from English to French goes deeper than one might think. To replace the 'Stop' button with 'Arrête' at least involves enlarging the dialogue box to accommodate more letters. And just doing this for a whole range of commands involves altering the economy of memory and interface at a fairly deep level. Consider then the much larger problems involved with languages whose grammar differs markedly from English; that use other scripts, such as Cyrillic; that do not operate alphabetically or even syllabically; whose graphic modes are not simply additive; and so on. For some written languages, even typography provides problems for software. Now consider the material poverty of most societies whose written language differs markedly from English, and the disincentive to software companies to develop the software they would need to adjust the Net to their own culture. Cheaper by far to let English become the essential world language.[7] Of course, alphabetisation is a possibility for such languages. But is even that likely to come without the intrusion of English into the culture? Claims that the Net fosters cultural imperialism are not without technological foundation. How is a deeper level of study encouraged for those who have to use a foreign language to get much out of the Internet? Educationalists who promote the Internet should concern themselves with this unintended aspect of their interests.

It is obviously inadequate to see the Internet as a new device to be added to the repertoire of educational technology. Its advent raises multiple and interweaving philosophical questions. Given, on the one hand, an understanding of the deeper economic problems, and, on the other, the depth of understanding that we claim of the links between culture, language and society, philosophers of education should have much to say that is distinctive about the impact of the Internet across the globe.

TOWARDS DEEPER UNDERSTANDING

Anyone who has read the pages of the new technology supplements in the educational press will have been struck by their consistently upbeat and frequently uncritical tone. The chapters are characterised by a sense of common purpose, as unsurprising and apparently uncontroversial as it may be insidious. The kinds of issue that this Introduction has drawn attention to receive scant consideration in that literature. This points to the serious inadequacies of much contemporary debate about the Internet and education, and demonstrates the need for the kind of analysis that this book provides. The common purpose that unites the contributors to this book is their desire to deepen that debate. They do this in the belief that failure to address seriously the philosophical problems that online education raises is likely to lead to confusion in policy and practice and to a squandering of resources and opportunities.

In the opening chapter, Colin Lankshear, Michael Peters and Michele Knobel examine the specifically epistemological questions that online education raises. By way of a critical treatment of Paul Gilster's 1997 book, *Digital Literacy*, the chapter discusses implications for classroom-based learning through the Internet. Teachers are at present confronted with perplexing epistemological questions concerning teaching and learning. The authors urge the importance of addressing these in the prevailing climate of performativity.

For understandable reasons, most discussions of online education tend to take for granted the technologically advanced conditions of the Western world. The chapter by Anthony Lelliott, Shirley Pendlebury and Penny Enslin provides a different perspective by considering the prospects for such educational change in terms of access and inclusion in Africa. The chapter draws attention to the huge importance of disparity of wealth in relation to the use of the Internet at a time of globalisation. It carefully rejects the naïve optimism that is expressed by some while pointing to the real consequences of failing to try to develop this new technology.

Media philosophy is emerging as a field of study with obvious relevance to online education. In this context, Mike Sandbothe seeks to further understanding by linking the kind of analysis suggested by Jacques Derrida's *Of Grammatology* with the pragmatism of Richard Rorty. The value of this is illustrated through examples from the author's online teaching.

The educational significance of the interface is the subject of Steve Bramall's discussion. In order to illuminate some of the more profound educational potential of school children's use of the Web he focuses on the interface practices through which individuals connect to, and download information from, the Web. Such practices constitute, he argues, a profound change in our culture, one that is increasingly reflected in, and has the power to improve, the sense-making apparatus of that culture and of its individual members.

Webzines are mini-magazines published by the authors themselves. In Chapter 5 Barbara Duncan presents examples from such magazines to show the ways in which they raise questions of identity and community. In view of the way it has been taken up by a new generation of feminists, the Webzine helps to explain something of what being a feminist may mean at the start of the twenty-first century. Unlike many dominant forms of writing, the Webzine disrupts commonly understood boundaries of genre and form, constructing a pastiche or a collage-like subject. The chapter throws light on the tensions schools often face between the sustaining of a common culture and the inclusion of an increasing range of alternatives.

Credibility has become a crucial problem for the Web, and Bertram Bruce takes up this question by exploring how characteristics of the Web lead to its being simultaneously a great and a questionable source of information. In particular he considers the extent to which the Web can be compared to a library. Drawing on the work of Walter Kaufmann, he argues that a close analysis of the processes of Web reading heightens the need for critical inquiry in its traditional senses: he explores ways in which Kaufmann's 'dialectical reading' might be extended to meet the new challenges that the Web presents.

Jane McKie's 'Conjuring Notions of Place' examines the significance of practices of guidance and navigation in the use of the Internet. She draws parallels with the ways that tensions between guidance and autonomy and between planning and spontaneity are played out in adult education. The theme of navigation leads her to consider how far the Internet effects changes in conceptions of time and place.

The question of place is also prominent in the chapter by David Kolb. The bits of information presented by the Internet offer quick immediate intensities. A typical facet of such information is that it has been pulled out of its constitutive relations and contexts: whatever it presents is not encountered in its full reality. He argues for the need to explore how far that kind of contextual richness might be realised on the Web in order to dispel the illusory experience of immediacy and completeness. He considers the possibility of an education that might encourage the kind of critically aware habitation appropriate to such complex and ambiguous spaces.

James Marshall addresses questions concerning the relation between print and electronic text. Drawing on Mark Poster's writings on the 'mode of information', he ponders the question whether electronic writing will destroy or displace books and other printed material in learning and teaching. These matters are shown to have a bearing not only on matters of knowledge and authority but on the relationship between the self, others and the world.

Following recent work by Andrew Feenberg, Paul Standish explores the socio-cultural context within which online education is being developed, arguing that a fetishisation of effectiveness is an important aspect of that context. This highlights ways in which the Web is to be understood in terms of the metaphysics of presence. The chapter points to an alternative approach that down-plays the current emphasis on virtual realisation, in favour of an appreciation of the opportunities the Internet offers in terms of the written word.

Herbert Hrachovec is concerned with the change in the nature of 'text', 'paper' or 'book' in digitalised, networked environments. His chapter embarks on a phenomenological assessment of the actual differences between print and virtual rendering of print but puts this into question through a methodological reflection on the conditions of claims for novelty. What, he asks, are the criteria that allow us to speak of continuity or epochal change in this area, and what are the politics of such comparisons?

Finally, in 'Tutors and Students without Faces and Places', Nigel Blake explores the relationship between face-to-face teaching and learning, and one-to-one teaching and learning on the Internet, challenging the assumption that learning via the Internet should necessarily be regarded as second best. The chapter broaches the question of the ecology of the relation between the two: to what extent does either mode of learning feed into and enhance the other? The argument moves towards the suggestion that education ideally involves a proper mix of the two.

In their different ways then these essays help to place online education in its broader contexts. They unsettle some prevailing assumptions. They demonstrate the benefits of careful attention to its practices. And they show the importance and the value of addressing the philosophical questions that the Internet raises for education, questions we ignore at our cost. As we have seen, the potentials are rich and fascinating. The problems are real and serious too.

NOTES

1. i.e. 'hello'. 'The Net at 30', *Guardian*, 21 October 1999.
2. *Ibid.*
3. It is sometimes erroneously said that the Internet grew out of American military need for a 'survivable' computer network for nuclear war-fighting. It is true that the ARPANET, the prototype of the Internet, was a project of the Advanced Research Projects Agency, a Ministry of Defense initiative with offices in the Pentagon. But as John Naughton makes clear (Naughton, 1999, Ch. 5), there was oddly no pressure at all to bend the research to any military aims. The motive for developing a network was to maximise the usage of some very large and expensive early machines, for research purposes. What *is* true is that the mature Net was born when its architects co-opted the use of 'packet-switching', a data-transmission technique originally developed in response to the military need for a nuclear-survivable telecomms system (Ch. 6). Ibid.
4. Lyotard was even alert to an early prefiguration of the Internet/Personal Computer (PC) partnership in an article of *La Semaine Media* 16, 16 February 1979. He quotes one J. M. Treille: 'Not enough has been said about the new possibilities for disseminating stored information, in particular, using semiconductor and laser technology . . . soon everyone will be able to store information cheaply wherever he [*sic*] wishes, and, further, will be able to process it autonomously' (Lyotard, 1986, n. 12).
5. Foreword to *Connecting the Learning Society*, the British government's consultation paper on the National Grid for Learning (http://www.open.gov.uk/dfee/grid/index.htm). Of course, it is no surprise that Blair's words echo those of President Clinton's 'Technology

Literacy Challenge' of February, 1996, which asserts the goal of making all US children 'technologically literate' by the twenty-first century.

6. For a critique of current political interpretations of globalisation, see Blake (1999).

7. Issues relating to these technological problems were informally discussed in a session of the First International Conference on Cultural Attitudes to Technology and Communication (CATaC), at the Science Museum, London 1–3 August 1998, whilst the relations between culture, language and poverty were addressed by a panel discussion on 'Global culture, local culture and vernacular computing: the excluded 95% in South Asia' (Kenneth Kenniston (MIT, USA) and Pat Hall (Open University, UK)).

1

Information, Knowledge and Learning: Some Issues Facing Epistemology and Education in a Digital Age

COLIN LANKSHEAR, MICHAEL PETERS

AND MICHELE KNOBEL

INTRODUCTION

Philosophers of education have always been interested in epistemological issues. In their efforts to help inform educational theory and practice they have dealt extensively with concepts like knowledge, teaching, learning, thinking, understanding, belief, justification, theory, the disciplines, rationality and the like. Their inquiries have addressed issues about what kinds of knowledge are most important and worthwhile, and how knowledge and information might best be organised as curricular activity. They have also investigated the relationships between teaching and learning, belief and opinion, knowledge and belief, and data and information. For some a key issue has been how students can become autonomous knowers. This issue has often been bound up with questions about what count as appropriate standards for reasonableness or rationality, and the conditions under which we can properly regard understanding as having occurred. During the past decade renewed interest has been shown in what is involved in becoming an authority, expert or competent performer in a given area of knowledge, as well as in how we evaluate and critique different or competing beliefs, theories, points of view or paradigms.

Until recently, such activity was conducted under relatively stable conditions. We could assume that the printed word/book comprised the paradigm medium for knowledge production and transmission; that propositional knowledge and denotation comprised the principal mode and space of knowledge work; that educational activity was underwritten by ideals of progress, liberal enlightenment, and personal and collective enhancement made possible through knowledge; and that scientific pursuit of knowledge was based on secure foundations.

We are presently living through a period in which such assumptions have been undermined to the point where they are no longer tenable. The circumstances, conditions and the very *status* of knowledge, learning, teaching and researching are currently in a state of profound upheaval under the double impact of rapid and far-reaching technological change and the massive assault on long-standing narratives of foundation and legitimation.

In this context new work in epistemology for education assumes great urgency, and should be given very high priority by philosophers of education. Indeed, many of the very questions about knowledge that in the past have been fundamental to epistemological work no longer seem relevant. In an age which *fetishises* information (Poster, 1993), knowledge may seem either to be passé or in need of a serious reframing. What follows is an attempt to identify some areas and concerns we believe need close attention in the context of the burgeoning use of new communications and information technologies, including their rapid incorporation into school-based teaching and learning. One important dimension of this, although by no means the only one, is the exponential growth of public and professional participation in the Internet.

LIFE ONLINE: SOCIAL EPISTEMOLOGY AND PRACTICES IN SPACES ON THE INTERNET

One of the most difficult challenges facing attempts to think about epistemology in relation to 'the Internet' has to do with what we might call the Internet's spatial 'ontology'.

For some people the Internet can seemingly be understood as an elaborate infrastructure for transmitting, receiving and manipulating information. As such it may be thought of in terms of a number of more or less discrete but linkable 'technologies' including email, pre-print archives, and the World Wide Web. From this perspective, Paul Thagard (1997) talks of such Internet technologies as now being 'ubiquitous parts of scientific practice'. He describes a range of these technologies and then offers what he calls 'an epistemological appraisal of their contributions to scientific research'. This involves working from the assumption that 'science aims at and sometimes achieves truth understood as correspondence between beliefs and the external world'. Scientists increasingly use Internet technologies in their efforts to achieve 'truth', and Thagard provides typical everyday examples of such uses. He then takes Alvin Goldman's (1986, 1992) five 'epistemic criteria'—reliability, power, fecundity, speed and efficiency—and uses them as a framework for evaluating 'the largely positive impact of Internet technologies on the development of scientific knowledge'. So, for example, the criterion of power is treated in terms of measured ability to help people find true answers to their chosen questions. Thagard looks at various ways in which the World Wide Web (WWW) is 'powerful in helping scientists find answers to the questions that interest them'. He identifies the availability of video simulations, the hypertextual organisation of material, the availability of digital databases and their capacity 'to be searched quickly and thoroughly', the use of email and news groups 'to solicit answers to interesting questions', the ready availability of software on the Web which scientists can use 'to generate answers to statistical or other questions that would be unanswerable otherwise', the availability of electronic pre-print archives as sources of answers to questions and the fact that scientists with common interests can find each other and work collaboratively on the Internet. Thagard then works through the remaining criteria in the same way, typically beginning his accounts by showing how the printing press previously helped scientists in their pursuit of truth, and how the Internet now builds on and amplifies the power, fecundity, speed, efficiency and reliability enabled by print.

For Thagard the Internet seems to be just another facility for conducting business as usual. Scientists continue to practise the pursuit of truth much as they always have, but now they have new technologies to help them in their efforts. Thagard calls this 'Internet epistemology', understood as the contributions of new information technologies to scientific research (which he understands in scientific realist and objectivist terms).

In many ways Thagard's conception of the Internet illustrates what Weston (1994) refers to as 'Phase II of the old boys' operation . . . [of] remodelling the modern apparatus'—an operation codenamed the 'Information Superhighway'. Following a well-established line of argument within the analysis and critique of mass media, Weston claims that 'all social institutions have their relative certainties made possible by the centralizing power of the technologies of mass communication'. In other words, the operating logic of public media throughout history and exemplified in the broadcast mass media of late modernity has followed a familiar pattern, in which:

> successive public communication technologies either began as, or very quickly were made to conform to, the extreme send:receive imbalances that, somewhere along the line, we started calling the mass media, or simply the media . . . Public access to these media is simply not problematical. On the one hand, there are the media and, on the other, there are their audiences, consumers, constituents, and publics. (Weston, 1994)

Weston notes that the development of what is now known as the Internet was intended by those with the power to oversee such things to follow the same media operating logic. He says that by 'the information revolution' they only meant 'to digitize the modern industrial state'. The so-called 'information superhighway' was 'supposed to be about a five hundred, not a one hundred million channel universe'. And it was certainly *not* 'supposed to be about a technological adventure that would reconfigure social relations [of communication and media] or blur the well-constructed boundaries between the public and the private ground'. The intended 'model' would fit well with the picture of state and corporate scientific endeavour made more efficient by Internet technologies painted by Thagard.

However, as is now obvious, the Internet has to date evolved rather differently. It has so far defied centralisation and the restriction of channels that are controlled by a few. It is a truly distributed public medium. It is certainly inadequate to view 'it' (simply) in terms of an information infrastructure involving multiple discrete but connectable 'technologies'. Neither is it appropriate to think of the Internet in terms solely of information and data except, perhaps, in some trivial sense in which *anything* that is communicated can sooner or later be called data or information. Instead, we can envisage the Internet as a range of technologically-mediated spaces of communicative practice that are amazingly diverse—a multiplicity of language games that are by no means confined to informing, and that are not best understood solely in terms of content.

Weston notes that the exponential growth in participation within diverse spaces of practice on the Internet has occurred *despite* a range of well-known constraints—initially including difficulty of access, frustratingly narrow bandwidth, and continuing observations that much of what is to be found there is banal or otherwise offensive, and often disorganised. For perhaps a majority of people who actively participate in online activities the Internet, unlike conventional mass media, is 'less about information or content, and more about relations'. Weston argues that practices in the Internet are mainly about 'people finding their voice' and about 'speaking for themselves in a public way'. From this perspective the matter of the content carrying this new relationship 'is of separate, even secondary, importance'. It remains important, however, because people usually want to '[re]present themselves as well as they can' (Weston, 1994). Hence, if we are to understand the Internet in more than merely infrastructural and technicist terms, or as a massive conduit for information transmission, retrieval and manipulation—which we must—we need to understand the ways in which the relational aspects of the diverse kinds of practices and purposes played out there 'qualify and define what gets transmitted as content'.

At the same time, if we are seriously to address issues of epistemology in relation to the development of the Internet we need to sort out how the complex range of practices engaged in on the Internet relate to epistemology—what, if any, the epistemological implications of particular practices are; and within this field of possible epistemological implications we have to work out which ones are (most) educationally relevant (which will involve difficult questions about the extent to which education should be about preparing people for lives and futures that will seemingly be increasingly lived out in cyberspace). This means at least three things. First, we have to recognise that the way academics understand and approach the Internet is only one way, and that it may differ greatly from the way non-academic publics understand and use the spaces and technologies in question. Second, to make plausible judgements about social practices on the Internet we need to know a lot more about what people actually do there than we know at present, and we need to look for patterns of practice and purpose and 'production' that go far beyond our current knowledge. Third, we must problematise our limited and often mystified understandings of the Internet which, to use an analogy from Chris Bigum (in personal communication), may be more like a chameleon than an elephant. If, to continue the analogy, we are like blind persons trying to discover the nature of the beast by fumbling for parts of it, the fact is that it will be even more difficult to do this if the beast is a chameleon than if it is an elephant! And this makes epistemological work especially difficult.

Nonetheless, as educationists we neglect investigating the possible epistemological significance and implications of practices involving new Information and Communications Technologies (ICTs) at our peril. This would be to hand the game over completely to the 'visions' of neo-liberal policymakers, techno-scientists and corporations who stand to gain from technologising educational provision in the image of computing hardware and software. What follows is a tentative preliminary exercise in considering some 'patterns', features and issues of social practices that have been associated with the rapid growth of electronic ICTs generally and Internet-based practices more specifically, and how these might call for rethinking episte-mology in a digital age. This rethinking might conceive of epistemology in social terms as practices of knowing that reflect a range of strategies for 'assembling', 'editing', 'processing', 'receiving', 'sending', and 'working on' information and data to transform 'data' into 'knowledge'. We might think here of Ludwig Wittgenstein's (1953) 'performative' epistemology, an epistemology of performance—'Now I know how to go on!' (Wittgenstein, 1953, p. 105)—that conceives knowing as making, doing and acting. This account is based on the relation of knowing to the 'mastery of a technique'. Such a view of performance epistemology might be usefully applied to a range of emergent practices. These include 'bricolage', understood as assemblage of elements, and 'collage', understood as the practice of transferring materials from one context to another. They also include 'montage', construed as the practice of disseminating borrowings in a new setting (Ulmer, 1985b).

PATTERNS AND PRACTICES OF THE NEW COMMUNICATIONS AND INFORMATION TECHNOLOGIES

Knowledge in the postmodern condition

In *The Postmodern Condition* Jean-François Lyotard (1984) advances what has proved to be a highly prescient and compelling account of scientific (as distinct from narrative) knowledge in so-called 'advanced' societies (Peters, 1995). His analysis resonates powerfully with the experiences of knowledge workers in modern neo-liberal states over the past 10–15 years. Lyotard's working hypothesis is that:

> the status of knowledge is altered as societies enter what is known as the postindustrial age and cultures enter what is known as the postmodern age. (Lyotard, 1984, p. 3)

Lyotard's analysis of the postmodern condition is a report on the status of knowledge under the impact of technological transformation within the context of the crisis of narratives—especially Enlightenment meta-narratives concerning meaning, truth and emancipation which have been used to legitimate both the rules of knowledge in the sciences and the foundations of modern institutions. His concept of the postmodern condition describes the state of knowledge and the problem of its legitimation in the most 'highly developed' countries, in the wake of 'transformations which, since the end of the nineteenth century, have altered the game rules for science, literature and the arts' (*ibid.*, p. 3).

By 'transformations' Lyotard means particularly the effects of new technologies since the 1940s and their combined impact on the two main *functions* of knowledge: namely, research and the transmission of acquired learning. He argues that the leading sciences and technologies are all grounded in *language-based* developments—in theories of linguistics, cybernetics, informatics, computer languages, telematics, theories of algebra—and on principles of miniaturisation and commercialisation. This is a context in which:

knowledge is and will be produced in order to be sold, and it is and will be consumed in order to be valorized in a new production: in both cases, the goal is exchange. (*ibid.*, p. 4)

Knowledge, in other words, 'ceases to become an end in itself'; it loses its use value and becomes, to all intents and purposes, an exchange value alone. The changed status of knowledge comprises at least the following additional aspects.

- Availability of knowledge as an international commodity becomes the basis for national and commercial advantage within the emerging global economy.
- Computerised uses of knowledge become the basis for enhanced state security and international monitoring.
- Anything in the constituted body of knowledge that is not translatable into quantities of information will be abandoned.
- Knowledge is exteriorised with respect to the knower, and the status of the learner and the teacher is transformed into a commodity relationship of 'supplier' and 'user'.

Lyotard sees some important implications and corollaries associated with this changed status of knowledge. In particular:

- As the principal force in economic production, knowledge 'effects' include radically changing the composition of the workforce.
- Mercantilisation of knowledge widens the gap between 'developed' and 'developing' countries.
- Commercialisation of knowledge and emerging new forms of media circulation—including, par excellence, the Internet—raise new ethico-legal issues including intellectual property rights, the state's role in promoting and providing learning, issues of decency, offence and censorship and issues concerning the relationship between the state and information-rich multinationals.

Lyotard's critique frames the central question of legitimation of scientific knowledge in terms of its functions of research and transmission of learning within computerised societies where meta-narratives meet with 'incredulity' (*ibid.*, p. xxiv). In his critique of capitalism Lyotard argues that the state and company/corporation have found their only credible goal in power. Science (research) and education (transmission of acquired learning) as institutionalised activities of state and corporation are/become legitimated, in de facto terms, through the principle of *performativity*: of optimising the overall performance of social institutions according to the criterion of efficiency or, as Lyotard puts it, 'the endless optimization of the cost/benefit (input/output) ratio' (Lyotard, 1993, p. 25). They are legitimated by their contribution to maximising the system's performance, a logic which becomes self-legitimating—that is, enhanced measurable and demonstrable performance as its own end.

The implications for the education function of knowledge are especially pertinent here. In terms of status, education—until recently regarded as a universal welfare right under a social democratic model—has been reconstituted in instrumental and commodified terms as a leading contributor to and sub-sector of the economy: indeed, one of the main *enterprises* of the post-industrial economy. The focus of educational work and provision is no longer based on questions of educational aims and ideals in the old sense that drew on language games involving values, aspirations, conceptions of and beliefs about humanity, potential, personal worth and autonomy, emancipation and dignity and the like. Rather, attention has moved from aims, values and ideals to a new focus on 'means and techniques for obtaining [optimally] efficient outcomes' (Marshall, 1998a, p. 8). That is to say, the education language game has been forced into commensurability with the varieties of technicist language games, and is required to play—to perform—according to the technological criterion of efficiency. The problem of legitimation, which is ever a problem of rationalising *power*, is addressed by making efficiency the basis of legitimation and then extending this logic across *all* the language games of the public–social institutional domain.

At the level of daily practice, performativity in education at all levels calls for our schools and universities to make 'the optimal contribution
. . . to the best performativity of the social system' (Lyotard, 1984, p. 48). This involves creating the sorts of *skills* among learners that are indispensable to maximum efficiency of the social system. For societies like our own, this is a system of increasing diversity and is seen as being composed of players competing in the marketplace of global capitalism. Accordingly, two kinds of skills predominate: first, skills 'specifically designed to tackle world [economic] competition', which will vary 'according to which "specialities" the nation-states or educational institutions can sell on the world market', and second, skills which fulfil the society's 'own needs'. These have to do with maintaining the society's 'internal cohesion'. Under postmodern conditions, says Lyotard, these cohesion skills displace the old educational concern for *ideals*. Education is now about supplying 'the system with players capable of acceptably filling their roles at the pragmatic posts required by its institutions' (see Lyotard, 1984, p. 48).

As Marshall notes:

> educational institutions . . . will be used to change people away from the former liberal humanist *ideals* (of knowledge as good in itself, of emancipation, of social progress) to people who through an organized stock of professional knowledge will pursue performativity through increasingly technological devices and scientific managerial theories. (Marshall, 1998, p. 12)

What are the implications for the content and processes of education so far as knowledge is concerned? Lyotard identifies several with specific reference to higher education, although these implications can readily be extrapolated downwards to elementary and secondary school levels. We will look at five of these implications which are especially relevant to our topic.

First, transmitting the 'organised stock of established knowledge' required for professional training may increasingly be left to new technologies. That is:

> to the extent that learning is translatable into computer language and the traditional teacher is replaceable by memory banks, didactics can be entrusted to machines linking traditional memory banks (libraries, etc.) and computer data banks to intelligent terminals placed at the students' disposal. (Lyotard, 1984, p. 50)

Second, from a pedagogical perspective, didactic instruction by teachers would be directed to teaching students 'how to use the terminals'. Lyotard identifies two aspects here: (a) teaching new languages (e.g., informatics, telematics), and (b) developing refined abilities to handle 'the language game of interrogation'—particularly, to what information source should the question be addressed, and how should the question be framed in order to get the required information most efficiently?

A third implication noted by Lyotard is of particular concern here. He suggests that a primary concern of professionally-oriented students, the state and education institutions will be with whether the learning of information is of any use—typically in the sense of 'Is it saleable?' or 'Is it efficient?'—not with whether it is *true*.

A fourth implication that runs parallel to the third is that competence according to criteria like true/false, just/unjust has been displaced by competence according to the criterion of high performativity.

Finally, under conditions of less than perfect information the learner–student–graduate–expert who has knowledge (can use the terminals effectively in terms of computing language competence and interrogation) and can access information has an advantage. However, the more closely conditions approximate to conditions of perfect information (where data are in principle accessible to any expert), the greater the advantage that accrues to the ability to arrange data 'in a new way'. This involves using imagination to connect together 'series of data that were previously held to be independent' (Lyotard, 1984, p. 52). That is, in the final analysis, imagination becomes the basis of extra performativity.

We need to emphasise two important points here with respect to Lyotard's analysis. First, his working hypothesis and the exploration based on it were not intended to have predictive value but, instead, strategic value in relation to the question of the status of knowledge in advanced societies. Nonetheless, Lyotard's account is very close to what has emerged in developed neo-liberal states. Second, we do not see Lyotard as advocating or endorsing the values and orientation emerging from his analysis. Instead, we see him as reporting the direction in which exploration of his hypothesis points.

Our own view is that Lyotard's investigation of his working hypothesis has, in the event, proved to be disturbingly accurate. His account of the changed status of knowledge corresponds closely to the lived experience of many teachers and researchers working in reconstituted and increasingly professionalised universities. Moreover, with the current strong push to technologise school classrooms we can already see at least the second, third and fourth of the implications described above applying increasingly to school learning contexts (cf. Lankshear, Bigum *et al.*, 1997; Lankshear and Snyder, 2000).

We would argue that Lyotard's investigation of the implications for the status of knowledge of computerisation occurring under conditions of incredulity toward meta-narratives is massively important. At the same time, it is at most a part of a much larger story so far as epistemology and education in a digital age are concerned. Lyotard's work predated the dramatic developments in and uptake of new ICTs during the 1990s. Practices involving new ICTs—and, notably, the Internet—occurring within non-formal and non-educational sites have crucial significance for how we think about knowledge and truth, and about their relationship to educational work. It is high time that educationists tried to 'tell the larger story as it is', and to face square on its implications for established epistemological positions, and for educational practices and emphases predicated on these. At the same time, it is important in the context of what are confused and confusing times not to give too much away too easily so far as epistemological principles are concerned. The rapid and far-reaching changes in which we are embroiled may have thrown into serious doubt some substantive epistemological theories, and various educational priorities, values, assumptions and practices associated with them. This, however, is *not* to argue against the importance of trying to get clear about the nature of knowledge, the significance of truth and the distinctions between and relationships among knowledge, truth, belief, information and the like, under changed and changing conditions. Our argument is not so much with the principles and concerns of conventional epistemologies as with some substantive theories that have been dominant throughout modernity.

It seems to us very likely that the relationship between education and knowledge needs to be rethought in profound ways within the mode of information (Poster, 1993). There are at least two important aspects to this inquiry. One will involve considering the extent to which education will henceforth be concerned with knowledge under foreseeable conditions. The other will involve asking the question: 'to the extent that education will still be concerned with knowledge, what kind or kinds of knowledge will be most important for schools to address, and what substantive changes in educational emphasis will this entail?'

We are aware that in much of what we have to say it may appear we believe that there is no longer any truth or any knowledge beyond what circulates as information. This is *not* our position. Rather, we think three things here. One is that new conditions require us to look again and, perhaps, in different ways from those we are used to, at what counts as knowledge and truth. The second is that we need carefully to consider the extent to which everyday practices—including many on the Internet—simply are not concerned with knowledge and truth as we have often understood them, but instead 'play' on quite different terrain. Third, we need to consider the extent to which education must help prepare learners for successful participation in such practices.

The superabundance of information

The Internet marks the current high point of what Mark Poster (1995) calls the second media age, or the second age of mass communications to emerge in the twentieth century. The first age, comprising film, radio and television, was based on the logic of broadcast. Here 'a small number of producers sent information to a large number of consumers', transcending earlier constraints of time and space by initially electrifying analogue information and, later, by digitising it. The integration of satellite technology with telephone, television and computer media has brought the emergence of a many-to-many logic of communication, which is Poster's second media age. This is a logic in which boundaries between producers, distributors and consumers of information break down, and where social relations of communication are radically reconfigured under conditions of infinitely greater scope for interactive communication than in the broadcast model (Poster, 1995, p. 3).

There is more to matters here than simply an analytic distinction between operating logics: one-to-one versus many-to-many. In addition, there are important contingencies associated with the development of the Internet that are relevant to our purposes. Three in particular are worth noting briefly here. These will already be familiar to readers and are rehearsed here for subsequent analytic purposes.

First, there is the now notorious issue of the sheer volume of available information. While the phenomenon known as info-glut (Postman, 1993; Gilster 1997, p. 6) or data smog (Shenk, 1998) is by no means confined to the Internet, it certainly reaches an apex here. In part the superabundance of information can be seen simply in gross quantitative terms. There is a mountain of the stuff in the ether, so to speak, which presents serious challenges to negotiating this mass to find what one wants or needs. In addition, however, the information resources of the Internet are readily *customisable*. Services and software are available that enable users to have gigabytes of data on identified topics 'dumped' direct onto their hard drives on an ongoing basis. Once the parameters of interest have been set the data dumping operation is automatic (until one decides to end it).

Second, the Net is a radically 'democratic' inclusive medium where information is to a large extent unfiltered. Paul Gilster (1997, pp. 38–39) notes that even with the introduction of cable television, conventional mass media are nonetheless exclusive. Certain categories of content are excluded through the filtering decisions and actions of programming executives and the like. While many information sources on the Internet (especially on the WWW) filter and otherwise moderate content in accordance with their perceived interests and purposes, this is in no way the norm.

Third, a great deal of information on the Internet is *presented*. Two aspects must suffice here. First, Gilster (1997, pp. 2–3) notes that with the tools of electronic publication being dispersed practically on a global scale, 'the Net is a study in the myriad uses of rhetoric'. In this context, says Gilster, the ability to distinguish between content and presentation in order to achieve a balanced assessment is crucial. The importance of presentation and the incentives to present information in maximally compelling ways should not be underestimated in the context of what Goldhaber (1997) calls 'the attention economy' (see below). Second, on the WWW much information is hyperlinked in ways that reflect conceptions of interrelatedness, relevance, emphasis, significance and values of the presenters. The information texts available on the Web are intensely mediated/interpreted, and this is further iterated through the operating logics and assumptions of search engines. As Standish observes:

> the links we encounter are ready made. As such they are the products of the author or designer of the hypertext and so reflect in some degree that person's biases and preoccupations. The facility one easily acquires in clicking on icons enhances the appearance of naturalness that the links so quickly come to have and so covers over the more or less idiosyncratic nature of the connections they supply. (Standish, 2000; see also Burbules, 1998.)

Of course, we find similarities in other media—for instance, author choices of key sources and references in print texts. But on the Internet the hypertextual, hypermediated nature of information sources is more complex and profound than in other media. This is largely a function of the ease of creating hyperlinks and the speed and facility with which linkable resources can be mobilised online. It is also partly a function of the logic of the attention economy and the desires of Web publishers to create (potential) associations with other presences on the Web. Other matters related to image and identity also operate to generate information presentation effects that are much more complex and ambiguous than typically occur in, say, print texts.

Writers have identified numerous issues associated with the potential constraints to sound information retrieval and processing practices resulting from the logic of many-to-many communication and contingencies like those we have raised here. One such issue is that of *credibility in cyberspace*. Nicholas Burbules and Thomas Callister (1997), for example, address the issue of how Internet users can assess the credibility of particular items of information and of information providers, and how they can acquire credibility in their own right as informers. They argue that the Internet poses important challenges to our more traditional ideas of how to assess and gain credibility in relation to information and knowledge. Traditionally, they say, our criteria for credibility have emphasised qualifications and characteristics of identifiable knowledge and information agents (and for all the fallibility this may entail). On the Internet, however, it may be impossible to identify original sources of information— seemingly much more so than in the more finite world of print-based information. In such cases we (may) have to rely on a range of commonplace proxies. Judgements must rely on such indicators as 'the avenues though which that information was gained'—drawing on the idea of the Internet and, particularly, the WWW as 'a vast network of credibility relations' within which 'the people who establish active links to reliable information, and whose information or viewpoints are in turn identified as and recommended by others, gain credibility as both users of information and providers'; the links that 'others who are better known' have made to the information; how frequently the information has been accessed (e.g. page visitor counters) and so on.

Burbules and Callister emphasise that these are indirect and imperfect measures of credibility, yet they may be all that Internet users can draw on to evaluate information that is beyond their experience and expertise in a field. Clearly, traditional epistemological concepts, criteria and practices—particularly, those adhered to by knowledge 'professionals' like academics—are put under considerable strain here.

A second issue concerns *the quest for perspective and balance*. Paul Gilster (1997, Chapter 7) describes a practice he calls 'knowledge assembly' which he sees as a necessary new literacy in and for the information age. He asks how one builds knowledge out of online searching and catching, and how specific items of information are to be evaluated. He seeks open, non-prejudiced inquiry, which strives for balance, goes where the evidence leads, and aims to get at the heart of the themes or issues in question. For Gilster, knowledge assembly is 'all about building perspective'. It proceeds by way of 'the accretion of unexpected insights' (*ibid.*, pp. 195, 219). When it is used properly, says Gilster:

> [n]etworked information possesses unique advantages. It is searchable, so that a given issue can be dissected with a scalpel's precision, laid open to reveal its inner workings. It can be customized to reflect our particular needs. Moreover, its hypertextual nature connects with other information sources, allowing us to listen to opposing points of view, and make informed decisions about their validity. (*ibid.*, p. 196)

Knowledge assembly is about targeting issues and stories using customised newsfeeds and evaluating the outcomes. It is the:

> ability to collect and evaluate both fact and opinion, ideally without bias. Knowledge assembly draws evidence from multiple sources, not just the World Wide Web; it mixes and distinguishes between hard journalism, editorial opinion, and personal viewpoints. [It] accepts the assumption that the Internet will become one of the major players in news delivery . . . but it also recognizes the continuing power of the traditional media. (*ibid.*, p. 199)

Gilster describes the tools and procedures of knowledge assembly using the Internet in terms of a five-step process. The first step involves developing a customised, personalised electronic news service—a personal newsfeed. Subscribing to an online news service and entering keywords that define the topics or issues you want to receive breaking stories about does this. The service—often fee-charging, depending on the range of information sources it culls—then sends you by email or via a Web page which can be tailored for personal use stories on topics of interest as they break. (For more detailed descriptions of the kinds of services available, see Gilster, 1997, pp. 201–208.)

The second step augments the first (which draws on formal 'published' information or 'hard news'). In the second step one subscribes to online newsgroups and mailing lists that deal with the subject(s) of interest. These offer the personal viewpoints and opinions of participants on the issues in question, providing access to what (other) netizens make of the topic. Some newsgroups make their own newsfeeds available, which helps with focused searching by sub-topics and the like among the myriad postings that occur across a range of lists on daily and even hourly bases.

In Gilster's third step one searches the Internet for background information—e.g. by going to the archives of online newspapers to get a history of the build-up of the story or issue thus far. Gilster also mentions using search engines to find Internet links to sites covering key players in the story or issue. These may provide related stories or other information that helps contextualise the issue or topic, providing additional breadth, variables and angles.

The fourth step involves drawing together other helpful Internet news sources, such as radio archives accessed by software like RealAudio, interactive chat sessions, video archives and so on. Although the facility should not be abused, direct email links might also be used to verify or disconfirm information.

The final step in the assembly process takes us beyond Internet sources of information and involves relating the information obtained from networked sources to non-networked sources such as television, conventional newspapers, library resources and so on. This is indispensable to seeking balance and perspective, since it puts the issue or story being worked on into a wider context of news and information—including prioritised contexts (e.g. where newspapers consistently run the story on page 1, or on page 12).

These steps toward 'filling the information cache' entail diverse understandings, skills and procedures—many of which are only acquired through regular use and 'practice'. For example, learning to find one's way around the innumerable mailing lists, news groups and discussion lists; identifying the 'predilections' of different search engines, and which one to use (and with which other ones) for particular areas or topics; how to narrow searches down by refining keyword checks; how to use Boolean logic, and which search engines employ which Boolean commands and protocols, and so on. Gilster also mentions specific 'tools' of content evaluation that one uses along the way to filling one's information cache, item by item: for instance, the credentials of the sources, the probable audience a source pitches at, the likely reliability of the source, distinctions such as those between 'filtered, edited news', personal opinion and propaganda (*ibid.*, p. 217).

Constitutive effects of how we interrogate the world

In a chapter called 'Logic and intuition', Michael Heim (1993a) explores some constraining influences on how we interrogate the world of information—and, indeed, the world itself—that can be seen as associated with normalised practices of a digital regime. He focuses on Boolean search logic, since nowadays to a large and growing extent we 'interrogate the world through the computer interface' and 'most computer searches use Boolean logic' (*ibid.*, pp. 14–15).

Heim's underlying point is that to live within the digital regime means that using Boolean search logic and similar computing strategies rapidly becomes 'second nature'—something we take for granted (Heim, 1993a, p. 14). He is interested in how this will 'affect our thought processes and mental life and, to that extent, how we will be constituted as searchers, thinkers, and knowers'. He builds on two key ideas: the types of questions we ask shape the possible answers we get, and the ways we search limit what we find in our searching.

For reasons of space we must bypass here many interesting details in Heim's account of the shift from traditional Aristotelian logic based on direct statements/propositions to abstract, system-oriented symbolic logic based on algebra, originating with Boole and Venn and associated more recently with philosophers like Quine. And we must bypass details of the implications of this shift Heim identifies for ontology, worldview and relations of knower to known. Three fragments may suffice, however, to evoke the flavour of his argument:

> With modern logic:
> systemic consistency became more important than the direct reference to things addressed in our experience.
> When system precedes relevance, the way becomes clear for the primacy of information [since] . . . For it to become manipulable and transmissible as information, knowledge must first be reduced to homogenized units.
> In its intrinsic remoteness from direct human experience, Boolean search logic [facilitates] a gain in power at the price of our direct involvement with things . . . Placing us at a new remove from subject matter, by directing us away from the texture of what we are exploring. (*ibid.*, pp. 178–18)

This part of Heim's argument concerns objects of knowledge and the relationship between knower and world in addressing the world. By easy extension, we can see how the way contemporary modes of system-based relationship to the world can make it possible for policy-makers, corporate chiefs and other powerful shapers of destinies to frame and enact policies and measures that impact so dramatically (and painfully) on the material lives and experiences of (other) people. When materiality is dissolved away, real effects may be a small (since invisible) price to pay for enacting the elegance of a logic, so that matters of epistemology, ethics and politics are profoundly imbricated.

Returning more directly to Heim's account of the relationships between question types and answers, and between search modes and what our searches turn up, we arrive at the operating mode of the search engine. On the surface it may appear that search engines have already moved beyond using Boole's tools: the use of AND, NOT, OR, NEAR and so on, in conjunction with 'key words, buzz words and thought bits to scan the vast store of knowledge' (*ibid.*, p. 22). Some search engines now invite us simply to ask them a question or enter a few words. (The 'initiated', of course, still prefer to work with key words and Boole.) But beneath the surface of our natural language questions or phrases the software is still operating on largely Boolean lines. The point is that *all* such searching makes use of logics that presume pre-set, channelled, tunnelled searching: *pointed* rather than *open* searching. Invitations from the machine to refine our search (as when too many data sources are identified) are invitations to further sharpen/focus 'an already determined will to find something definite'; to 'construct a narrower and more efficient thought tunnel; to create still finer funnels to sift and channel "the onrush of data"' (*ibid.*, pp. 22–23).

Heim contrasts this kind of information scan with what he calls 'meditative perusal'. He distinguishes his notion of meditative work from that recommended by numerous advocates of online searching. For the latter, 'meditating' means no more than engaging in reflective efforts to find sharper and more discriminating key words. From this perspective, information scanning is pre-conceived, focused, highly goal-directed and treats texts as data. The key values of information scanning are speed, functionality, efficiency and control. The answers we get from scanning are bounded and defined, comprising data which falls within overlapping circles in Venn diagrams. We can then use what we get in accordance with our knowledge purposes.

In contrast to this, Heim describes 'meditative perusal' as the kind of 'contemplative, meditative meander along a line of thinking' that we might engage in by slowly reading a book and keeping 'the peripheral vision of the mind's eye' open. Here the reader is open to unexpected connections, meaning and interpretation, options that were taken and others that were not, authorial hunches, tensions and contradictions and so on. This is an approach to knowledge/getting to know (about) something which privileges intuition, the unexpected, openness to 'discoveries that overturn the questions we originally came to ask' and to 'turning up something more important than the discovery we had originally hoped to make' (*ibid.*, pp. 25–26). Insofar as spaces on the Internet can, like books, be browsed in this mode, doing so will require us to resist the wider web of values and purposes to which search logics are recruited or, at the very least, to be and remain aware of wider options that may exist.

Economies of information and attention

The superabundance of information has been linked to the hypothesis of an emerging attention economy in ways that have important epistemological implications. The fact that information is in over-saturated supply is seen as fatal to the coherence of the idea of an information economy, since 'economics are governed by what is scarce' (Goldhaber, 1997). Yet, if people in post-industrial societies will increasingly live their lives in the spaces of the Internet, these lives will fall more and more under economic laws organic to this new space. Numerous writers (e.g. Lanham, 1994; Thorngate, 1988, 1990) have argued that the basis of the coming new economy will be attention and *not* information. Attention, unlike information, is inherently scarce. But like information it moves through the Net.

The idea of an attention economy is premised on the fact that the human capacity to produce material things outstrips the Net capacity to consume the things that are produced—such are the irrational contingencies of distribution. In this context, 'material needs at the level of creature comfort are fairly well satisfied for those in a position to demand them' (Goldhaber, 1997)—the great *minority*, it should be noted, of people at present. Nonetheless, for this powerful minority, the need for attention becomes increasingly important, and increasingly the focus of their productive activity. Hence, the attention economy:

> [T]he energies set free by the successes of . . . the money-industrial economy go more and more in the direction of obtaining attention. And that leads to growing competition for what is increasingly scarce, which is of course attention. It sets up an unending scramble, a scramble that also increases the demands on each of us to pay what scarce attention we can. (Goldhaber, 1997)

Within an attention economy, individuals seek stages—performing spaces—from which they can perform for the widest/largest possible audiences. Goldhaber observes that the various spaces of the Internet lend themselves perfectly to this model. He makes two points of particular relevance to our concerns here. First, gaining attention is indexical to originality. It is difficult, says Goldhaber, to get new attention 'by repeating exactly what you or someone else has done before'. Consequently, the attention economy is based on 'endless originality, or at least attempts at originality'.

Second, Goldhaber argues that in a full-fledged attention economy the goal is simply to get enough attention or to get as much as possible. (In part this argument is predicated on the idea that having someone's full attention is a means for having them meet one's material needs and desires.) This becomes the primary motivation for and criterion of successful performance in cyberspace. Generating information will principally be concerned either with gaining attention directly, or with paying what Goldhaber calls 'illusory attention' to others in order to maintain the degree of interest in the exchange on their part necessary for gaining their attention.

Multimodal truth

Since the invention of the printing press the printed word has been the main carrier of (what is presented as) truth. Mass schooling has evolved under the regime of print, and print has more generally 'facilitated the literate foundation of culture' (Heim, 1999). Of course various kinds of images or graphics have been used in printed texts to help carry truth (such as tables, charts, graphs, photographic plates, illustrations). However, Web technology merges pictures and print (not to mention sound) much more intricately and easily than has ever been possible before. As Heim puts it:

> The word now shares Web space with the image, and text appears inextricably tied to pictures. The pictures are dynamic, animated, and continually updated. The unprecedented speed and ease of digital production mounts photographs, movies, and video on the Web. Cyberspace becomes visualized data, and meaning arrives in spatial as well as in verbal expressions.

This situation now confronts the primary focus within classroom-based education on the linguistic–verbal–textual resources of reading, writing and talk. Teaching and learning have been seen throughout the history of mass education as principally linguistic accomplishments (Gunther Kress, personal communication). Recently, however, teachers and educationists have become increasingly interested in the role of visual representations in relation to teaching and learning. 'The importance of images as an educational medium is beginning to be realised, as text books, CD ROM, and other educational resources become increasingly reliant on visual communication as a medium for dealing with large amounts of complex information' (*ibid.*).

SOME IMPLICATIONS FOR EPISTEMOLOGY AND EDUCATION

The patterns, features and issues associated with social practices involving new ICTs sketched here are by no means the only ones we could address. They are, however, quite diverse and well-subscribed, and they provide a reasonably broad-based 'catalyst' for considering how much and in what ways we may need to rethink epistemological matters in relation to educational theory and practice. This final section will identify some of the issues and challenges we believe should be taken up as priorities by educational philosophers (among others).

We can begin by identifying in a broad sweep some of the key elements of the epistemological model that has underpinned education throughout the modern-industrial era. We can then go on to consider how far these elements may be under question in a digital age where more and more of our time, purposes and energies are invested in activities involving new communications and information technologies.

Throughout the modern-industrial era of print, learning has been based on curriculum *subjects* organised as bodies of content which are in turn based on work done in the disciplines (history, mathematics, natural science and so on). The primary object of learning was the content of subjects. This was based on the premise that what we need to know about the world in order to function effectively in it, and that is to be taught in formal education, is discovered through (natural and social) scientific inquiry. Even the very 'practical' or 'manual' subjects (such as cooking, woodwork) contained a considerable 'theory' component.

School learning has also been based on the idea that by participating in curriculum subjects derived from the disciplines learners could come to see how this content gets discovered and justified by experts, in addition to learning (about) the content itself. To use a once-common formulation from Anglo-American educational philosophy, knowledge has both its literatures (content) and its languages (disciplined procedures), and successful learning initiates learners into both (cf. Hirst, 1974). Of course, it is another matter as to how far this ever actually occurred in practice within schools. The fact remains, however, that for educational philosophers as otherwise different as John Dewey, Israel Scheffler, Maxine Greene, Paul Hirst and Kevin Harris, the epistemological ideal for education has always been to promote the development of *knowers* as well as to transmit *knowledge*.

The broad epistemological model which has dominated school education since its inception has been the standard view of knowledge which has dominated Western thought since the time of Plato. This is widely known as the 'justified true belief' model. According to this epistemology, for A (a person, knower) to know that *p* (a proposition) A must *believe* that *p*, *p* must be *true*, and A must be *justified* in believing that *p* (see, for example, Scheffler, 1965).

This general model allowed for many variations, for instance in theories of truth (correspondence, coherence, pragmatist), in theories of reality (realism, idealism) and so on. But beneath all such variations, justified true belief has been the epistemological standard for two millennia, and has been applied (in a more or less particular way) to school curricular learning. The ideas canvassed in the body of this chapter pose a range of issues for this epistemology and for established educational practices based on it. We will identify and comment briefly on five points here, aware that what we have to say is at most a tenuous beginning to a pressing area of inquiry.

First, the standard epistemology constructs knowledge as something that is carried linguistically and expressed in sentences/propositions and theories. This is hardly surprising considering that for two millennia the modes for producing and expressing knowledge have been oral language and static print. To the extent that images and graphics of various kinds have been employed in texts their role has been, literally, to illustrate, summarise or convey propositional content.

The multimedia realm of digital ICTs makes possible—indeed, makes *normal*—the radical convergence of text, image and sound in ways that break down the primacy of propositional linguistic forms of 'truth bearing'. While many images and sounds that are transmitted and received digitally still stand in for propositional information (cf. Kress' notion of images carrying complex information mentioned above), many do not. They can behave in epistemologically very different ways from talk and text—for example, evoking, attacking us sensually, shifting and evolving constantly, and so on. Meaning and truth arrive in spatial as well as textual expressions (Heim, 1999), and the rhetorical and normative modes displace the scientific-propositional on a major scale.

Michael Heim (1999) offers an interesting perspective on this in his account of what he calls 'the new mode of truth' that will be realised in the twenty-first century. He claims that as new digital media displace older forms of typed and printed word, questions about how truth is 'made present' through processes that are closer to rituals and iconographies than propositions and text re-emerge in similar forms to those discussed by theologians since medieval times. Heim argues that incarnate truth as the sacred Word is transmitted through a complex of rituals and images integrated with text-words. In the case of the Catholic church, for instance:

> communal art is deemed essential to the transmission of the Word as conceived primarily through spoken and written scriptures. The word on the page is passed along in a vessel of images, fragrances, songs, and kinesthetic pressed flesh. Elements like water, salt, and wine contribute to the communication. Truth is transmitted not only through spoken and written words but also through a participatory community that re-enacts its truths through ritual. (Heim, 1999)

The issue of how truth is made present in and through the rituals of the community of believers/practitioners has been an abiding concern of theologians for centuries. Is the presence of incarnate truth granted to the community through ritualised enactment of the sacred word real, or should it be seen as symbolic or, perhaps, as a kind of virtual presence? (*ibid.*). Heim suggests that this and similar questions take on new significance with the full flowering of digital media. If truth 'becomes finite and accessible to humans primarily through the word', he asks, 'what implications do the new media hold for the living word as it shifts into spatial imagery?' (ibid.).

Heim casts his larger discussion of these issues in the context of avatar worlds being constructed by online users of virtual reality (VR) software to express their visions of virtual reality as a form of enacted truth. (Avatars are graphic images or icons adopted by users to represent themselves in three dimensional worlds which are inhabited and co-constructed by other participants represented by avatars. As such, avatars are graphic extensions of the textual descriptors for online identities adopted by participants in earlier text-based MOOs, MUDs and MUSHs.) Heim speaks of participants realising and transmitting their 'visions' of virtual reality—the worlds they construct online—through what he calls the 'new mode of truth'.

A second challenge facing much established epistemological thinking concerns the fact that knowing has generally been seen as an act we carry out on, and truth has been seen as pertaining to, something that already exists. In various ways, however, the kind of knowing involved in social practices within the diverse spaces of new ICTs is very different from this. More than propositional knowledge of what already exists, much of the knowing that is involved in the new spaces might better be understood in terms of a performance epistemology—knowing as an ability to perform.

At one level we can understand this in terms of procedures like knowing how to make and follow links when creating and reading Web documents. At another level it is reflected in Lyotard's observation that under conditions of the changed status of knowledge the kinds of knowledge most needed by knowledge workers include procedural knowledge of languages like telematics and informatics, and knowledge of how to interrogate information sources. Of particular importance to 'higher order work' and other forms of performance under current and foreseeable conditions—including performances that gain attention—is knowledge of how to make new moves in a game and how to change the very rules of the game. This directly confronts some dominant assumptions in conventional epistemological thought, such as those concretised in normal science which presuppose stability in the rules of the game as the norm and paradigm shifts as the exception. While the sorts of shifts involved in changing game rules cannot all be on the scale of paradigm shifts, they nonetheless subvert stability as the norm.

Once again, it is important to note here that Lyotard does not endorse the state of affairs he describes any more than we endorse the features and patterns of practice described earlier. Rather, the operating logic is: 'if this is how things are, this is what follows from them'. Accepting the way things are and accommodating to them educationally and epistemologically is one option. Problematising them, however, is a different option. And it is the option we favour. But in order to problematise them they need first to be *named*. Lyotard names some of them and we have tried to name others—as a basis for problematising them and working toward developing considered epistemological and educational responses.

Third, practices involving new media help to identify weaknesses in traditional individualistic epistemologies which, following Descartes, have always existed. Problems with the notion that knowing, thinking, believing, being justified and so on are located within the individual person (the 'cogitating' subject) have become readily apparent in postmodernity. Theories of distributed cognition, for example, have grown in conjunction with the emergence of 'fast capitalism' and networked technologies (Castells, 1998; Gee, Hull and Lankshear, 1997). A further aspect is apparent in the role and significance of multi-disciplinary teams in 'imaging new moves or new games' in the quest for extra performance. The model of multi-disciplinary teams supersedes that of the expert individual as the efficient means to making new moves (Lyotard, 1984). In addition, we have seen that in the information-abundant world of the Internet and other searchable data sources it is often impossible for individuals to manage their own information needs, maintain an eye to the credibility of information items and so on. Practices of information gathering and organising are often highly customised and dispersed, with 'the individual' depending on roles being played by various services and technologies. Hence, a particular 'assemblage' of knowledge that is brought together—however momentarily—in the product of an individual may more properly be understood as a *collective* assemblage involving many minds (and machines).

Fourth, it is important to recognise that the role and significance of knowledge in the social conditions of postmodernity have changed in ways that should not be ignored by epistemologists and educationists. For a start, none of the three logical conditions of justified true belief is necessary for information. All that is required for information is that data be sent from sender to receivers, or that data be received by receivers who are not even necessarily targeted by senders. Information is used and acted on. Belief *may* follow from using information, although it may not, and belief certainly need not precede the use of information or acting on it.

Furthermore, the 'new status' knowledge of the postmodern condition as described by Lyotard—knowledge that is produced to be sold or valorised in a new production—does not necessarily require that the conditions of justified true belief be met. This follows from the shift in the status of knowledge from being a use value to becoming an exchange value. For example, in the new game of 'hired gun' research where deadlines are often 'the day before yesterday' and the 'answer' to the problem may already be presupposed in the larger policies and performativity needs of the funders, the efficacy of the knowledge produced may begin and end with cashing the cheque (in the case of the producer) and in being able to file a report on time (in the case of the consumer). Belief, justification and truth need not come near the entire operation.

Even Gilster's account of assembling knowledge from news feeds stops short of truth, for all his emphasis on critical thinking, seeking to avoid bias, distinguishing hard and soft journalism and so on. The objectives are perspective and balance, and the knowledge assembly process as described by Gilster is much more obviously a matter of a production performance than some unveiling of what already exists. We assemble a point of view, a perspective, an angle on an issue or story. This takes the form of a *further* production, not a capturing or mirroring of some original state of affairs.

Once again, we are not endorsing, advocating or passively accepting the direction of these changes. We are identifying them as matters educationists have not to date taken sufficiently seriously. They prompt many questions. For example, if the accounts of features, patterns and growing significance of social practices involving new ICTs provided here are reasonably accurate, how are we to interpret and enact epistemological principles like commitment to truth, knowledge as a use value, the importance of following arguments and evidence where they lead and so on? What place is left for such principles in educational practices and everyday life, and do we need to shore up space for them? How should educationists respond to the fact that many teachers currently have no clear idea of what to do with the information new ICTs make available to learners? To what extent and in what ways should schools be seeking different operating conceptions of knowledge from those inherent in subject-based learning, and how do we decide what these are? What kind of mix and balance should we be seeking among propositional kinds of knowledge, procedural and performance knowledge, and how can curricula take account of this? What is the proper relationship between how learning is organised in school and 'insider' versions of social practices involving new ICTs occurring in the world beyond school?

Finally, so far as performances and productions within the spaces of the Internet are concerned, it is questionable how far 'knowledge' and 'information' are even the right metaphors for characterising much of what we find there. In many spaces where users are seeking some kind of critical assent to what they produce, it seems likely that constructs and metaphors from traditional rhetoric or literary theory—for example, composition—may serve better than traditional approaches to knowledge and information.

CONCLUSION

The digital age is throwing many of our educational practices and emphases and their underlying epistemological assumptions, beliefs, concepts and substantive theories into doubt. The relationship between what students learn in school and the ways in which they learn it and what people actually do and how they do it in the world beyond school in contexts increasingly mediated by new ICTs has become increasingly tenuous. There are many aspects of this which we have barely taken up here, including the extent to which mindsets associated with physical-industrial space and those associated with cyber-information space may be inherently different and, indeed, incompatible (Tunbridge, 1995; Bigum and Lankshear, 1998). Those aspects we have addressed here suggest that our capacity to understand what will be involved in making informed and principled responses to the conditions of postmodern life in computerised societies will depend greatly on our willingness to problematise and rethink *both* the role and significance of knowledge and truth within existing and emerging social practices and social relations *and* some of our longstanding epistemological investments. We need to rethink these each in relation to the other, and in relation to postmodern means of producing and enacting power. If this chapter does no more than encourage us to explore these claims further, it will have done its job.

2

Promises of Access and Inclusion: Online Education in Africa

ANTHONY LELLIOTT, SHIRLEY PENDLEBURY

AND PENNY ENSLIN

The promises and pitfalls of Information and Communications Technology (ICT) are tied to two quintessential motifs of our times: globalisation and the learning society. Both ideas have a rather different purchase in Africa than they do in Europe, North America and Australasia. So, too, do the promises of information technology.

Globalisation may be described as the process by which societies are connected through rapid, large-scale networks of political, social and economic interaction. Such temporal and spatial processes, James Bohman (1998) suggests, would not be possible without multiple networks of co-ordination and interaction, and a proper supporting communicative infrastructure. In other words, the international communications network is both a feature of globalisation and the very condition of possibility for the process of globalisation.

The learning society is a predominant contemporary myth (Hughes and Tight, 1995). Current political, social, economic and education problems, so the myth goes, may all be addressed through the development of a learning society. Four other interconnected myths sustain the myth of the learning society: the productivity myth; the change myth; the lifelong learning myth; and the learning organisation myth (Hughes and Tight, 1995). Information technology is a common theme in all these myths. To call these ideas myths is not to dismiss them out of hand. Rather it is to recognise both their power and the ways in which they either distort or obscure our understanding. The myth of the learning society, together with its sustaining myths, can at best offer only a partial basis for understanding the complex relations between life, learning and work, and for planning related educational policy and practice (see

Hughes and Tight, 1995). The very notion of learning is under-theorised, indeed taken for granted, in several of these myths and some of their pivotal concepts such as the recognition of prior learning. Yet, as a myth, the idea of a learning society may have a powerful role in enabling governments and industry, as well as communities and individuals, to take education and training seriously in developing alternative visions of a well-functioning society and in leading people through change. Part of the vision, we suggest, is to provide open access to educational goods and so to include those who have previously been excluded. On the face of it, information and communications technology has a crucial role in realising this vision.

Whereas the nature and likely consequences of globalisation are hotly debated (as are the nature and possibility of a learning society), the prevailing view is that the African continent, along with the rest of the developing world, needs wide access to ICT if it is to compete in a global economy (Djamen, 1995). This view is echoed, perhaps more cautiously, in South Africa's White Paper on Science and Technology (Republic of South Africa, 1996), as the following extracts show:

> Social and economic systems 'globalised' by world market forces, the information revolution and new communications technologies, require constant innovative planning and monitoring in order to function optimally . . . The ability to maximise the use of information is now considered to be the single most important factor in deciding the competitiveness of countries as well as their ability to empower their citizens through enhanced access to information. (p. 5)

While this White Paper stresses the economic benefits of information technology, visionaries such as Judith Chapman emphasise the benefits for democracy, social justice and education:

> The vision of a networked society with equal access to knowledge and information, made up of communities and individuals, themselves in charge of their own learning environments, and governments, educators and the private sector working in partnership, is fundamental to the evolution and achievement of a democratic, free, economically stable and just society in the 21st century. (Chapman, 1996, p. 52)

Although Chapman cautions that educational and social change should not be driven solely by technology, she is remarkably enthusiastic about the democratic and educational prospects of technology and about its benefits. Modern technologies are not only cost effective, she argues, but also offer possibilities for new approaches to learning in new kinds of learning organisations. Seductive though it may be, Chapman's interpretation of the political and educational significance and desirability of ICT assumes the perspective of the developed world. It is less appropriate to the developing world, as are assumptions about the effective maintenance and utilisation of information.

In Africa and the rest of the developing world, patterns of inclusion and exclusion, empowerment and disempowerment have differed from those of Europe and North America. So, too, have patterns of educational provision and styles of teaching and learning. Colonialism was a form of forced but only partial inclusion, accompanied by some particularly destructive forms of exclusion. Despite nascent democracy in parts of Africa and pockets of economic development under conditions of relative peace and prosperity, the African continent can hardly be described as a stable post-industrial context. Much of the African continent remains under-developed and poverty-stricken. Civil war and famine are rife and universal basic education a dream yet to be fulfilled. What place has ICT under conditions such as these? Or, to put the question in more graphic terms and from a woman's perspective:

> ...how can a woman be interested in Information and Communication Technologies (ICTs) on a hungry stomach with a child crying on her back for food and another she is carrying in her arms dying because of lack of medical care? (AFR-FEM Listserve, quoted in Ochieng and Radloff, 1998, p. 63)

In this chapter we explore an unavoidable dilemma concerning ICT in Africa—a dilemma from which, we argue, there is no escape. Without access to ICT, societies like those in Africa are in danger of exclusion from global development, although not immune from the effects of globalisation. But access to ICT brings new forms of exclusion and new risks. It also makes stern demands on distributive justice, for any money spent on developing ICT and its necessary systems of support will be money not spent on food, shelter, health-care and basic education.

First, we provide a brief overview of current patterns of access and relative costs. Second, we argue that while ICT might contribute to consolidating democracy in Africa, at the same time it can be used to subvert this process. Economic development and nurturing a strong civil society are the most important prerequisites for the growth of democracy in Africa. Our chapter attends to the second of these prerequisites, leaving the first to authors with a more robust understanding of economics than our own. We examine possible ways in which ICT, in education and more generally, may both promote and undermine the growth of civil society. Third, we question the prevalent touting of ICT as a means of education and argue that it cannot so serve unless there is already a basic level of education—a condition that, in most of Africa, has not been met. In other words, physical access is far from sufficient for epistemological access (Morrow, 1993/4). More seriously, enthralment to ICT may subvert the task of achieving universal basic education in countries that are still well short of this mark. Even where basic education is present, the advantages of ICT are not straightforward. Access to knowledge and understanding is inevitably both constrained and enabled by learning time and space. These are radically reconfigured in ICT and in notions of the learning society, as they are in the very process of globalisation.

TECHNOLOGY ON THE LINE IN AFRICA

A recent example of how ICT has been used successfully in Africa is the application of Geographical Information Systems (GIS) in the 1999 elections in South Africa. GIS is a newly emerging technology which consists of a geographical management and planning tool. It allowed the South African Independent Electoral Commission (IEC) to establish a spatial database for the entire country. Such a database enabled voting districts to be set up on the bases of previously collected census information (Nel, 1999). The IEC states that, without this technological tool, it is unlikely that the elections could have been held in the successful manner they were.

However, of all African countries, South Africa is the most technologically advanced. Jensen (1999a, 1999b) has produced a comprehensive summary of the networking constraints in the African continent. There is an extremely limited telecommunications infrastructure consisting of less than one phone line per 100 people in Southern Africa. Further, it is estimated that Internet users in Africa number approximately 1.5 million. Of these, 1 million are in South Africa, leaving the remaining 500, 000 among the 734 million people on the continent. This equates to one Internet user for every 1500 people compared to a world average of one user for every 38 people, and a North American average of one in every four. Despite this limited connectivity overall, there are only two countries in Africa which do not have any Internet access. These are Congo (Brazzaville) and Eritrea. As this chapter goes to press, Somalia has opened its first Internet service provider (ISP). The installation fee is the equivalent of the monthly income of many Somali families. It is a cruel irony that the most recent country in Africa to be connected is worth less than Bill Gates.

Connectivity *within* African countries is minimal and is usually confined to the capital cities. Direct connectivity between countries within the continent is almost non-existent. This means that for African countries to link with each other via the Internet, they have to connect through a European or American 'hub', sometimes provided as part of an aid package. Generally in Africa, international bandwidth is insufficient due to high cost and lack of digital circuits. This results in slow connections throughout the continent when compared with developed countries.

Access to the Internet is also reliant on service providers (hosts), who provide connections for their clients. In Africa, there is only one service provider for every 30,000 people. The total number of African hosts is approximately that of Latvia, which has a population of only 2.5 million compared to the African population of approximately 780 million. African service providers consist of 0.06% of the world's 43 million hosts. However, the African host growth rate is 36% per six months (measured to December 1998), which is double the world average. In Africa, the cost of access to the Internet is high: 5 hours per month costs approximately $60. Comparative costs in USA and Britain are $6 and $16 respectively. It is important to stress that the cost in Africa is ten times that of the USA, while per capita income is at least ten times *less*.

As would be expected, usage of the Internet is relatively limited. Jensen (1999a) summarises users and usage as follows:

> The average use is one incoming and one outgoing email message per day, most often with people outside the continent rather than between African countries. The World Wide Web, which is now almost synonymous with the Internet in developed countries, is still a relatively under-utilised resource in Africa. Relatively few institutions use the Web to deliver significant quantities of information, and very few use it for their activities, other than to provide descriptive and contact information. While many government ministries have access to email, very few have a Web-site. With the exception of national (as opposed to provincial) government in South Africa, there is little government use of the Internet for administrative purposes.

The majority of Internet users belong to non-government organisations (NGOs), private companies and universities. Most users are well-educated males and in South Africa belong to the previously advantaged sector of the population. Universities initially pioneered the development of Internet usage across the continent. However, even now, full access is usually restricted to staff. Early in 1999, only 20 countries had universities with full Internet access. Schools have even less access than universities and most is restricted to private schools.

DEMOCRACY ON THE LINE

> . . . recent sociological analyses of the process of globalisation emphasise the two-sidedness of the political phenomena that it produces: it presents new opportunities, as well as unparalleled risks;

it opens up prospects for new forms of governance, as well as threatens existing democracy to the core. Although globalisation spreads through the escalation of power in larger and larger social systems and institutions, it has also produced an increase in the power of transnational civil society. (Bohman, 1998, p. 200)

If globalisation has—as Bohman puts it—an upside and a backside, ICT offers both a means of joining commercial networks for economic gain, and the danger of being sucked into a globalised market in which neo-colonial interests are served, which in turn can deepen the politico-economic crisis in Africa, so undermining democracy's fragile foothold on the continent.

Recent developments in democratic theory reflect on the implications of ICT for promoting new dimensions of, and new opportunities for, democracy. Primary among these new dimensions is the opening of deliberative space both within and across nation states. Where new technologies prevail, even Benjamin Barber's strong democracy seems possible (Barber, 1984).

Can an international democratic movement be strengthened by ICT? John Dryzek (1999), exploring the 'discursive sources of international order', explores several sources of discursive democratic control which are open to international actors, showing how campaigns on biopiracy and whaling are waged in 'a transnational civil society' in which fairly unrestrained communication between actors is possible. Here networks can play a role in fostering deliberation unconstrained by the state. In spite of well-founded fears that the Internet is a male preserve and the danger that women will be marginalised in the area of ICT, Ochieng and Radloff (1998) survey some of the ways in which women are making increasing use of ICT, both in Africa and globally. ICT provides tools for disseminating information, participating in decision-making and for mobilisation. For example, at the Fourth World Conference on Women in Beijing in 1995, delegates were able to use electronic media networks to pass information back to organisations in their countries and to receive responses from them. In Africa a network called the Gender in Africa Information Network (GAIN) provides an 'electronic meeting place' by linking networks across the continent, collecting and disseminating information on gender issues. Some such networks set out to provide training in the use of ICT for communication. In developing countries in general, ICTs are being used to track malaria, and are assisting through email discussion groups in promoting women's reproductive health and in combating HIV/AIDS. Beyond these examples of environmental, gender equity and health campaigns, to what extent can such electronic democratic fora be used to challenge state power and how broad a public can they include? Are they bound to remain limited campaigns involving a relatively small number of people or might they have some efficacy in building civil society?

The growth of democracy in Africa is hindered by its history of colonialism, dependency and post-colonial political repression. The prerequisites for the growth of a democratic public sphere in Africa include the creation of a freer and more vibrant public sphere. Can ICT contribute to this project, both within the African continent itself and by enabling African democrats to join a global public sphere, which could offer alliances with activists and organisations? While Bohman warns that 'we are quite far from anything like a global public sphere, especially with regard to the political institutions and associations in civil society that might support it' (*ibid.*, p. 201), he concedes that the creation of a cosmopolitan global public sphere, with forms of publicity broader than the European model, is possible. His caveat is that it is possible only on condition that the organisation and institutions of civil society already exist.

But the forms of publicity introduced by global media structured around anonymous and large-scale networks 'do not establish the same degree of responsiveness, reflexivity and mutual accountability typical of communication in the public sphere' (*ibid.*, p. 210).

Electronic media produce a different kind of public space from speech or writing. The type of large audience created by electronic media is unstructured and less likely to require public reason. Its audience is more liable to anonymity, both to one another and to the authors of the messages conveyed by the media. Electronic communication creates a social space characterised by anonymity and a lack of responsiveness and accountability; a lack which extends to accountability about the networks themselves. This is a serial space, in which individuals are interconnected but do not interact as members of a communal forum, rather than a public sphere:

> We can expect that under proper conditions and with the support of democratic institutions, a vibrant public sphere will expand and become open to and connected with other public spheres. Members will develop the capacities of public reason to cross and negotiate boundaries and differences between groups, persons and cultures. Certainly, the global media may help foster this process. However, the mere availability of widely distributed messages, texts and communication formed in other public spheres is not the same as the creation of contexts of mutual responsiveness and accountability required for the self-conscious identification of a public that crosses boundaries of social and cultural space. (Bohman, 1998, p. 213)

We contend that it is more important to develop civil society and the public sphere in Africa than to get its citizens into ICT. Until African countries have been able to create 'contexts of mutual responsiveness and accountability', not only is ICT unlikely to foster an extensive civil society, but it could be used by governments and the military as an instrument of repression. Education has a crucial role in developing contexts of mutual responsiveness and accountability. Apart from basic literacy and numeracy, citizens need the capacity for critical judgement and deliberation for democracy to grow. Under the current conditions of dependency and demoralisation in much of Africa, all these are demanding tasks.

EDUCATION ON THE LINE

Judith Chapman rightly suggests that the question to be asked about ICT is 'how society can exploit technology in order to provide the most effective education for a democratic, socially inclusive and economically advanced community' (Chapman, 1996, p. 51). The betterment of society, then, becomes the criterion for whether, when and how to use technology in education. As we have indicated, with some risk of generalisation, Africa is in dire need of societal betterment. With a few exceptions, the countries of Africa are undemocratic, economically unstable and both excluded and excluding. Within countries, the practices of social exclusion run along the lines of class, ethnicity, gender, religion, language and location.

Not to put too fine a point on it, education in Africa is in a mess. A selection of facts and figures from a recent needs assessment study of countries in eastern and southern Africa serves to illustrate the point (see Chisholm *et al.*, 1998). Angola, probably the worst off of these countries, spent 10% of its national budget on education in 1990 and only 4% in 1997. Over the past decade enrolments have fallen sharply. In 1993, school enrolment was estimated to be about 53% of children in the age-range 5–14, with average dropout and failure rates estimated at 50%. Tanzania has the lowest rate of secondary school enrolment in eastern and southern Africa—only 5% of the relevant age group. The Musoma Resolution of 1974 committed the Tanzanian government to achieving universal primary education for all children between the ages of 7 and 13 by 1997. By the early 1980s the goal was well within reach with a 90% enrolment but since then there has been a sharp decline both in primary enrolments and in educational quality. HIV/AIDS has been a significant factor in primary and secondary enrolment patterns, as well as in the dwindling pool of qualified teachers. In Botswana, one of the more prosperous and stable countries in Africa, 90% of primary age children were enrolled at school in 1993 and in 1994 there was an 80% progression from primary to junior secondary school. However, only about 10% of those who complete primary school gain university entry. Despite its economic prosperity, wealth is unevenly distributed in Botswana, with nearly 47% of the population living below the poverty datum line in 1994.

The language of educational policy in these and other African countries reflects the new global scripts of social justice and economic efficiency, partly as a result of the power of western democracies, and partly as a consequence of dependency (*ibid.*). It is a language 'that speaks universally to local problems' through its commitment to access and equity, to social justice and the right to education and, simultaneously, to quality and efficiency. Chisholm and her co-authors warn that despite its power to address educational problems, this language also 'hides the enormous difficulties of providing and assessing access, equity, quality and efficiency' (*ibid.*, p. 19). In particular, they worry about how such language, and the policies that use it, either deny or obliterate the complex and differentiated meaning of local needs and experiences. One of the effects of globalisation is that African countries that were alive with educational experimentation in the 1960s 'now search for the eldorado of western innovation' (*ibid.*, p. 19).

Many of the promises of ICT, like those of lifelong learning, come couched in the language of access and equity, appealing both to social justice and to efficiency. On its own, this gives us no reason for rejecting the promises as false or misleading. Information technology clearly does have the capacity under appropriate circumstances to reach large numbers of learners through a few well-qualified teachers using materials developed by specialists. In places where both books and qualified teachers are scarce, ICT may indeed have the capacity to provide learning resources where there are none. Its capacities are especially alluring in curriculum areas like mathematics and the natural sciences which are widely valued for their contribution to a stable economy, yet notoriously ill catered for in schools throughout Africa.

Nonetheless, in many respects, the promises are both false and misleading. They are false because the prerequisites for an educationally sound and inclusive access to ICT can be met by very few African countries at present. They are misleading because they may divert attention from other more pressing concerns and other more viable solutions. The gung-ho version of ICT in education shares some of the features that Hughes and Tight (1995) ascribe to myth. It offers a simplistic 'truth' that 'captures the imagination in a populist and transmittable form', yet in practice its claims are neither self-evident nor strong. Gung-ho promises for ICT, like those underpinning the myth of the learning society, proffer a superficially simple solution to complex economic, educational, political and social issues. Whatever their mobilising powers—and they are no doubt considerable—myths can also block solutions to problems. Once a 'consensual idealisation' is seen as the solution it may serve to deny the possibility of other or better solutions (Hughes and Tight, 1995, p. 300).

Consider, first, the prerequisites for educationally sound and inclusive access to and use of ICT. Baldly stated, inclusive access requires that every educable person has access to ICT regardless of gender, class, language, locale or age (with the obvious exception of the very young and, possibly, the very old). More is involved than access to hardware. As Chapman argues, inclusive education requires new information technologies to open up and increase access to educational establishments and agencies for open learning and dual-mode instruction. Obviously this does not mean a computer for every household. What it does require is a properly-equipped learning centre within walking or cycling distance from every household, no matter how remote. The telecottages piloted in parts of Africa as well as Asia provide a model (Mansell and Wehn, 1998). This is still a long way from Chapman's ideal, in which educational pathways and institutions are not rooted in space and time but could be accessible electronically 'from anywhere and available at any time' (Chapman, 1996, p. 53). While institutions constituted by a mix of physical and remote access points could indeed meet the needs of groups previously constrained from furthering their education, this is much more likely in developed countries than in war-torn, economically unstable countries in Africa.

As we have indicated, physical and institutional access are important prerequisites for inclusion in the educational use of ICT. We will not consider here the many obstacles to meeting these prerequisites. Instead let us assume that the provision of physical access is feasible, if not now then some time in the foreseeable future, and if not in all African countries then at least in those that are relatively stable. The point is that physical access is not sufficient for epistemological access (Morrow, 1993/4). Charles Taylor's well-known argument against negative liberty is pertinent here (Taylor, 1979). Where people lack the capacities to exercise an opportunity, the opportunity is empty. At the very least, epistemological access to the educational goods of ICT requires students (and their teachers) to become computer literate as well as conventionally literate and numerate. They should be able to handle information technology at a level appropriate to different fields of study and be equipped to employ it appropriately to further their cognitive development in the future. In any case, information on its own is not the same as education (Marshall, 1998b).

Epistemological access is enabled or impeded by the placement and organisation of learning activities in space and time (Pendlebury, 1998). Educational practices, like other social practices, are conducted within spatio-temporal settings that are partly constitutive of the actions and interactions that occur within them. ICT radically reconfigures space and time, creating an extended present which softens the boundaries between public and private, between local, national and international. It delineates a new and much more open kind of pedagogical space in which learners and learning, teachers and teaching, all take on new identities. For instance, Chapman speaks of 'new possibilities offered by the emphasis on student-centred and self-directed modes of progression' (Chapman, 1996, p. 52). She also suggests that time-delayed exchanges by electronic mail and computer conferencing will enhance access because many types of students seem to participate more fully in learning opportunities offered in this medium. This construes learners as responsible, self-directed individuals who have already acquired habits of critical judgement. It is not clear how educational programmes that use ICT will deal with longstanding habits of learning bred under the authoritarian and narrowly didactic approaches that are characteristic of schooling in many parts of Africa. Little attention seems to have been given to the question of how best to prepare teachers in Africa for the educationally-sound use of ICT.

As a form of mass communication, ICT involves the institutionalised production and diffusion of symbolic goods. While extending the availability of such goods in space and time, it also constitutes a fundamental break between their production and reception (Thompson, 1990). We think this break has quite profound implications for the educational deployment of ICT, especially where the context of reception differs radically from the context of production, as is the case of most African countries using ICT. Much of the content and style of the materials produced in developed countries is unsuited to social and cultural traditions in the least-developed countries and may have the effect of excluding people who are already severely disadvantaged. Mansell and Wehn (1998) acknowledge the usefulness of ICT in overcoming such obstacles as geographic remoteness and scarcity of teachers, but warn of major difficulties associated with ICT use in the least-developed countries. These include conflicting agendas in curriculum content and about the cultural and linguistic dominance of the Western English-speaking world. To date ICT applications for education in developing countries have had three serious weaknesses: they have been unsuited to the technological and organisational infrastructure of the countries concerned, they have been over-specified in terms of their technological sophistication and they have been insufficiently focused on the problem-solving environment (Mansell and Wehn, 1998). The educational possibilities of ICT are constrained or enabled both by the technology and the curriculum it transmits and by the context in which it is received. One of the challenges is to ensure that the 'world's stocks of information' are combined effectively with local knowledge. Another is to transcend mere information and to transform it into a range of learning activities that meet educational ends. There is also the challenge of institutional change in places where schools and other institutions are only minimally, if at all, functional. In the absence of institutional change, ICTs are likely to be used within traditional educational programmes by traditional and often poorly qualified teachers. Under such circumstances, ICTs are unlikely to make very much difference to the educational opportunities of marginalised people.

In considering the possibility, viability and desirability of ICT as a means of education in Africa it is crucial to examine how political, social and individual interests are differently served by different patterns of deploying technology in schools and other institutions concerned with education and training. As we have suggested, debates about ICT in education pivot on much more than technical and financial capacity. Writing about the use of computers in schools, C. Paul Olson notes that 'the computer as a tool *does fundamentally reorganise material relationships and organisations of production* and our thoughts about what production is' (Olson, 1987, p. 83). Over a decade later his arguments, we think, are pertinent to the wider set of debates about ICT in Africa, especially his claims about the relationship between new technology, new social forms and older patterns of success and failure:

> With the retooling for a new technological season, some social forms are sure to change too. But the newness can be overdone. The *patterns* of older players often stay the same and the strong are better equipped to play than the weak. The societal track record should give us clues as to who will maneuver what and how they will fare. (Olson, 1987, p. 185)

CONCLUDING REMARKS

In conclusion, we turn once more to Chapman's vision of a learning society which is both just and economically stable. 'The vision of a networked society with equal access to knowledge and information . . . is fundamental to the evolution and achievement of a democratic, free, economically just society in the 21st century' (Chapman, 1996,

p. 52). We do not doubt the necessity of education for democracy, nor do we doubt the importance of ICT in shaping the global economy. We accept that ICT, effectively deployed, can contribute to economic development in Africa's least-developed countries. But we worry that idealistic uptake of the idea of a networked society obscures the very real challenges involved in accomplishing inclusive education and a sustainable civil society in most African countries. It also obscures the dilemmas of justice that must be addressed by nation states with severely limited resources and populations living below the poverty datum line. ICT can only contribute to education and democratisation in Africa if social capacity is developed to a sufficient level on the continent. The context of reception needs to become a context of production that is responsive to local requirements and accountable to citizens. This in turn calls for teachers and citizens who have the skills, understanding and confidence to engage with national policy and strategy deliberation and implementation. In the absence of these conditions, the educational and democratic goods of ICT are a chimera.

3

Media Philosophy and Media Education in the Age of the Internet

MIKE SANDBOTHE

When, as a philosopher, you concern yourself with issues of media theory, you are often confronted with the largely rhetorical question as to what philosophy has to do with media. That logical, ethical, aesthetic and epistemological issues, or questions concerning the philosophy of science and of language, are genuine philosophical questions seems self-evident to us today. The neologisms 'philosophical media theory' or 'media philosophy', however, sound unaccustomed, irritating, suspect. To some they may even appear to be a *contradictio in adjecto*. In the following considerations I would like to demonstrate that in the conditions of the transformation of media currently taking place it is important and meaningful to construe the question of media as a philosophical question. My considerations are organised in three sections. In the first section some fundamental sets of media-educational problems with regard to the Internet will be outlined, to whose solution media-philosophical reflections can make an essential contribution. In the second section, two different conceptions of the currently evolving discipline of media philosophy will be introduced. Finally, in the third section, it will be shown how these conceptions, if they are sensibly combined with one another, could make a fundamental theoretical contribution to the clarification of important problems arising today in a media-educational perspective.

THE CHALLENGES TO MEDIA EDUCATION THROUGH THE CURRENT MEDIA TRANSFORMATION

A transition is currently taking place from an educational culture shaped by the printed word and spoken speech to a form of educational practice in which working in the Internet's multimedia environment assumes central importance. This transition puts in question four idealised basic assumptions in the self-understanding of traditional education. The *first* basic assumption is that the knowledge to be conveyed in schools and universities is to be localised, detached from its concrete contexts of use, and relocated in a specifically academic realm of theoretical knowledge transfer. The *second* basic assumption is that lessons are to take place as communication among people who are present. The voice here appears as the distinguishing medium of an educational transfer process which is conceived of as face-to-face communication. Within the framework of this process—according to the *third* basic assumption—teachers are vested with the authority of omnicompetent knowledge administrators. They play the role of living encyclopaedias, they speak as if in print, and have a preordained pigeon-hole, a binding definition and a fixed evaluation to hand for every question and every piece of knowledge. The *fourth* basic assumption follows from the preceding three. It relates to the structure of the knowledge that is to be taught or learned. In the conditions of traditional educational culture this knowledge is understood as a stock of established facts, standing in a hierarchically arranged context of order, and is represented paradigmatically by the institution of the library catalogue system.

In the context of debates on educational philosophy throughout the twentieth century, all four assumptions have been repeatedly discussed and partially problematised from varying perspectives. Nonetheless they may be considered as the implicit guidelines for actual educational practice in most schools and universities in the USA and Europe. Under the influence of the media transformation that is currently taking place, it is practice itself which problematises the basic assumptions mentioned above, and in a sense directly relevant to school and university. Once educational activities reorient themselves to the dynamics of knowledge itself, as found in the new medium of the Internet, educators begin to need a more experimental understanding of their own practice, within whose framework they can scrutinise the basic assumptions of an educational culture shaped by the world of the printed book and oral culture.

The *first* of the four reconstructed basic assumptions of traditional educational culture—the notion of a closed realm of theoretical knowledge—is put in question in the open semiotic world of the Internet in two ways. This occurs, on the one hand, with regard to the physical space of knowledge, literally the classroom or seminar room. As soon as teachers begin to incorporate the Internet into work with students or pupils, the school class or seminar group enters a virtual space that transcends the limits of the class or seminar room. On the other hand, there are alterations in the symbolic knowledge space brought about by this transcending of borders. The complex networked character and unobservable intertwinements of theoretical knowledge, as well as its pragmatic binding to practical contexts of usage, clearly come into view in the light of experience in the Internet (cf. Sandbothe, 1996).

The *second* basic assumption of traditional educational culture also becomes problematic with the use of the Internet in education. In conditions of Internet-oriented teaching and learning, face-to-face communication no longer appears to be distinguished in some particular way as the model or paradigm of educational communication. Rather, synchronous and asynchronous communications possibilities between people who are not present come along—in the form of mailing lists, news boards, IRC, MUDs and MOOs—assuming equal value with conversation between people who are present and relativising its traditional primacy as the paradigm for the mediation of sense and meaning. The experiences of computer-mediated communication have a twofold feedback effect on face-to-face communication itself—on the one side decentralising, on the other revalidating it.

This has consequences for the *third* basic assumption. The incorporation of the Internet into lessons leads to a transformation of the educational communicative structure that furthermore affects the inner constitution of the face-to-face conversational relationship of conventional lessons. This happens in the form of decentralisation, such that teachers no longer stand at the hub of the learning situation as omnicompetent knowledge administrators. The restrictedness and short half-life of the teacher's individual knowledge stock is immediately made clear to the students through the Internet's collective knowledge network. This calls into question the traditional legitimation of the teacher's authority and the classical structure of direct lessons. Teachers no longer appear to be sovereign administrators of a hierarchically organised framework of knowledge, which is to be imparted in direct teaching. Instead, faced with the 'information overload' manifested on the Internet, they acquire new educational responsibilities for evaluation and communicatively pragmatic navigational tasks.

The notion of a hierarchically structured framework of knowledge is also questioned by the Internet, and with this the *fourth* basic assumption of traditional educational culture. In its place we find the experience of a hypertexually networked, interactively evolving and potentially infinite referential context of graphical, pictorial and acoustic signs. No intrinsic order or immanent systematism is discernible which would unite these data to a comprehensive bibliographical knowledge cosmos, such as shaped the world of ideas of the Gutenberg age. Instead there is a continually increasing demand on users to introduce order to the data chaos themselves, relying on reflexive judgement and using the corresponding Net tools (bookmarks, search engines, intelligent agents and so on). Knowledge is changing from supposedly being an objectively pre-given stock of intrinsically ordered facts to a constantly changing artefact of intersubjectively mediated judgement. It proves to be a process, open to constant revision, and in whose realisation the skills of associative networking, independent evaluation and pragmatic coupling to individual and collective interest are foremost.

How can the foundational principles of an Internet-oriented educational culture be developed in the light of the transformations described? How is one to secure the continued commitment of this new culture to the democratic ideals of political Enlightenment, whilst improving and extending the conditions for realising that commitment? How is the realm of educational knowledge to be conceived when we no longer apprehend it as a closed academic realm of theoretical representation of knowledge, which cognitively mirrors or constructs reality? How is educational communication to be understood when it is no longer to be characterised by the priority of spoken language and the guiding function of face-to-face conversation? How is the altered constitution of the authority of teachers to be described, when teachers can no longer be legitimated as opaque arbiters of selection and authoritative evaluation, personalising a preordained canon of knowledge in an institution-specific manner, and making this appear as an ordered and examinable system of factual matters? And finally, in what new way is the structure of knowledge itself to be understood in the changed media conditions? What is knowledge if it is not a system of hierarchically ordered facts? How do sense and meaning come about in a networked world in which there is no Archimedean point of reference, no ultimate reference text, no uniform systematism?

It is the task of media philosophy to respond to fundamental theoretical questions of this type, which form the point of departure for the development of media education in the Internet age. Media philosophy has to develop concepts which can help provide answers and open new horizons of action. Until now media philosophy has hardly any standing as an independent discipline within the framework of academic philosophy. But both in Europe and the USA there are a multitude of endeavours suggesting that this will change in the future. In the following pages, I will be concerned to move on from already existing departure points for the development of a contemporary media philosophy, and to relate these to one another in a productive manner such that fundamental philosophical principles for an Internet-oriented educational culture can be developed.

To this end I will draw upon two differing conceptions of media philosophy which at first glance appear heterogeneous and incompatible: theoreticist and pragmatist conceptions of media philosophy. Both emerge from philosophical camps that determine contemporary thinking in a decisive manner. The theoreticist conception of media philosophy was developed by Jacques Derrida in the framework of his deconstructionism. The basic ideas of the pragmatist conception of media philosophy have their origin in the work of the founder of neopragmatism, Richard Rorty, including Rorty's pragmatist reinterpretation of Donald Davidson, the avant-garde thinker of analytic philosophy.[1]

Derrida's deconstructionist media philosophy can help us to understand that the current media transformation does not undermine the constitution of sense and meaning, but rather allows the laws already valid for face-to-face communication to become transparent. Against this background the American computer sociologist Sherry Turkle has spoken of the way in which the Internet brings basic ideas of philosophical deconstruction 'down to earth' (Turkle, 1995, p. 17). By this is meant that through the forms of communication characteristic of the Internet, the epistemological insights and intuitions of deconstructionism are increasingly becoming an implicit constituent of common sense. To get to the bottom of the media-philosophical significance of these transformations taking place at the level of our everyday epistemology, it is helpful to review the media-philosophical essence of Derrida's thinking.

The same applies to the media-philosophical implications of the neopragmatism founded by Rorty. The Internet not only allows sense and meaning to appear in a different epistemological light: at the same time, our dealings with interactive data networks also lead to a reassessment of the status and the function of sense and meaning itself. Knowledge no longer appears primarily to be a copy or construction of a reality that is to be cognised, but turns out in its pragmatic function to be a tool for the active and experimental changing of reality and shaping of the world. With recourse to Davidson, Rorty has suggested trying to understand our theories and vocabularies as means that serve to optimise our interaction with our environment in an intelligent manner. As the goal on the horizon for this interaction, he emphasises the idea of a gradual improvement and extension of the democratic form of life, which for us today is binding precisely on account of its contingency. Both aspects of Rorty's neopragmatism make an important contribution to the reconstruction of the media-philosophical transformations that are taking shape at the common sense level in the Internet age.

In the following pages, I will demonstrate how the deconstructionist constitution of sense and meaning on the one side, and the pragmatic-political project of democratic Enlightenment on the other, are to be conceived of as fitting together. To this end, the varying conceptions of media philosophy which can be reconstructed with recourse to Derrida on one side and Rorty on the other will be introduced in more detail.

MEDIA PHILOSOPHY BETWEEN THEORETICISM AND PRAGMATISM

In the context of contemporary media-philosophical reflections, we can distinguish two different conceptions of media philosophy. On one side, media philosophy is understood as a new fundamental discipline within the canon of academic philosophy, linking onto the foundational projects formulated in the nineteenth and twentieth centuries by epistemology, philosophy of science and philosophy of language. On the other, the project of media philosophy is linked with a new orientation of philosophical self-understanding that Rorty has called the 'pragmatic turn' (Rorty, 1979, p. 149). By this is meant the transition to a form of philosophical activity whose focus is no longer the theoreticist question of the representational or constructivist reference of our linguistic cognitive achievements to reality, but instead the pragmatic question of the utility of our thinking in contexts of action, contexts to be determined morally, politically and socially. Both conceptions of media philosophy can be reconstructed by reference to their relation to the 'linguistic turn' (Bergmann, 1954, p. 106; cf. also Rorty, 1967) taken by modern philosophy in the twentieth century.

The central claim of the theoreticist conception undercuts the linguistic turn by media-theoretical considerations, and sets it on deeper foundations. Two foundational movements can be distinguished: one horizontal and one vertical. The *horizontal* undercuts the linguistic turn by placing a plurality of pictorial, graphic, tactile, motoric, acoustic and other semiotic systems on an equal footing with spoken language, itself the focus of linguistic philosophising. These systems are presented as other and further dimensions of mediative constitution of meaning. The *vertical* foundational movement undercuts the linguistic turn by consideration of the material constitution of the media-based sign systems in which human beings generate meaning and interpret reality, a material constitution obscured by linguistic philosophers. Both strategies for a media-philosophical deepening of the linguistic turn can be paradigmatically illustrated using the example of Jacques Derrida's *Of Grammatology* (Derrida, 1998; French original: 1967).

I begin with the vertical foundational movement. The basic critical thesis of Derrida's major early work relates to the special status spoken language has always implicitly enjoyed in occidental thinking, eventually quite explicitly in the enactment of the linguistic turn in philosophy. On Derrida's view, the upshot is the thesis, a thesis to be media-theoretically problematised, of the philosophical priority of spoken language. Speech has this priority because of the specific materiality or, better, the supposed immateriality of that medium in which speech takes place. In his analysis of the medium of the voice, Derrida proceeds in two steps. Each of these two steps thematises a different aspect of the mediative materiality of spoken language. The first step is concerned with its obviously phonic character, the second with its hidden written signature.

To highlight the specific peculiarity of the phonic character of spoken language, Derrida emphasises that when we articulate a sentence, we not only externalise what is said as a message for a partner in communication, but always hear and understand the articulated sentence ourselves too. Derrida calls this phenomenon, characteristic of the human voice, a 'system of "hearing (understanding)-oneself-speaking"' (*ibid.*, p. 7). According to Derrida, occidental philosophy's one-sided orientation towards the phenomenology of this system means that the medium of 'phonic substance' in which speech takes place appears 'as the nonexterior, nonmundane, therefore nonempirical or noncontingent signifier' (*ibid.*, p. 7f.). In this interpretation however, the actual externalisation—which occurs not only in the act of communication addressed to a conversational partner, but in the very instance of hearing and understanding oneself speak—is blended out, replaced by hypostatisation of an inner and immediate presence of meaning. This hypostatisation, criticised by Derrida as 'phonocentric' (*ibid.*, p. 12f.), systematically obscures the mediative complexity that is proper to human speech. The second step of the vertical foundational movement reveals this complexity by displaying spoken language's hidden written signature.

'Phonocentrism' implies a degradation of writing as a supplementary 'signifier of the signifier' or a tertiary 'sign of a sign' (*ibid.*, pp. 7, 43). In these conditions the written sign is understood as a merely technical representation of the phonic sign that itself is understood as closely related to a supposed media-neutral realm of pure meaning. Derrida takes this phonocentric definition of writing, and uses it in a deconstructionist manner as a model for the functioning of spoken language itself. On this basis one obtains a 'modification of the concept of writing' which Derrida speaks of as 'generalized writing' or 'arche-writing' (*ibid.*, pp. 55, 56). 'Arche-writing' denotes a semiotic (referential) structure, in which the sense of any sign—and therefore the sense of the spoken word as well, the meaning of *logos*—is a function of its relation to other signs taken as signs of signs of signs and so on (without any reference to a media-neutral domain of pure meaning). This relational semiotic referential structure, which Derrida also calls '*différance*' (Derrida, 1982), at the same time serves for him as the point of departure for the second, horizontal foundational movement.

According to Derrida the word 'writing' is used in contemporary thinking 'to designate not only the physical gestures of literal pictographic or ideographic inscription, but also the totality of what makes it possible; and also, beyond the signifying face, the signified face itself. And thus we say "writing" for all that gives rise to an inscription in general, whether it is literal or not and even if what it distributes in space is alien to the order of the voice: cinematography, choreography, of course, but also pictorial, musical, sculptural "writing"' (*ibid.*, p. 9). The internal logic and independence of the pictorial, graphic, tactile, motoric, acoustic and other semiotic systems, but also their equal primordiality and intertwining, are the focus of the 'horizontal' move which Derrida carries out, after having deepened 'vertically' the linguistic turn. Both moves undercut phonocentrism by deciphering the conditions of possibility for the constitution of meaning as the interplay of differences—an interplay due to the formal figure of *différance*, which in itself has no meaning, since it results from the material contingency of those media in which and as which it occurs.

I call the problem area taken up and further developed in a deconstructionist manner by Derrida 'theoreticist' because it abstracts from all *concrete* contexts of interest and all *determinate* targets set by human communities. The theoreticist demarcation of the tasks of media philosophy addresses the constitution of our understanding of both self and the world, and hence a domain beyond all practical horizons of utility, a domain that is supposed to produce, found or legitimise those horizons. In contrast to this theoreticist version, the pragmatist definition of the tasks of media philosophy emerges from culturally and historically given practical contexts of interest and socio-political targets. This can be illustrated by taking as examples selected considerations set out by Richard Rorty, the American figurehead of neopragmatism.[2]

Unlike Derrida, Rorty is not concerned with the deconstructionist *deepening* of the linguistic turn. Instead, following on from Donald Davidson, Rorty takes the linguistic turn more as an occasion for a change of subject and a side-stepping of the issues of the epistemological tradition in their linguistic reformulation. He does this by developing a pragmatic vocabulary (Rorty, 1991b). In the conditions of the linguistic turn as further developed by Sellers and Quine, linguistic competence was apprehended as the ability to form content, and hence to individuate things and identify them, within a differentially structured and holistically conceived conceptual network, or semiotic scheme. Davidson confronts this view with the provocative thesis that 'there is no such thing as a language' (Davidson, 1996, p. 475). This radical implication follows from Davidson's rejection of the 'dualism of scheme and content, of organising system and something waiting to be organized' (Davidson, 1984, p. 189). According to Davidson this dualism can be traced back to Kant. It underlies not only the different readings of the linguistic turn from Carnap and Bergmann through to Quine and Sellars, but is even presupposed in Derrida's general semiotics of *différance*. Against this Davidson suggests erasing the 'boundary between knowing a language and knowing our way around in the world generally' (Davidson, 1996, p. 475) and 'thinking of language as a kind of know-how' (Rorty, 1994a, p. 976), as a collection of pragmatic instruments allowing us to interact with other people and the non-human environment.

Following Davidson, Rorty pleads in favour of an instrumental concept of media. Media are not, however, to be reduced to neutral tools in the mere transmission of pre-existing information, as in the phonocentric tradition criticised by Derrida. Rather, the determination of the function of media is extended beyond the narrow realm (specific to theoreticism) of the conditions of possibility of knowledge to the wider realm of human action. In this sense Rorty emphasises: 'For even if we agree that languages are not media of representation [of external reality—M.S.] or expression [of inner reality—M.S.], they will remain media of communication, tools for social interaction, ways of tying oneself up with other human beings' (Rorty, 1989a, p. 41). Human action is understood by Rorty in the practical and political terms of the goods and aspirations according to which people in the Western democracies have learned increasingly to organise their public conduct in the last two hundred years, in spite of all relapses. These goods and aspirations are the socio-political ideals characteristic of the Enlightenment's political project, those of an increase of solidarity and a decrease of cruelty and humiliation in human coexistence (Rorty, 1991a, 1994b, especially pp. 67–89; 1998b).

Against the contingent, but for us today increasingly binding, background of Euro-American liberalism, the pragmatist determination of the tasks of media philosophy answers to the efforts of democratic societies 'to incorporate ever more people in their own society' (Rorty, 1994b, p. 80). In order to increase solidarity and decrease cruelty and humiliation, there is no need for a profound philosophical moral justification. For 'the moral development of the individual and the moral progress of the human species as a whole is based on the reshaping of human selves so that the multitude of relationships constitutive of these selves becomes ever more comprehensive' (Rorty, 1994b, p. 76). In Rorty's view the media play an important role in the pragmatic implementation of this project of democratic universalisation. Central to this is the practical efficacy of narrative media such as 'the novel, the movie, and the TV program' (Rorty, 1989a, p. xvi). Rorty is concerned here primarily with the contents, the concrete narratives offered by the media. They are to contribute to bringing forward the 'process of coming to see other human beings as "one of us" rather than as "them"' (Rorty, 1989a, p. xvi).

If one attempts to go beyond Rorty, making use of his comments on media for an exacting conception of pragmatist media philosophy, a modified view of the entire fabric of different types of media results. The system of media in a broad sense comprises sensuous perceptive media (such as space and time), semiotic communications media (such as images, language, writing and music) as well as technical transmission media (for example, print, radio, television and the Internet).[3] Whereas the emphasis of the linguistic, grammatological or picture-theoretical research of theoreticist media theories is mostly in the realm of semiotic communications media (or in the realm of spatio-temporal perceptive media), pragmatist media philosophy accentuates the peripheral realm of technical transmission media. From a pragmatist perspective, the media-political shaping of precisely this outer realm proves to be the central point of departure for those who want to foster long-term changes in the realm of perceptive and communications media.

The close definition of the relationship between philosophy and politics expressed in these considerations takes a decisive step beyond Rorty. In Rorty's view the public–political sphere of technical transmission media is to be sharply delineated from the esoteric vocabularies of philosophy. Philosophical vocabularies are, according to Rorty, to be understood as their author's private self-creation projects, about whose relevance for common sense little can be said. And if philosophical vocabularies do after all find their way to the common man once in a while, which according to Rorty can indeed happen in exceptional cases, then this takes place 'in the long run' (Rorty, 1993, p. 445), that is, on the horizon of historical developments which are to be measured on the temporal scale of centuries. In the age of the new media technologies, corrections need to be made to this conservative assessment of the meaning of philosophy. For, although Rorty himself notes in the first chapter of *Contingency, Irony, and Solidarity* the 'process of European linguistic practices changing at a faster and faster rate' (Rorty, 1989a, p. 7), this in fact leads to faster and more radical transformation of the philosophical fundaments of common sense than Rorty is prepared to admit (see Sandbothe, 1998b, 2000c).

If one interprets the technical media of modernity as machines with whose help whole societies can acquire new ways of perceptual and semiotic world-making in relatively short time, then it becomes clear that media-political issues have genuine philosophical dimensions and that philosophical media theories have eminently political aspects. Although pragmatic media philosophy in this exacting sense distances itself from the theoreticist programme of providing philosophical foundations for our socio-political contexts of action, this does not mean that it abstains from philosophical depth of focus altogether. Rather than this abstention (suggested in Rorty's plea for a 'post-philosophical culture' (Rorty, 1982, p. xi)), it attempts to use the analytical instruments made available by Derrida's theoreticist media philosophy in a pragmatic fashion. The project of a media philosophy that integrates the two approaches in this way aims at making the media-induced alterations in common sense accessible to experimental research. Thus, these mediative changes in our everyday epistemology can be related to the political–practical purposes of a democratic shaping of human coexistence. What this looks like in detail will now be demonstrated paradigmatically, with regard to the media-educational questions set out at the beginning.

MEDIA-PHILOSOPHICAL FOUNDATIONS OF AN INTERNET-ORIENTED EDUCATIONAL CULTURE

The graphic user interface of the hypertextually structured World Wide Web stands at the heart of the Internet today. The World Wide Web is to be distinguished from the older Internet services, which are linear textual applications and include services ranging from email and Talk, Net News and mailing lists, through to Internet Relay Chat (IRC), MUDs and MOOs (see below and in Sandbothe, 2000b). I will begin with linear textual services and concentrate on the synchronous communications services of MUDs and MOOs (Rheingold, 1993). MUD is the abbreviation for Multi-User Dungeon, which is a virtual gaming 'haunt'. A number of participants log in simultaneously to a fictional text-based game landscape in order to collect so-called 'experience points' in combat with other players and programmed robots, and to advance in the respective game's hierarchy to being a 'wizard' or 'god'. Wizards and gods have the power to alter the game landscape and to program the problems which the other participants must solve. MOO stands for Multi-User Dungeon Object Oriented, which—in contrast to the strictly hierarchically organised, and sometimes quite violent, adventure MUDs—are games in which co-operation, solidarity, education and science are central. Every participant receives programming rights from the start, that is, he or she can create rooms and objects in the medium of writing and independently contribute to the shaping of the text-based educational and game landscape.

The binding of writing to synchronous conversation in one-to-one or many-to-many communication creates a pragmatic recontextualisation of the use of writing in MUDs and MOOs. With the help of written signs, speech acts are performed between people in MUDs and MOOs which it would be difficult to carry out in the technical medium of print: people fall in love, make promises to one another, argue with each other and make up again, laugh, cry, flirt with each other, and do all those things that we can also do in face-to-face communication or on the telephone. In the synchronous interpersonal communications characteristic of MUDs and MOOs, writing does not serve exclusively, or even primarily, to make descriptive statements or truth claims. Rather it is utilised as an instrument for the co-ordination and execution of communal social activities.

In MUDs and MOOs even those actions which are not speech acts in the classical sense, but actions which in real life we would apprehend as non-linguistic actions, are also carried out in the mode of writing. This is because in interactive writing, as a form of communication which is restricted to the medium of writing, it is only that which takes place as a written act that functions as real communication. My smile only becomes present in a MUD or MOO when I write the sentence 'Mike smiles' or the equivalent emoticon ':-)'. (An emoticon is a graphic device combining simple punctuation marks in conventional combinations, to express simple emotions non-verbally in text on the Internet.) The same applies when I drink a beer in a virtual bar or sit on the desk in the virtual office of a colleague in MIT's Media MOO. In all these cases, it is irrelevant whether some independent reality is represented by the letters I type in. It does not matter whether I am really smiling, really drinking a beer, really sitting on the desk, or if I merely construct these actions. Rather what matters is that, by formulating these sentences online, I carry out actions in the respective MUD or MOO, that is, modify the conversational situation through my actions.

The pragmatisation of our sign usage that is taking place in the Internet becomes even clearer when we turn to the hypertextual constitution of the World Wide Web. It is characteristic of hypertexts that they point to intertextual references not merely in the mode of footnotes, but by using active links which make these references constituent parts of those texts. The idea of a closed meaningful content, already suggested at the material level by the closed unit of a manuscript bound between two book covers, is made problematic by the hypertextual constitution of textual elements presented and interconnected with one another in the Internet. The positive side of this change, in hypertextuality, consists in the explicit and technically manifest opening of signs to other signs and to virtual as well as real actions. In the hypertextual World Wide Web, letters and graphical signs become programmable. Pragmatically, signifiers, as icons, generate, with a mouse click, no longer a merely symbolic, but a real connection to what they designate. So in the digital bookstore Amazon.com, a click on the button with the inscription 'Buy 1 Now With 1 Click' suffices and—assuming that I am registered with address and credit card number as a customer on the server—I immediately receive the following answer: 'Thank you for your 1-Click order! (Yes, it was that easy.) One copy of the book you ordered will be sent to you as soon as possible'.

Of course, the fact that we can order books through the exchange of written signs is not a distinguishing characteristic of the World Wide Web. We can also carry out such an ordering process by post or fax. The distinguishing feature is that, through the Web, the pragmatic dimension of our use of writing is made explicit and salient by the immediate answer which our order elicits in an interactive system. This brings me to an important point, which I may not have highlighted clearly enough until now. Of almost all the properties distinguishing our sign usage in the Internet as something particular in relation to our everyday, non-digital sign usage, it can be said that these properties are in no way things radically new, but rather that they make explicit and vivid things which happen implicitly and unconsciously in everyday sign usage. In summary one can say, with recourse to Derrida and Rorty, that against the background of pragmatic embedding of sign usage in the Internet, the deconstructionist constitution of sense and meaning appears as directly ratifiable and evident, while it would otherwise be systematically concealed by the presence of voice and the (derivative) authority of the printed word. How can the transformations being experienced by the basic assumptions of traditional educational culture in the Internet, as reconstructed at the beginning of this paper, be redescribed against this background?

In an Internet-oriented educational culture, the *first* basic assumption of the givenness of a closed academic realm of theoretical knowledge representation is replaced by the deconstruction of academic knowledge spaces (Ulmer, 1985a). Deconstruction has two aspects, one destructive, one constructive. The destructive aspect is emancipation from the fixedness of the educational communication process in the world of the classroom or seminar room. With the integration of the Internet into the educational process, the virtual world opens up as a space of shared learning. This opening at the same time constitutes the constructive aspect. In the design of a university's or school's own MOO, or in working together on a seminar's or a school class's own homepage, learners experience the learning space in a quite literal sense as the product of their co-operative imagination and collective design capabilities.

These self-designed and permanently evolving knowledge spaces can at the same time be networked with other knowledge spaces and virtual, as well as real, action spaces. In this way possibilities for transcultural communication are revealed which contribute to the realisation of learning in a transnational context. On the Internet, it becomes possible for students and learners who are spatially and geographically separated from each other, and to this extent live in different worlds, to live together virtually in a common world whose basic spatio-temporal co-ordinates they can co-operatively construct in a deliberative process of negotiation. In this way, globality as a form of life becomes tangible and ingrained as a basic everyday attitude in a playful, matter-of-course manner. Furthermore, on the level of everyday epistemology, the deconstruction of academic knowledge spaces leads to a conscious awareness of the interpretative and constructive nature of our experiences of space and time. The recognition that comes with this, of the contingent character of even our deepest convictions and epistemological intuitions, represents a further important basis for transcultural dialogue which is concerned precisely with the intertwining of contingent convictions and supposedly self-evident intuitions of different origins.

The *second* basic assumption of traditional educational culture is also deconstructed by the incorporation of the Internet. In this case, the destructive aspect consists in the fact that voice-centred face-to-face conversation no longer functions as the dominant paradigm of the educational communication process. Instead, interactive writing undergoes a characteristic revaluation. In Internet conditions, writing no longer functions—as in the printed book—solely as a medium of knowledge storage, but (in MUDs, MOOs and IRC) becomes usable interactively as a synchronous medium of communication. The constructive aspect is that, in interactively writing a conversation, we experience the constitution of sense and meaning as always mediated by signs which themselves refer to other signs (as signs of signs of signs and so on). In this way, the inner written signature of our thought and communication becomes immediately ratifiable. Common sense changes. Under the influence of the Internet, our everyday epistemology is becoming increasingly deconstructionist.

This applies not only to our use of alphabetic writing, but also to our use of pictures. If one considers the internal data structure of digital pictures, then it becomes clear that in terms of their technical structure, images composed of pixels have the character of 'writing' in Derrida's sense. By using editor programs, the elements of the digital image can be exchanged, shifted and altered, just as the letters of a system of writing can be. Images thus become flexible scripts which can be edited. In the digital mode, the image loses its distinguished status as a representation or construction of reality. It proves to be a technological work of art whose semiotics arise internally from the relations between pixels and externally through the hypertextual reference to other documents (Mitchell, 1992).

Moreover, the deconstruction of the educational communication process where the Internet is used has profound repercussions for the status of face-to-face communication, effects of both decentralisation and revalidation. I will discuss decentralisation later. The revalidation effect consists in the sharpened perception of the characteristics proper to the real conversation situation in real space, a sharpened perception made possible by the experience of its difference from virtual communication in virtual space. The anaesthetic reduction of communication to the medium of interactive writing—as takes place in IRC, MUDs and MOOs—also renders the visual, acoustic and tactile evidence that we subconsciously presuppose in face-to-face communication the object of conscious deconstruction in the medium of writing. The appresent presence of participants in online chat means that in order to be present at all as a chat participant, we must describe to the other participants what we look like, what our voice sounds like, how our skin feels, in which spaces and times we move, and altogether what kind of beings and in which kind of world we are. Out of this there arises a deconstructionist awareness of the body through which we become sensitive in a new way to the specific gestural and tactile signatures of everyday face-to-face communication in real space.

The decentralisation effect that arises from the experience of the inner written signature of our thought, speech and communication is closely linked with the transformation which affects the *third* basic assumption of traditional educational culture. In an Internet-oriented educational culture, the authority of the teacher is no longer grounded in the authoritative personalisation of theoretical knowledge stocks in the figure of the omnicompetent teacher. Instead, the authority of the teacher is now grounded in her competence to use language in a pragmatic way and in her ability to make transparent use of different sources of knowledge, heterogeneous interpretations and divergent interests. Where the teacher has these abilities, the integration of the Internet in lessons no longer presents a problem. On the contrary, teachers who are already prepared to disclose to learners the sources, contingencies, relativities and openness, as well as the developing character, of their own knowledge in the framework of decentralised face-to-face lessons will also use the Internet to enter into a shared media-based learning process with their pupils. The authority of the teacher is preserved here, above all, by helping the learners to learn the art of independent, reflective and intelligent learning themselves (which is decisive for success in their own lives). The teacher's advantage thus no longer consists primarily of possessing preordained curricular reserves, but rather of the competence to channel the constantly growing flows of information in an understandable, pragmatic and co-operative manner, and to transform them, in co-operation with the learners, into situated knowledge that is useful and beneficial to the learning community.

In Internet conditions, the *fourth* basic assumption of traditional educational culture, that knowledge is to be understood as a fixed stock of hierarchically ordered facts, is replaced by a process concept of knowledge. The intersubjectively mediated faculty of reflective judgement is central here. This faculty comprises those pragmatic and deconstructionist abilities whose intelligent interplay is decisive for media competence in the use of the Internet. In traditional media practice, the spectator or reader can usually pre-judge the value of an item from its association with a particular publisher, a particular TV or radio station, or a particular newspaper editor—that is, to something already known and general. On the Internet, things are different. Through the use of search machines and work in the various databases accessible via the Web, users are confronted with a broad spectrum of quite disparate information in relation to a given keyword. The origin of the information is not always transparent and its attributability is often difficult to ascertain. While the classical media system was based on the development by viewers or readers of stable long-term preferences for programmes or newspapers that appear trustworthy, on the Internet we have to deal with an information overload. Even with the use of search machines and intelligent agent programmes, this overload can ultimately only be channelled through the reflective judgement of the individual user. The comprehensive and systematic development of reflective judgement at all levels of the population and on a global scale is the central task for a democratic educational system in the twenty-first century.

I conclude by providing two examples from my own work with the Internet at the universities of Magdeburg and Jena. Within the framework of a seminar in Magdeburg on 'Philosophical Media Theory' that I offered in the summer term of 1996, I stressed the deployment of interactive communications services like MUDs and MOOs for academic use. We began by reading a book and an essay by the American media theorist Jay David Bolter of the Georgia Institute of Technology (Atlanta) in a sequence of four sittings, without computer support. In the course of the reading we worked out questions together, some straightforward questions of textual understanding, but also some which problematised Bolter's basic theses. The second seminar sequence took place in a computer room. Two students sat at each PC, with all the PCs being connected to the Georgia Institute of Technology's Media-MOO in which Jay Bolter had invited us to a discussion. By reference to the communicative situation that developed, one can demonstrate very well what I mean by a deconstructionist decentralisation and pragmatic de-hierarchialisation of the teaching situation.

The characteristic communicative situation of the first seminar sequence should first be briefly described. The conversational situation was structured so that I, as the teacher, worked together with the students on the development of an open understanding of Bolter's texts, an understanding which admitted questions and uncertainties. The point was not to cover up my own problems of understanding, but rather to articulate these problems as clearly as possible so that students were encouraged by my example to express their own problems of understanding in the same manner. My function in the seminar was thus not to present the students with a binding and true textual understanding for them simply to reproduce. I did not offer them a standard interpretation, comprehensive and general, with which they would have been able to subsume the text definitively. Instead, I entered with them into a targeted process of reflective judgement, in the course of which we communicated with each other about the uncertainties, different interpretative possibilities, open questions, manifold references and associations which turn up in the process of reading an academic text. At the end of this deconstructionist process, we had a list of questions of understanding and interpretation which we thought we could not settle amongst ourselves, as well as a second list of questions which seemed to us to problematise certain of Bolter's basic ideas. Equipped with these two lists, we began our march into the Internet and our visit to Bolter's Media-MOO.

What was interesting above all about the communicative situation in online discussion with Bolter was that the decentralisation and de-hierarchialisation which had implicitly characterised our work in the computer-free text-reading sessions, expressed itself in conversation with Bolter as a peculiar experience of solidarity. In conversation with Bolter we experienced ourselves as a thinking and reflective community which posed questions, formulated objections, followed up, changed subject, brought up new problems and so on, in a co-ordinated and co-operative manner. The technical boundary conditions contributed to this. Bolter could only see what we wrote, but we ourselves could communicate orally at all times to discuss what we were writing and our continued argumentative procedure, without Bolter hearing. The weak degree of determinacy or, more positively formulated, the deconstructionist openness which we had allowed ourselves in the first seminar sequence, now proved to be our strength. The author, who had been brought back from the anonymous world of the printed book to the virtual conversational reality of online discussion, could now be confronted step by step with our specific problems of interpretation and critical objections. In the transposition from the world of the printed book to the interactive world of written conversation, the seminar participants experienced with clarity the way that, in a successful reading, one reflective judgement leads on to another. Bolter answered those of our questions that went beyond textual understanding by incorporating them into his own reflections and thus helped us understand how published knowledge is the momentary take of an open thought process, a process in which good texts invite their readers to participate, by thinking for themselves.

I now describe my experience of Internet use in philosophy seminars at the Friedrich Schiller University in Jena with the example of a *Proseminar* on Aristotle's *Nicomachean Ethics* which I led in the 1999 summer term. In the framework of this seminar I tried to utilise the World Wide Web collectively in a targeted way to improve the seminar discussion and the ability of students to take themselves and their fellow students seriously as writers, that is, as text authors. The participants prepared themselves for the respective Aristotelian sequences that were to be dealt with in the seminar by writing short summaries and comments on the corresponding passages before the sitting. A week before the relevant sitting, these summaries were made available to all by publication on a seminar homepage set up for this purpose (http://www.uni-jena.de/ms/seminar/) so that each participant could already form an image of the published state of reflection of all their fellow students before the sitting. The procedure in the seminar was that one participant then offered a so-called 'survey-presentation'. These survey presentations reconstructed and interpreted the Aristotelian text to be thematised and in so doing incorporated the summaries and comments of the other participants as secondary literature.

In this way the authors of the summaries and comments experienced early on what it means to be received and taken seriously as an author. They sensed, as it were through the example of their own publications, how a text alienates itself from its author in the medium of publication and how deconstructionist processes of reflection are necessary to reconstruct the openness of thought in reading. Through this form of collective writing and publication, they learned new forms of reflective reading that no longer apprehend the text as a pre-given general stock of knowledge that is to be subsumed under a certain heading, but which recognise in the text an instrument which it is important to learn to use pragmatically and meaningfully by means of reflective judgement in an open, interactive and participatory intellectual exercise.

The two examples from my own teaching experience show that the Internet not only means a great challenge for media theorists and media educationalists, but also, and precisely, that it can provide creative impulses to teaching in subjects as seemingly media-independent and withdrawn as philosophy. In addition, the examples make it clear that in educational policy it no longer suffices to acquire new computer technology, set up network connections and install intelligent educational software. Technical use of new media is by no means a sufficient condition for the development of reflective judgement. This false optimism, disseminated by many educational policy-makers today, is based on deterministic assumptions about media. Against this prejudice, it must of course be emphasised that the targeted development of reflective judgement has its educational place not only and not primarily in the computer laboratory or in front of the Internet screen. Rather it begins in the everyday communication situation of normal, non-computerised face-to-face lessons, which at the same time as its deconstructionist decentralisation, is pragmatically revalidated in an educational world shaped by the new media.

The central challenge which current and future educational policy is confronted with is how the revalidation of face-to-face classroom practices is to be combined with the reshaping of knowledge promoted by the emergent information network technologies. Here, I have taken the Internet as a paradigm to set out the need it presents to revise important basic assumptions about the nature of knowledge and education, and I have argued that a blend of deconstruction and pragmatism accounts theoretically for the phenomena currently emerging. The salient point for educational policy is that the Internet is currently our best paradigm for the topology of information in the future, and that there is every reason to believe that this is just the tip of the iceberg. History has taught us what fate awaits those who are too late in identifying and circumnavigating icebergs.

Translation by Andrew Inkpin

NOTES

1. Cf. here Sandbothe, 2000c; a shortened version of the text has appeared online as Sandbothe, 1998b. For an introduction to deconstruction see Rorty, 1989b; for an introduction to (neo)pragmatism see Rorty, 1998a.
2. For an account of the prehistory of pragmatic media philosophy in Peirce, James, Dewey, Nietzsche and Wittgenstein, see Sandbothe, 1998a and Sandbothe, 2000a.
3. On the inner differentiation of the media concept see Sandbothe, 2000a and 2000b.

4

The Educational Significance of the Interface

STEVE BRAMALL

INTRODUCTION

Children of school age routinely garner information from the Web-sites and homepages of the World Wide Web (WWW). For the foreseeable future increasing numbers of children will be doing more and more of this. These children will generally be in classrooms for much of the time, although their school-based learning will be supplemented by the use of home computers. The content and quality of information gathered by children will continue to be circumscribed by the demands of the curriculum and by the parameters and guidelines provided by for example anti-pornography filtering software or, more positively, the National Grid for Learning.[1] For the foreseeable future too, teachers will remain in a position to enable, guide and regulate children's Internet use. It is and will be the job of teachers to help children to employ the resources of the WWW in order to become well informed, and to help them to reflect intelligently on the structures and processes involved, and on the significance of their learning to wider human concerns. But what specifically do children learn from using the WWW? Furthermore, is it possible that using the WWW and reflecting on the engagement with it could provide an opportunity for children to learn something new and significant? If so, what is it, and what is the role of teachers in this learning?

At one level it is clear that educated Internet use can lead to the desirable educational objective of intelligent information gathering, management and processing by pupils. Although there may be problems and dangers associated with using this new technology, the access to and dexterity with data that it enables can make a positive contribution to the well-being of individuals. If, however, we were to restrict our thoughts to these immediately apparent benefits, we would run the risk of telling an impoverished story of the educational potential of learning via the WWW. To generate a richer account we should also keep our ears open to the hidden possibility that accessing information on the WWW might enable more open-ended and perhaps more significant educational processes. In order to illuminate some of the more profound educational potential of school children's use of the WWW I focus here on the interfaces and interface practices through which individuals connect to, and download information from, the WWW. My contention is that drawing information from the WWW via interfaces constitutes a profound change in our culture that is increasingly reflected in, and has the power to improve, the sense-making apparatus of our culture and its individual members.

CHILDREN'S USE OF THE INTERNET

Before proceeding further it may be valuable to pause here for a brief empirical description of the content of the WWW and its usage by children. The sheer scale of this information resource and the rate of its expansion should not go unmentioned. According to OCLC research,[2] the WWW is now home to a total of 3.6 million sites. The number of publicly available sites is not only large but has grown rapidly, with no signs of this growth slowing. In 1997 some 800,000 sites were publicly accessible. Research carried out in 1999 found that this number had increased to 2.2 million. These sites together contain nearly 300 million individual pages. The average Web-site is made up of 129 pages, up from 114 pages in 1998.

Publicly available Web-sites have become a standard source of information for children producing schoolwork. According to the latest findings from NPD Online Research,[3] two out of three children who have access to a computer at home use it to help them do their homework. In a survey of 2 143 parents the NPD found that, on average, children with household PCs use them for one hour every night to do their homework. Half of this time is spent online, with parents monitoring Internet access. 19% of children said they 'always' found information for assignments online, 65% said they found information 'most of the time' and 17% said they got information 'some of the time'. 88 % of children use their computers to access special reports and research, 85% use their computers as a reference source, 54% use them for educational software and 50% use them for nightly homework. 73% of parents said their children used a computer at school. 85% of children used a shared PC while 15% used their own personal PCs.

The routine use of the resources of the WWW by school-age children appears set to continue to expand. In surveys presented under the heading 'Meeting Generation Y' in July 1999, Nua Ltd. confirmed what most people have long suspected: that teenagers and children constitute one of the fastest-growing Internet populations.[4] Nua's findings indicate that globally 77 million under-18 year-olds are expected to be online by 2005. In Britain, a study by National Opinion Poll Research found that Internet users are held in high esteem by teenagers and children, regardless of whether they themselves have Net access. Internet users were described as 'clever', 'friendly', 'cool', 'trendy' and 'rich' by both users and non-users. 79% of British children say that the Internet helps them to learn. Pulling together these empirical strands we can weave a picture of school children's learning where, in our society, and in both the school and the home, accessing information increasingly involves looking on the Web. Downloading has become the norm and as natural for children, if not more so, as looking in a library.

Of course there are those who would argue with some justification that any analogy with a library is inadequate in that it misses the interactive quality of Internet activities. Those who focus on the interactive possibilities of the Internet—the bulletin boards, multi-player games, chat-rooms, online communities and so on—might want to characterise the Internet as (putting it crudely) most interestingly a communicative technology rather than an informational system. The educational promise of the interactivity of the Internet is clearly great, and clearly in need of greater understanding. However, here I want to restrict the focus to what constitutes perhaps the bulk of online activity, the finding of information. My contention here is that if we understand the nature of the informational system imaginatively, and in particular the means of accessing information, we might find that accessing is not a passive activity and that an important lesson about human understanding lies hidden behind the seemingly simple idea of getting hold of data.

UNDERSTANDING THE INTERFACE

The central claim of this chapter, that the interface has educational significance, is grounded in the idea that the interface between members of our culture and the web of information to which it grants us access is of cultural significance. It is therefore to the task of revealing the hidden significance of interfaces to our culture that we should now turn. Generating an adequate understanding of the interface implies giving an account of its cultural meaning and significance. One way of bringing this out is through a perspectival articulation, a 'look at it like this' approach aimed at revealing the phenomenon in an aspect that can illuminate. This is the sort of method employed at least in part by the writer Steven Johnson in his influential book *Interface Culture* (Johnson, 1997) and it is to this work that I will turn repeatedly in this section. First however we need to know what we mean by 'interface'.

In relation to accessing the Web, the word interface, as one might expect, refers to what comes between each of us and what is 'out there'. Specifically it is the active point of contact between an individual looking for information and the informational content stored on the Web. It has been described as (amongst many other things) a conduit, a portal, a translator and an interpreter. This range of descriptions probably reflects the plurality of interfaces that provide a variety of means of accessing Web-stored data. Often the differences in interfaces reflect the differences in the quality of information accessed and the purposes for which the information is sought. The collective noun 'interface' is used by convention in a generic way to refer both to all interfaces as well as in a specific way to refer to particular interfaces. This seems analogous to the way that the term 'novel' can refer to a literary mode as well as an individual text.

So much for how the term is used, but what are interfaces made of and what exactly is their function? In one sense the computer screen might be said to constitute an interface. Certainly the screen comes between us and the WWW and it affects the way in which information comes to us. For example, data from the Web comes in a two-dimensional format, are backlit and are framed within a rectangular viewing area. However, it may be helpful to think of the screen as significantly different from software interfaces. One way to articulate the distinction is to understand the screen not as an interface but rather as the place where interfaces are displayed. Another is to see the screen as a physical, in contrast to a software, interface. Whichever way the distinction is made, I should make clear here that my concern here, like that of Johnson, is with software interfaces.

In fact Johnson identifies the interface as software. He writes 'In its simplest sense, the word refers to software that shapes the interaction between user and computer' (Johnson, 1997, p. 14). Perhaps the most ubiquitous example of a software interface is the desktop, the familiar visible spatial artifice through which we manipulate the programs and files stored in digital form in our computers. However, when we are talking about accessing the Web, the significant interface items are those which enable us to get the information we seek: windows, browsers (such as Netscape Navigator), search engines (such as Alta Vista), links, filters and so on. These are programs designed by software technicians which aim to satisfy our information-gathering desires. 'Our only access to this parallel universe of zeros and ones runs through the conduit of the computer interface, which means that the most dynamic and innovative region of the modern world reveals itself to us only through the anonymous middlemen of interface design' (*ibid.*, p. 19). Understood this way, interfaces are the software means of transferring information from elsewhere, where it is stored as zeros and ones, to here, where it is re-presented in intelligible form.

The function of interfaces is however not simply to carry messages. Rather they have an important role in helping to select what we see. The sifting or filtering function of interfaces is a necessary part of accessing information because of the vastness of the sea of information held on the Web. In the absence of a selection process, information would be impossible to access because it is a huge, ever-expanding mass of unorganised data. This can be illustrated with reference to the recent development of 'magic lenses', interface software designed to focus on specific aspects of a set of data. 'Like the original window, the lens sounds like a tool for revealing things, for opening up new data landscapes, but in practice it turns out to be more useful for shutting things out. The lens is a tool for discriminating. It filters out, and in doing so it keeps many things opaque. The lens acknowledges that surplus information can be just as damaging as information scarcity' (*ibid.*, p. 88). Direct apprehension of the information of the WWW would, if it were possible, result in the unintelligibility of information overload, the so-called 'blizzard of senselessness'.

The reducing and filtering function of interfaces is carried out in a variety of ways and it is in terms of this function that the different types of interface are differentiated. Search engines typically indicate sites and pages narrowed down to those containing key words and phrases, while browsers filter through the use of common categories. In the latter case what individuals select from is information that is pre-selected and pre-classified. This is like having a helping hand to guide us through the chaos. Although much is made of the fragmentary nature of information on the Web and of the *anomie* of Web experience, it is apparent that order and structure, as prerequisites of intelligibility, are necessary features of information gathering. The achievement of intelligibility through the generation of structure and order is the province of interfaces.

The work of interfaces in delivering information that is selected and structured to meet the needs and desires of school pupils is surely valuable in educational terms. However we should note that perhaps as with all technology it is a double-edged sword. Whilst rapid access to information may in itself be desirable, the interface has the potential to act as a force for passivity rather than creativity. In delivering information pre-packaged according to the categories of a browser, interfaces have the potential to reduce the need for creative investigation: they could be described as failing to stimulate young minds adequately. Furthermore, with the recent developments of interfaces that deliver to an individual information pre-selected according to categories which reflect the past choices of that individual, there is the potential for counter-educational conservatism.

In each of these examples the information provided through the interface could be said to reinforce a pupil's current beliefs and interests rather than to challenge them. Similarly the sort of choice offered to a pupil on the menu of an interface may be a simple choice, a means of 'getting what you want' rather than one challenging enough to generate educational puzzlement or confusion. In response to the educational deficit of the simple choice model of learning, interface technicians are increasingly trying to find ways of designing interfaces that stimulate change in the information-gathering patterns of Web users. As a recent Web article has it:[5]

> Education has a concept called 'the teachable moment', the point when a learner is ready to learn, willing to change, and can act. For Web-sites, the parallel is something we call 'the seducible moment'. This is the point at which designers can entice users off the path to their original goal with the lure of something else.

The description so far of the structures, processes and mechanisms by which we get information from the Web then could already have some value in helping us to think about educational activities and aims in the world of 'onliners'. Clarity about the functions and utility of a variety of interface technologies could serve the aim of bringing up children to be adept and intelligent in their information seeking and manipulation. It could also help perhaps in the development of more open and creative use of information and information systems and in alerting us to pitfalls. Using and understanding the Web can therefore help young persons to become better informed and better informers. However, this has been only one characterisation of the phenomenon before us. The description thus far has been technical, describing in literal terms the potential of the person-interface-Web information system to extend our current informational practices. The greater and riskier productive promise, where the interface might reveal genuinely educational insight, requires metaphor.

The grand metaphor created by interface designers is that of space. Following McLuhan's early descriptions of computer power as extending bodily powers (McLuhan, 1996), the metaphor of space has now come to dominate the way we orient to computer-mediated information so completely that it has lost the lustre of metaphor. Windows are no longer the marvellous fictional inventions they once were: they seem to us merely an efficient, traditional means to access data. But the whole system of representation of interfaces is metaphorical, as is much of the enabling language of cyberspace, a place where people surf and navigate and browse through sites with rooms and bulletin boards. The now clichéd question is not what information do you require, but rather where do you want to go.

This spatial metaphor is the principal means by which we represent the world of dataspace, a world which we find difficult even to refer to without talking spatially. Going back to the words of Johnson:

> As our machines are increasingly jacked into global networks of information, it becomes more and more difficult to *imagine* the dataspace at our fingertips, to picture all that complexity in our mind's eye—the way city dwellers, in the sociologist Kevin Lynch's phrase, 'cognitively map' their real-world environs. Representing all that information is going to require a new visual language, as complex and meaningful as the great metropolitan narratives of the nineteenth-century novel. (Johnson, 1997, p. 18)

The construction of the fiction about the layout of cyberspace, the architecture, the transportation networks and so on, in short the narrating of the expansion of cyberspace, is already well under way. It is not absurd to think of the interface designer as the narrator. Already the design of the representation of globally accessible information is coming to resemble the mythologies of the USA and the UK. Cyberspace presents itself in terms both of American mythology of frontiers and open landscapes to be explored and the British urban mythology of a nation of shopkeepers putting their goods on public display.

It is true that to many the experience of cyberspace echoes the Wild West, or rather the Hollywood evocation of the Wild West. It presents itself as new space ready to be colonised with an absence of state regulation and censorship, with the opportunity for anyone to post information and few mechanisms to check on the veracity of content. That said, one of the striking features of the WWW is the increasing amount of self-regulation. Cyberworld is not simply a site of anarchy and destructiveness. There is law and law enforcement, there are protocols, there are communities that include and exclude. There are systems of money, churches, welfare centres, hospitals, schools and shops. The story we tell ourselves about this very large collection of information stored as zeros and ones is a tale of the building and inhabiting of a parallel culture.

PHILOSOPHY

The philosophical tradition that I would suggest might enable us to understand and work productively with the person–interface–Web system, understood thus, is that of German phenomenology, not only Kant and Hegel, but Heidegger, Ricoeur, Gadamer and Schutz. The reason for conceiving these thinkers as providing appropriate intellectual resources is that the interface, understood as an enabling artifice, is manifestly a cultural construct. Johnson's account of the experience of Web culture reflects the necessarily phenomenological character of interface experience and alerts us as to the possibilities for understanding this experience in phenomenological terms. The new space which he lyrically describes is unmistakably a human achievement, and an achievement moreover that is made possible only through the construction of the metaphorical medium of the interface. His book is littered with echoes of phenomenology; nothing of the Web can be experienced in the absence of mediation through time and narrative, and space is the form of Web experience.

The experience of cyberspace can further be usefully understood as hermeneutical in character. Johnson's account is indeed in some ways Heideggerian. Woven into his narrative is an unspoken ontology of human finitude, a presumption of the limitations of human understanding. At one level the claim that the interface is a hermeneutic device is straightforward. Making the information of the Web intelligible requires mechanisms of selection and inter-pretation that are in a sense analogous to those attributed in legend to Hermes the Greek interpreter of the messages of the gods or to the biblical hermeneutics of the Reformation. However in under-standing the Web it seems that what we are engaged in here is a double hermeneutic. We attempt to make sense and speak truth about a world, and this is enabled only through both our own experiential categories and the categories supplied by interfaces.

In Heideggerian terms we might say first that information from the Web comes to us already fore-structured, and second that our understanding of this fore-structured reality proceeds only through the mediation of our own fore-structures of understanding. The latter fore-structures are, for Heidegger, what makes experience possible at all. It is fore-structures that enable us to understand reality 'as something'. Understanding for Heidegger is never a presupposition-less apprehension of anything, rather it proceeds as interpretation within the parameters of what we are already prepared to comprehend. To use his words, 'In every case interpretation is grounded in "something we see in advance"—in a fore-sight. This fore-sight "takes the first cut" out of what has been taken into our fore-having, and it does so with a view to a definite way in which this can be interpreted' (Heidegger, 1962, p. 191). Hence our fore-structuring mechanisms go before us, categorising and presenting reality in an intelligible form.

The encompassing fore-structures of the information on the Web are categories of space and place; the sub-categories are those listed in the browser and directory. The fore-structures of our understanding are the media of understanding: the language, concepts, categories, narratives and metaphors through which we channel the infinity of the noumenal into finite intelligible thought. The contribution to phenomenological hermeneutics of Gadamer is the thesis that our specific fore-structures are supplied by our specific history and tradition. It is cultural 'prejudice', understood as a particular set of beliefs, interests and concepts, that goes before us and conditions experience, pre-selecting the aspects in which the world reveals itself to us. 'In fact, the historicity of our existence entails that prejudices, in the literal sense of the word, constitute the initial directedness of our whole ability to experience' (Gadamer, 1989, p. 284). Understanding on this account is perspectivalist. The 'view from nowhere' that had a place within some Enlightenment thinking is rejected as a model for achieving an understanding of meaningful human reality. Instead what is embraced is the necessity and positivity of understanding through views from particular cultural and historical places. As Gadamer writes (*ibid.*): 'We accept the fact that the subject presents itself historically under different aspects at different times or from a different standpoint'.

The thesis that all human understanding is necessarily perspectival contributes to the coherence of phenomenological hermeneutics but also indicates limitations on human understanding. Perspectival understanding is necessarily partial and incomplete. It can only ever be one view of reality, revealing a limited aspect of the world which will be always open to rethinking. (Again this has an analogy with the workings of the interface where we might say that the metaphors and categories condition what we see on the Web.) Gadamer uses the metaphor of 'horizon' to make the point. 'We define the concept of "situation" by saying that it represents a standpoint that limits the possibility of vision. Hence essential to the concept of situation is the concept of "horizon". The horizon is the range of vision that includes everything that can be seen from a particular vantage point' (*ibid.*, p. 302).

For Gadamer, the productive moment in human understanding comes through the overcoming of one's limited horizon and the opening up of new horizons. What this promises is a significant modification of the fore-structures of understanding such that a new perspective on reality is enabled. It might be described metaphorically as changing the lens through which reality is viewed such that new phenomena can come into focus. This change of perspective is, for Gadamer, made possible through the 'fusion of horizons'. This is the process whereby those with different horizons attempt to understand one another. In attempting to render the other intelligible we are called on to stretch and modify our fore-structures such that, in the dialectical interplay of 'genuine conversation' a new, shared horizon is created. Along with this modified viewpoint comes the potential to reveal the world in a novel aspect, to re-understand. Furthermore, Gadamer argues that through the fusion of horizons the parochiality of one's horizon, (normally unnoticed, a 'given') comes into view. Through 'genuine conversation' one's own 'prejudice' itself can come into view and so be understood in its specificity as a limited, historically and culturally located, human achievement. Pushing the argument further, Gadamer speculates that it is then a short step from here to developing an enabling awareness of the nature of human understanding which includes metacognition of the frame-work of human understanding, what he calls 'effective historical consciousness'.

From this post-Enlightenment characterisation of the structures and processes of human understanding we can derive both a description of human learning and an account of the mechanism through which learning takes place. Clearly, learning in this story does not occur only through the accumulation of knowledge and understanding. Rather, an integral part of the process is the development of the language, concepts, categories, narratives and metaphors through which the world may be comprehended. Initiation into our culturally dominant 'prejudice' may therefore stand as an apt description of an educational process, but it is not the whole of the story. If it were then our children would at best receive a conservative education and at worst suffer the fate of those who try to understand the new in ways that are inadequate to the task. Better understanding requires appropriate and novel fore-structures of understanding.

Understood thus, the intelligent agency of the coming generation relies on the possibility for changing purposively the categories through which its members represent reality to themselves and whereby the selection of what is significant takes place. This facility of reinterpretation can be argued to be a necessary moment in the democratic process of constructing the cultural, political, moral and intellectual practices and institutions to which they aspire. It may also be said to be a necessary feature of retaining a belief in the progress of human understanding. In liberal terms it may be thought an important corollary of liberty and thereby of personal autonomy. The change in perspective does not result from education as initiation but from the process of unearthing, recognising, challenging and modifying one's own cultural presuppositions through attempting to understand others in their alterity. One way of describing an educated person (or perhaps an educated generation) is then in terms of their being cognisant of the possibilities of, and adept at, changing for the better their categories of understanding. They will to a degree recognise 'prejudice' as such, alter their perspective, and understand the methodological framework of understanding. To repeat Gadamer's phrase, they will develop 'effective-historical consciousness'.

THE EDUCATIONAL SIGNIFICANCE OF THE INTERFACE

One way of judging the educational significance of the interface then is in terms of its efficacy in aiding the achievement of the educational aims of the model of learning outlined above. Perhaps the principal educational promise of the interface lies in its potential value as a device which can help pupils and teachers to bring into the open and alter for the better their fore-structures of understanding. Further to this it could be judged in terms of its role in helping to develop pupils' understanding of the sort of being that they are, and of understanding itself. But in what ways might the use and understanding of the person–Web interface aid the development of educated persons hermeneutically conceived? What would make us believe that it could help us to help the coming generation to change the way they think?

One sense in which the interface educates is by example. The developing of novel categories through which information is presented to us is routine at the interface. It is the stock trade of a host of Internet-based companies. An example is 'lastminute.com', the site of an interface provided by a commercial company dedicated solely to supplying information about events that can be attended and that occur in the next three days. This is a categorisation of information into a specific time-slice that acts like a set of temporal car headlights illuminating that which is just far enough ahead. This company is a beacon of Internet success which has generated for itself a market value in hundreds of millions of pounds in a few years. The lesson being learned by those aiming to exploit the Web financially, and which is undoubtedly filtering down to school children, is that one route to success is through the development of novel categories of information.

Related to this is the potential to raise awareness of the existence, character and malleability of fore-structures that is supplied by the challenge to standard informational categories found in some interfaces. Categories can be personalised: 'Today's browsers alter the look-and-feel of the data they convey; tomorrow's will alter the meaning of that data by emphasising certain stories over others that are particularly relevant to the reader' (Johnson, 1997, p. 102). In addition, the seeking of information on the Web is routinely carried out using clusters of themes put together in a loose category that exists only briefly. This is the creation of temporary and pragmatically conceived informational conduits. Categories for the young onliners can be new fluid configurations, a long way from the idea of pigeon holes into which we fit new experiences. Categories at the interface are items through which children can experiment and play.

The experience of using interfaces to access the Web is already throwing up new questions about how we describe the identity of the cluster of items that we want to see. It is surely also filling the heads of school pupils with metaphors and symbols that transfer into their understanding of themselves and their reality. Just as the widespread use of computers granted us the metaphor of hardware, software and data with which to describe our brains and minds and memory, so the metaphors of the interface seep into the descriptive apparatus of youth. Physical landscape can now be described in terms of the fictional landscape of cyberworld and the desktop. Those who navigate cyberspace also navigate their way through life.

On this account it can be argued that the use of interfaces may help pupils to recognise the possibility of seeing that they might usefully understand themselves as operating through categories, and it may be seen as helping pupils to develop transferable skills and dispositions of categorical open-mindedness. However it is in the generating of reflective understanding about the structures and processes of understanding that much of the educational promise of the interface lies. Some of the advantages of reflecting on human understanding by using the interface as prompt derive from its novelty and popularity. It is an additional medium through which we represent ourselves to ourselves and thereby another opportunity for revealing the perspectival and interpretational character of human cognition through media study. It also has the advantage over other cultural forms, for example the novel, that it is currently in vogue and therefore pupils are highly motivated to find out about it.

A more specific way in which the interface may be thought to have an advantage over other media in helping to achieve the ends of hermeneutically conceived learning is that it is inescapably experienced phenomenologically and reveals the necessity of metaphor and artifice in all understanding. We already know what the fake landscape of the interface presents to us—it is information put on the Web by someone else. We also know that between being produced and being accessed the information was stored as a string of zeros and ones held electronically on a disk. There is nothing mysterious here, but we find that we still have to employ metaphor to make things appear from the chaos of the vastness of information.

Enlightenment scientific method, even as an ideal, is exposed as inadequate, potentially misleading children with an impoverished account of human understanding. The literalism of the objective mirroring or ever closer modelling of what is 'really out there' is not a tenable account of the structures and processes through which we access Web-based information.

Reflection on the perspectival nature of the interface may also help to reveal the perspectival nature of human understanding per se, and may act as a vehicle for showing the positive contribution of perspectivalism to understanding in general. Johnson writes of the development of interfaces as providing new perspectives.

> The most fertile historical analogy for this process is the invention of perspective in painting... perspective, however, turned out to be more than just a minor enhancement to the painter's repertoire. The mathematical studies of Alberti and Leonardo transformed not just the spatial language of European painting but also the role of the artist itself, elevating painting to a higher cognitive stature—closer to science or philosophy... it eventually helped produce what we now call the renaissance. (*ibid.*, p. 214)

Johnson's argument is that the perspectivalism of the interface centres the visual field on the human point of view, and that the experience of looking through and at the myriad of interfaces as perspectives is conducive to raising the cognitive stature of the interface designer and improving the cognitive abilities of the users.

Generally speaking, the claim being made here is that the attempt by schoolchildren to understand the Web and its interface can be understood as a 'genuine conversation' between two horizons that has the potential to fulfil some of the Gadamerian educational aim of changing the ways in which they can see the world. Cyberworld, mediated by interfaces, constitutes an example of alterity, the understanding of which requires the generating of novel categories of interpretation. Anyone who has tried to describe the Web to those as yet uninitiated will know that there is an ever-changing textual and symbolic language to be learned and a ever renewable story to be told. As Johnson concludes, 'Our interfaces are stories we tell ourselves to ward off the senselessness, memory palaces built out of silicon and light. They will continue to change the way we imagine information, and in doing so they are bound to change us as well . . .' (Johnson, 1997, p. 242). In trying to understand the stories, we are asked to question what sorts of stories are significant, and we are called on to stretch and modify our means of understanding.

In contrast to some accounts of the effects of Internet technology in the classroom, this description of the lessons that the coming generation can learn from their engagement with the Web puts teachers at centre stage. The importance of teachers in this story is not exhausted by their role as technical guides and mentors in use of the Web, nor by their capacity as aids to genuinely critical and creative information accessing and use. The full realisation of the educational promise of the use and understanding of Web interfaces requires specific forms of engagement and more importantly reflective understanding. The initiation into productive modes of Internet engagement and the stimulating of appropriate reflection on the experience and its wider implications are directed activities. They are unlikely to occur in the absence of teachers. Drawing on them helps us to describe some of the tasks that teachers must perform if they are to bring about genuine understanding in pupils.

The task of teachers on this model is twofold. First, teachers have the responsibility to help children to become adept at information accessing and processing and to ensure that the information resources of the Web are used wisely, creatively and progressively. Second, it is the job of teachers (by stimulating and guiding reflection on the structures and processes of accessing the Web via interfaces) to help children to overcome the limitations of the fore-structures bequeathed to them by their tradition and to help them to develop the capacities for generating new fore-structures that will enable them to flourish in a rapidly changing cultural and epistemological environment. Part of the latter job of teachers involves teaching children how to think in new categories; part of it involves teaching children how to think about categories. This will mean teaching children how to think metaphorically where appropriate and, ideally, how to engage with, and reflect on, the totality of these experiences in ways that reveal the structures, processes and frameworks of human understanding itself.

Such educative tasks are beyond the current remit of teachers of information and communication technology, and perhaps beyond that of teachers currently charged with teaching media studies. The use of Web experience as the key to wider and deeper understanding on the part of children would imply also wider and deeper understanding on the part of teachers. Teachers intent on using a phenomenological account of Web interfaces and Web experience in order to help to reveal, challenge and change categories and categorical frameworks of understanding would themselves need specific sorts of knowledge, skills and understanding. This would place particular demands on teacher education. Teacher education would need to cover a broad range of knowledge including that pertaining to information and communications technology, to media studies and to sociology, and taught such that they could be brought together synthetically. Teachers would benefit from learning more about the characteristics and methods of different forms of knowing, reasoning and understanding, especially about the perspectival, narrative and metaphorical aspects of understanding. In practical terms teachers would need to be taught how to initiate dialogues of the form that Gadamer terms 'genuine conversation' and to recognise and be able and willing to act at the appropriate 'educable moment'.

These initial and sketchy suggestions about teacher education are contentious and tentative. In this they reflect the speculative quality of the arguments made here as to the educative promise of the Web. However, if there is something in this story the speculation may be worth the effort. In terms of promoting human understanding the interface may have the potential to be as productive as the chalk-face.[6]

NOTES

1. Information on the National Grid for Learning can be found at www.ngfl.gov.uk
2. Statistics generated from the Web Characterisation Project in June 1999 carried out by OCLC (Online Computer Library Center, Inc.). The report can be found at http://www.oclc.org/oclc/press/19990908a.htm
3. NPD Online Research can be found at http://www.npd.com/corp/press/press_990817.htm
4. Nua Ltd. can be found at http://www.nua.ie/surveys/analysis/weekly_editorial/archives/issue1no84.html
5. The full chapter can be found at http://world.std.com/~uieWeb/
6. I should like to thank John Turner for his important contributions to the development of the ideas and arguments contained in this chapter and Nigel Blake and Paul Standish for their helpful contributions and comments on an earlier draft.

5

Writing Feminist Webzines and the Confusion of Identity

BARBARA J. DUNCAN

To return to last week's yammering, I want to say that I've been getting some interesting responses to the personal/political/feminist article, responses that are underlining for me the fact that I'm still pretty conflicted about defining feminism. A lot of you have said that feminism is a belief set like a religion, and that because of this there will naturally be a certain amount of disagreement among feminists and feminisms. I agree on the second point: debate is essential to learning, to be sure. And I certainly wasn't arguing that there should be any sort of unchanging rule-book. Quite the contrary—I believe feminists *should* disagree with one another, debate one another, learn from each other. (Can you say feminist praxis?) (3.5.98)[1]

This short excerpt is an example of the short daily 'yammer' sections from the webzine, *Miss Melty* (http://www.melty.com) in which the author addresses some of the responses to one of her essays on feminism. This form of writing is becoming an increasingly popular mode of communication among a number of young feminists on the Internet who write about personal and social issues in daily, journal-like publications. Some webzines are collections of writing from a number of different authors who collectively produce the webzine, such as the popular *Geekgirl*, an Australian webzine (www.geekgirl. com.au) while others are personal webzines and are designed and written by one author. *Miss Melty* is an example of the latter and is updated about every few days or so with a journalistic entry concerning recent events in the media, or in the life of the author. The idea of the webzine is an extension of the 'zine' which, due to cheap and plentiful reproduction technologies, were produced and dissemi-nated primarily among a small group of US punk-music fans in the 1980s. These zines varied from a couple of pages copied and stapled together to larger pamphlet-like publications with elaborate graphics and layout. Paper zines are distributed through an underground network of zine writers who often exchange zines with each other or hand them out at concerts and other gatherings.[2] Zines have become more popular and read among a wider audience on the World Wide Web (the Web) and are known as 'webzines', covering topics such as work, popular culture, thrift store shopping and girl culture. Webzine writing is notable for its style in that 'anything goes' due to the lack of publisher demands. Taboo topics, such as pornography, homosexuality and erotica are freely explored for an audience that is anonymous and global in nature. Different genres of webzines have begun to emerge, with girl webzines as one such genre that explores feminism in the 1990s as well as other more feminine-oriented topics. In particular, feminists and the cyberfeminist movement have created a space for themselves through their writing in webzines and have transformed dismal projections of modern technological control into possibilities for expanded identities.

Philosophically, webzines raise questions as to the nature of authenticity. These self-published documents disrupt the idea of an author and complicate the notion of an essential or authentic self because they seem to encourage a hybrid and contradictory notion of identity. For feminists, as well as other marginalised groups, this is a crucial issue because being feminist infers that one is locatable or authentic due to beliefs, style or other identifiers. But writing on the Web constructs a subject that is not completely attached to a 'real' person in the usual way, and thus the idea of being a feminist is more complex and a cause for some confusion. While other forms of writing can be viewed in this way, Web writing highlights this separation, suggesting a kind of slippage between the author and the writing that is made manifest by the digital realm.

In this chapter I examine the nature of webzine writing, arguing between notions of hybridity—the idea that it contains many different fragments, genres and elements that construct a disconnected subject as a kind of cyborg—and notions of niche feminism where many different populations of feminism are coming to exist as a result of communications technology. Unlike many other forms of writing, the webzine disrupts commonly understood boundaries of genre and form, constructing a pastiche or a collage-like subject. Because this form of writing has been taken up by a new generation of feminists, it serves to explicate what being a feminist means in the 1990s and beyond. Self-published webzine writings demonstrate how feminists are constructing themselves online through their writings and interactions with others. Toward this goal, I examine the feminist webzine known as *Miss Melty* to understand what is happening to feminist identity in the context of communications technology. Assuming that feminist identity is a good indication of the nature of identity in general, these trends suggest two somewhat contradictory trends for the state school. On the one hand, while schools need to be a place for teaching common values and the encouragement of tolerance and dialogue, they instead mirror a trend toward proliferation of educational alternatives. Moreover, the state school is itself becoming more specialised in response to a society that is becoming ever more divided and splintered in terms of identity.

In the webzine *Melty*, disconnected or fragmented excerpts are juxtaposed to create a sense of textual collage and a sense of a disconnected and fragmented self. For example, *Melty*'s Web pages on Martha Stewart, a popular and controversial figure among US feminists due to her interest and devotion to crafts, home repairs and other housewifely kinds of activities, explore two different contradictory opinions. Ann, the author of *Melty*, interestingly shows how Martha is somewhat divided day-to-day on whether or not she likes or accepts what Martha stands for.[3] On the one hand Ann likes to be homey and fix things up, but on the other hand she realises that Martha stands for a superficial and consumer-based TV personality, which does not easily fit into the traditional feminist mindset. The following two essays are placed as links next to one another on the same page. So, one sees at the same time the links: 'Why I love Martha', and 'Why I hate Martha'. This gives the impression that, despite the fact that they were written at different times, Ann is somewhat ambivalent about her feelings toward this pop icon and wants to hold on to both positions despite the feminist implications and contradictions:

> I love Martha. Okay? Let's just get that out in the open. Personal Web pages are all about voyeurism, after all—and what's more voyeuristic than reading a dirty little confession like that?
>
> But seriously. Martha is love. Sure she's rich, sure she's a shallow icon of American consumerism. Who cares? The gal can cook. And garden. She can even build a shed—it says so in her magazine. Oh, her magazine. It's beautiful. It really is. And her books! The craft ideas to be found in her books! I'm telling you, you just need to get over it and start loving her. There's nothing wrong with a little domestic bliss, okay? When was the last time you cooked a meal that won you the love and affection of all the beautiful people you invited to your table? Sounds nice, doesn't it? Well Martha can HELP you with that. She'll get you action. Really. What do you have to lose? GIVE IN. MARTHA IS CALLING YOU. (Obsessions, 11.3.96)

Next to this entry is the following on 'Why I hate Martha':

> To be perfectly honest, I'm getting a little sick of Martha Stewart. She's gotten to be too much of a media phenomenon. I know, I know, she was always a media phenomenon: her fakeness is the basis of her charm. But something in her has changed. Maybe it's those new Kmart commercials she's doing. Maybe it's her move from NBC's

TODAY show to CBS Morning. But even her magazine, which I've always adored, has begun to bother me. I've barely glanced at the March issue and it's been on my coffee table for at least 3 weeks.

Maybe I'm the one who's changed. Maybe my problem is that I've let too many people know about my affections for her. It's like when I was in junior high and mentioned to a few people that I thought cows were kinda cute, and all of a sudden everyone I knew was buying me cow junk. Every fucking holiday, more cow paraphernalia. That really sucked. Well, the same thing is happening with Martha. Whenever she comes up in conversation, all eyes knowingly shift onto me. I've gotten all the Martha Stewart jokes emailed to me at least a dozen times each. My parents send me her newsclippings. And friends call up late at night just to let me know she's going to be on Letterman. I don't want to seem ungrateful. I appreciate the media alerts, I really do. (And her spot on Letterman was a classic!) I'm just suffering from Martha overload, that's all. I just need a little distance from her, a little time to think.

In the meantime, you can . . .

Visit the <u>Web Guide to Martha Stewart</u>.

Learn about Martha and her <u>gay friends</u>.

Or, you can read about why I used to <u>love</u> Martha. Sniff. (Obsessions, 3.12.97)

Her opinion of Martha has obviously changed over the course of a few months but, as is the nature of webzines, the previous essay is left to exist alongside the Martha-loving one, giving one the impression that, despite the Martha-hating essay, Martha is still loved in some way. At the bottom of the 'Why I hate Martha' essay are a few links to her 'beautifully designed magazine' and a 'Web Guide to Martha Stewart' demonstrating that the love affair is perhaps not completely over. Another indication of Ann's ambivalence is her inclusion of the link to the 'Why I love Martha' essay at the bottom. As she puts it, 'you can read about why I used to love Martha. Sniff.'—which suggests that she still feels torn about her decision to hate Martha and is still fascinated by her amazing ability to cook and decorate the home. The webzine allows her to express an ambivalence toward a non-feminist figure in the form of juxtaposition and links and brings out the contradictory impulses of being a feminist and living a lifestyle that is not traditionally feminist. While being interested in crafts, cooking, and home-maintenance is not necessarily diametrically opposed to feminist ideals, Martha does symbolise traditional family values and a return to more role-appropriate behaviours for men and women. Most feminists in the US would probably not want to be associated with such a popular TV icon. Nevertheless, Ann does not discuss feminist issues here and has either divorced her love of Martha from her feminist self or does not perceive this as a contradiction. In any case, it is an interesting juxtaposition for a feminist webzine to highlight.

Webzines also facilitate the discussion and exploration of taboo subjects that have been noticeably absent from much feminist discourse of the 1960s and 1970s. If not absent, the discussions of, for example, pornography have traditionally focused on how it degrades women without an assessment of how it works in different contexts. But the webzine has changed this to a certain extent. Confessions and personal revelations abound in the webzine world. Feminism in the 1990s is more about discovering the lost pleasures of such radical topics. For instance, discussions of pornography often have to do with confessions of its appeal and the delight of discovering an erotic self. In the following entry, Ann writes about her discovery and fascination with cheap drugstore novels as a young girl:

> In sixth grade my girlfriends and I would dare each other to look inside copies of Playgirl at the Waldenbooks store in the mall. The hunky-beefy photo spreads were so gross, though, that we outgrew the game after just a few peeks. I was much more of a soft-core romance fan, anyway. I started out by reading goofy Foxfire love stories and graduated to cheap drugstore novels. My friend Terry and I would steal her mom's trashy books and hide them up in her room until the coast was clear. Then we'd race through them, searching for all the dirty parts, comparing one to another. ("This one says 'Throbbing Member'!" "Ohmygod, this one calls it a 'Sword of Love'!") *Clan of the Cavebear* and Judy Blume's nasty *Wifey* were big favorites. ('My History of Porn', 2.1.97)

Later in this essay, she includes images from various sources and contexts concerning the idea of pornography, but in the context of the essay she disrupts some common assumptions about these images without referring to them directly, by creating a new meaning from her assemblage of text and 'found' image. In particular, she includes the picture of a beautiful young phone-sex worker who is gazing out, holding a phone, obviously engaged in fantasy role-playing with a client. The image is cropped, but one does see that a piece of advertisement is clearly visible with the words 'Live' and 'fantasy' written over her forehead. Underneath the image is the following text:

> My first college boyfriend had a stack of old porn mags hidden in his bedroom. When I found them I cried and he had to apologize to me for being 'such a guy'. By the time I left him for my first college girlfriend, though, I had discovered Susie Bright and lesbian porn and couldn't care less about what he was reading. *On our Backs* was so amazing to me. It was playful and dirty and tough and feminist, and full of naked pictures of cute, real-looking girls. From it I learned

about all these other great smut rags, like <u>Taste of Latex</u>, <u>Bad Attitude</u>, <u>Future Sex</u>, <u>Black Sheets</u>, and <u>Frighten the Horses</u>. Reading them made me realize that pornography wasn't necessarily something bad. There was more to it than just the typical newsrack men's fare. ('My History of Porn')

At this point in the essay one does not expect the typical feminist response to such an advertisement. Indeed Ann is not reading the images in the usual feminist way. The inclusion of taboo topics such as pornography suggests a subversion of the typical feminist response to phone-sex workers. While others such as Jill Nagle (Nagle, 1997) have also helped to pave the way toward a new feminist understanding of sex work, feminist/girl webzines have brought the issue to another level—one that addresses a lay person's context. Feminist webzines discuss the issue in a very personal and intimate manner (as a confession) and lead the way toward defining a new kind of hybrid feminism. Ann understands that pornography victimises women at the same time that it can give pleasure in a very grounded and human way—one to which a variety of different people can relate.

Another taboo topic that webzine writers and feminists in the 1990s (or third-wave feminists) have taken up is the issue of race. Again, while feminists in the second wave also dealt with this issue to a certain degree, the movement was largely motivated and controlled by white middle-class feminists. While feminism today is still dominated by white feminists there does seem to be a new awareness of the exclusion of women of colour as suggested by the creation of magazines such as *HUES*[4] and the discussion of the idea of liberal feminism as in the following excerpt of *Melty*:

> Here we return to the issue of false universals, and whether or not feminism should address 'non-feminist' issues like racism or poverty. Liberal feminists tend to argue that feminism should 'stick to the basics' and let other movements deal with 'their' issues, not-so-tacitly promoting the idea that feminism 'belongs' to white women. Liberal feminism strives for a world where women are equal to men, although *which men* they refer to remains unanswered. But if you look at liberal reform goals—ending domestic violence, reproductive freedom, affordable childcare, decent jobs free from sexual harassment, good healthcare—you see that these issues are not just about gender alone. In order to achieve them, feminism *must* address racism, feminism must address economic exploitation—because each of these dynamics is inextricably linked to the others. ('Personal vs Political vs Feminist', 3.1.98)

In other essays Ann also addresses the issue of whiteness and privilege and expands her construction of a feminist self to address those who are not always accepted in feminist circles.

These kinds of discussions are more common among webzine writers and other online spaces that deal with feminist issues, but have been noticeably absent from popular magazines for girls such as *Seventeen*. The lack of publishing constraints has facilitated a proliferation of discussion on topics that were normally considered too controversial, and thus has expanded the range and breadth of what feminism is all about.

Other aspects of a hybrid and expanded feminism brought out by webzine writing are the blend and juxtaposition of genres and styles. *Melty* is a combination of styles of writing, both serious and frivolous. Even her serious essays on international politics or feminism have a personal touch that is reminiscent of oral forms of communication. This blending of the formal and informal, serious and pleasurable, facilitates a unique hybrid style of writing that runs against the tide of many forms of writing. The webzine provides a space to step into many different genres without restriction. As a feminist form of writing it also coincides with the notion that feminism in the 1990s is as much about politics as it is about irony and pleasure. For instance, in the following excerpt she writes about the pleasure she gets from watching the TV show *Buffy the Vampire Slayer* at the same time as she feels disgust with sexual stereotypes on another popular television show.[5] In this excerpt she demonstrates a writing style that is very informal but the issue is a serious one, and one which she feels strongly about:

Just enjoyed two evenings straight of pure Buffy viewing pleasure, and I'm thrilled to learn that the show is moving to Tuesday nights, since that means I can watch it again. Buffy is so uncompromising, I dig her mightily. Unfortunately, I couldn't motivate to get off the couch before 'Dawson Creek' or whatever the hell it's called came on next: THE biggest piece of shit I've watched on teevee in a long, long time. When a show is *that* bad, I lose all motor skills—I can't run away, I can't turn the channel, all I can do is sit there and scream at it. (It's kinda fun, in a sick way, but nevermind that. I'm busy ranting here.) It was like some women's-studies professor had invented the show as a hypothetical example of sexism in media – it was a *caricature* of itself! EVERY female character was either virgin or whore. EVERY two seconds there was a gratuitous shot of some girl's babydoll dress wafting up daintily to reveal her crotch. Or another skinny chick's backside, conveniently poised and tilted slightly upward for our gazing pleasure. ARG! And the 'pretty' boy lead character, blathering on constantly about what a genius Speilberg is, looked like someone carved his face out of a pumpkin. It was all hyped up on the radio and in the paper today as 'a program that can be enjoyed by teens and their parents'. What!? I would have *never* watched that show with my parents – not at 16, not now. It was all about sex, and in the worst possible way! Every other word was 'hormones' or 'hump' or 'size queen' or 'genitalia'. Seriously! Totally gratuitous. Totally insulting. (1.20.98)

However, in another essay on feminism she writes with a seriousness and formality that is quite different:

> Challenging the division between the personal and the political, the public and the private, was a radical move that revitalized the feminist movement during the 1970s. But it carried mixed implications for the movement itself. On the one hand, steering public attention towards once private issues enabled feminists to raise awareness and initiate action around social problems that previously had been either ignored or quietly accepted. The Roe v. Wade victory and the proliferation of domestic violence shelters are but two examples of such successes. However, the strategy of connecting the personal with the political, when used as an organizing technique, often proved counterproductive and divisive. ('Personal vs Political vs. Feminist', 3.1.98)

Miss Melty is an amalgam of academic-style writing and fun, chatty forms of writing that blend into a representation of a feminist Ann who is multi-dimensional and diverse. Webzines offer opportunities for sharing and interacting with others on many different levels all within the same writing space and work to connect feminism, a serious and important political issue, with fun and pleasure. The proliferation of webzines is an indication that in some sense feminists may be accepting a blend of various styles of thinking and acting. They are using technology to further their project and to understand what feminism means in a world dominated by global and diversity issues. Not only are they expanding what it means to be a feminist in the sense of an occupation or style, but the expansion extends to race, class, and physical disability as well as many other attributes. As the authors of *A Girl's Guide to Taking Over the World: Writings From the Girl Zine Revolution* write:

> What threads these zines together is that they are all very real and very much from the heart. They don't have advertisers to please, and they weren't created for financial success. They originate from a need for expression, a need girls have to discover and create the truth about themselves and their lives. Through zines, we can see young women uncensored and free to discuss their realities. (Green and Taormino, 1997)

A problematic issue, however, is access. If only an élite, educated number of feminists with access to computers are able to write and read webzines, then it does not seem like the nature of feminism as a whole could be expanding that much. But this ignores the 'trickle down' effect where webzines are being reproduced in other forms and other forms of writing inspired by webzines and zines are created and distributed. Webzines and the third-wave feminist movement have gained national attention, both good and bad, as suggested by the recent *Time* magazine article which identifies and publicises the third-wave feminist movement (Bellafante, 1998). There is still a participation issue, but print zines as well as other books alleviate this to a certain degree. A recent swell of books on girl power and feminist thinking acknowledge this style of thinking and suggest that it is more than a phase, but rather an important part of defining oneself as feminist from an expanded point of view.[6] For example, one essay from a collection of women's writing, titled *Listen Up: Voices From the Next Feminist Generation*, discusses how the author felt she could be a feminist despite this apparently non-feminist occupation.

> Just saying my title is enough to make most people laugh: feminist aerobics instructor. Huh? It's like being a fascist poet. People think you just can't. One day several years ago as I impelled my step class to eat whatever they wanted whenever they wanted, to love their thighs no matter what size, I was overwhelmed by all the uniquely American, female contradictions confronting me. The women in the class just stared at me with these blank, nearly hostile eyes. Hello? What part of 'low-fat' didn't I understand? Couldn't I see how fat they were? What kind of aerobics instructor was I, anyway.
>
> The answer was easy: a twenty-something, lower-middle-class musician/writer/social critic cum feminist aerobics instructor with big college loan payments, and, therefore, a big, two-sided problem. (Valdes, 1995, p. 12)

Webzines are indeed having a larger effect not just by themselves, but as a part of a larger movement that is trying to redefine feminism in a way that is more relevant to the needs and issues of the current political climate.

Another issue to address is that webzine writing does not seem all that different from other forms of writing. For instance, there are many examples of fragmentary and collage-like writing in novels like Emily Brontë's *Wuthering Heights*, or in texts such as Deleuze and Guattari's *A Thousand Plateaus*. What is unique though is the possibility for massive distribution. Furthermore, webzines have been produced by many people who do not normally consider themselves writers. Because the nature of writing on the Web tends to be much more informal and more like oral communication, many potential writers find themselves in a comfortable and familiar writing environment where they can express themselves, not in a formalistic way, as in worrying about spelling, punctuation and grammar, or the flow of argument, but rather in a way that they feel suits their style— one that is not necessarily accountable to the structures and limitations of formal writing.

A third issue suggests that it is not clear what being a feminist means if the notion is so fragmented that anyone or anything can be a feminist. It might be argued that the Web and/or postmodernism have obliterated any meaningful distinctions that might provide feminism with a political voice. It suggests a kind of confusion of identity and with feminism in general. In particular, it is not immediately clear what the difference is between expressing a hybrid self as opposed to a fractured self. One might suggest that these webzines represent a fractured self that is searching for a sense of wholeness—a way to fit the pieces together that makes sense and feels right. The idea of hybridity suggests a union of two different parts to make something that is different from either of the two parts yet which has some of the characteristics of both. Hybridity implies that the new entity created from the parts is in some ways even better than the parts by themselves—that this new creation has the strength of both parts in one organism. Hybrid crops are created because they have, for example, the insect-resistant properties of one strain while also having the desirable taste of another. So implying that feminism is a kind of hybrid suggests an unproblematic way of being. This implies that there is one kind of feminism that is a hybrid collection of disparate thought and practice blended together in a unified way. While many are indeed expanding and blending their conceptions of feminism, this new feminist self perhaps more closely resembles the cyborg in its uneasy blend of elements.

The cyborg contains both the idea of the hybrid and the monster, as in Frankenstein's creation where all the appropriate parts are in place but everything is slightly off, slightly grotesque, and sewn together with rough and crude stitches. Similarly, the cybernetic cyborg is a blend of human and machine, but it is not a fluid or smooth blend. There are parts that are clearly machine attached to other body parts that are clearly organic. The cyborg metaphor contains both the idea of hope and danger, constructing the self as neither an unproblematic, improved entity involving a smooth blend of attributes nor a disjunct, barely functioning collection of disparate parts that do not really fit together. *Melty* is a collection of disparate facets of feminism, seemingly uniting popular culture, politics, and different genres of writing in a single cyborg publication. *Melty* writes as both an academic and political feminist as well as a TV-watching and homemaker feminist. While these aspects are not always assembled in a neat and tidy package, it is something like a hybrid, or better yet, cyborg representation of feminism.

Yet while the webzine *Melty* represents a kind of cyborg feminism there is also a sense in which it represents a small, isolated niche feminism. For example, *Melty* can be considered a kind of intellectual academic feminism that does not have much value for working-class feminists. Or, put another way, *Melty* is a very American webzine that refers to popular culture and politics that is only of interest to US feminists. While many feminists are trying to expand their identities on the Web, there is a larger tendency where feminists are able to find a group that more closely represents their own unique interests, such as post-structuralist feminists, liberal feminists, post-feminists, cyberfeminists and so on. What was once understood as feminism, while it was never a united and unified community, has now become even more splintered and divided. This is why many refer to feminism today as 'feminisms' as a way to describe the fractured and disconnected nature of affiliations. Despite the real possibilities for interaction and discussion on the Web, the new communications technology is also creating a feminist identity that is much more niche-oriented.

If identity is best represented by the idea of multiple identities, then schools might emphasise one of two directions. Given increasing multiple and diverse kinds of niche identities, schools presumably might need to work even harder to create a sense of tolerance and understanding between diverse interest groups and cultural affiliations. Whether it is a sense of nation or 'imagined community', it seems that schools might be the appropriate place to create a sense of commonality. Another direction, however, is for schools to follow the trend of niche communities, catering to very specific kinds of identities. In the USA virtual schools, voucher programs, home-schooling, charter schools and magnet schools all suggest that public schools are becoming more specialised, catering to smaller more local groups of interest, and that the idea of the public is being undermined to a certain degree by the idea of 'publics' (Fraser, 1993). While Nancy Fraser calls upon the idea of many publics to further the project of democracy, the danger is that this can also recapitulate the splintering and alienation among disparate interest groups. It creates the tendency to develop and sustain isolated public spheres—none of which will necessarily talk to one another when necessity demands such dialogue. Fraser suggests that as long as these public spheres are not bracketed off from each other there will still be a possibility for dialogue, and suggests that 'insofar as these arenas are *publics* they are by definition not enclaves' (Fraser, 1993, p. 15). This notion draws upon a wider notion of the 'public at large' which she suggests is a way to reduce divisive kinds of separatism. It nevertheless may be the only viable alternative given, as Fraser argues, the existence of social inequity. So while she makes a case for the idea of many publics, it is also clear that she is holding on to some notion of larger community goals. But she is ambivalent about whether this wider public should be the nation-state, particularly in an expanding and globally interconnected world. If schools follow this trend then it seem imperative that some overarching goals need to be maintained in order to free up the possibility for multiple kinds of schools. Perhaps what this suggests is not a re-imagination of the nation, but rather a re-imagination of a democratic ideal, whether it is a nation or something larger. For example, the European Community is one such re-imagination that is a potential model for rethinking the space of public discourse in an increasingly interconnected and inter-dependent world. The writing of feminist webzines and the increasing proliferation of identities around the notion of feminism indicate that students' affiliations are becoming much more complex and varied. Assuming that schools need to address this issue, the idea of localised niche schools under a democratic umbrella might be one way to work with this trend.

NOTES

1. All excerpts from the webzine *Miss Melty* which have a link to another webpage will be underlined.
2. Zines are also publicised by a magazine called *Fact Sheet Five* which reviews new zines and is printed and distributed in the United States in many alternative book stores.
3. I will assume that *Melty* is authored by a person named Ann throughout this discussion. While there is good reason to believe that this person actually exists and is who she claims to be, the realm of cyberspace makes all this background information questionable.
4. *HUES* stands for 'Hear Us Emerging Sisters' and is a magazine devoted to the feminist interests of women and girls of colour.
5. The TV show *Buffy the Vampire Slayer* is a very popular series among girls in the USA and depicts a high school girl who was appointed to defend the world against vampires. Part of its popularity is due to the Buffy's strong and capable female role model. Buffy leads the fight against the vampires and organises the student revolt. In addition, she is also very feminine.
6. For instance, the following books were produced as part of the feminist webzine movement: Francesca Lia Block and Hillary Carlip (1998), *Zine Scene: The Do it Yourself Guide to Zines* (Girl Press); Trina Robbins (1999), *From Girls to Grrrlz: A History of Women's Comics From Teens to Zines* (San Francisco: Chronicle Books); Leslie Heywood and Jennifer Drake (eds) (1997), *Third Wave Agenda: Being Feminist, Doing Feminism* (Minneapolis: University of Minnesota Press); Laurel Gilbert and Crystal Kile (1996), *Surfer Grrrls: Look, Ethel! An Internet Guide for Us!* (Seattle, WA: Seal Press); Carla Sinclair (1996), *Netchick: A Smart-Girl Guide to the Wired World* (New York: Henry Holt); Lynn Cherny and Elizabeth Reba Weise (eds), *Wired_Women: Gender and New Realities in Cyberspace* (Seattle, WA: Seal Press).

6

Credibility of the Web: Why We Need Dialectical Reading

BERTRAM C. BRUCE

Many educators today recognise the importance of online data sources for all sorts of research and writing projects. Some now permit students to include online sources in their work and others actually require their use. There are abundant resources available online, including real-time video; radio stations from around the world; reference tools, such as encyclopaedias, dictionaries, thesauri and collections of quotes; libraries of poetry, short stories, images and music; critical studies and research articles on every conceivable topic; information about authors and historical figures; government and public policy data; current events; interactive software; and much, much more. At the same time, most users quickly see the problems that arise. Issues of privacy, plagiarism, pornography, hate sites, commercialism and simply wasting time arise regardless of the topic. The abundance soon yields thousands of Web-sites of dubious quality and relevance.

The World Wide Web is growing rapidly, unpredictably, unevenly and without the familiar guideposts of established publishers and vetting procedures. As the Web assumes ever greater importance in education, research and daily life, these phenomena deserve more critical examination. Is the Web a bountiful source of information and resources on every conceivable topic, as some claim? Or is it unreliable, ephemeral, and over-commercialised, as others warn? Do we need to develop criteria for evaluating Web pages to separate the good from the bad? Is the Web a fundamentally different medium that requires new modes of critique? This chapter explores how characteristics of the Web lead to it being simultaneously a great and a questionable source of information. The issue then becomes how we should read such a complex and contradictory text.

THE GROWTH OF THE WEB

Cyberspace appears at times to be lawless. But there are two descriptive laws that have shaped its destiny. Moore's Law and Metcalfe's Law define, at least metaphorically, the vast growth of the Web, with both its promises and its problems. The widely-cited law proposed in 1965 by Gordon Moore holds that the computing power of a microchip will double every eighteen months. This generalisation has held up for nearly four decades. As chips have become smaller, more transistors can be placed on each chip, allowing new features to be added. The speed increases because the distance between the transistors is reduced. The accumulation of these quantitative changes has brought about qualitative changes in what computers can do.

As more transistors are packed into smaller and smaller spaces, microchip technology is approaching natural limits. At the size under development today, atomic layers can be counted and identified. Even Moore (1998) himself says now:

> So at some time in the next several generations, we really start to get to some fundamental limits. But not before we've gone through probably five more generations of technology. If you extrapolate all those curves together . . . we run out of gas doing that in the year 2017.

Metcalfe's Law has an even more direct connection to the growth of the Web as a gigantic library. It states that the value of a network increases as more people use it:

> If you had the only telephone in the world, who would you call? Networks seem to grow more valuable to a user proportionately with the number of other users he or she can call. In a network with N users, each sees a value proportional to the N–1 others, so the total value of the network grows as N*(N–1), or as N squared for large N. (Metcalfe, 1995)

Just as with Moore's Law, this law about networks has natural limits. Metcalfe himself points out that once a critical mass is reached mere growth may not add much value. A telephone becomes valuable as more of the people one would like to call have a telephone, but there is a lesser increase in value once most of those people have a phone.

The production of inexpensive computers and the attraction of networks have fuelled the growth of the Web. This raises the question: How large is the Web today? Like many simple questions, this one turns out to be more complicated than it might at first appear. It hinges on the definition of terms such as 'large' and 'Web'. Different assumptions and different approaches to measuring the Web lead to varying results. Most of these numbers have been doubling every twelve to eighteen months. Various surveys estimate that there are roughly 200 million users of the Internet. This is about 3% of the earth's population. More than half of those users are in the USA and Canada. Other surveys calculate the number of active Internet addresses to be around 40 million.

A Web page can be anything from a few words, to a site with video, interactive software, music files or extensive text. Thus when we say that there are so many pages on the Web, it is not quite the same as saying so many pages in a book. Still, if we knew how many Web pages there were, we would have some idea of the size of the Web, at least relative to what it has been. By comparing the pages returned by various search engines,[1] Steve Lawrence and C. Lee Giles (1999) derived 800 million pages as a lower bound for the size of the publicly accessible Web. This means the Web contains at least 800 million pages, probably somewhat more. They estimate further that these pages contain six terabytes of data versus the twenty terabytes of the entire Library of Congress.[2] Lawrence and Giles found that the best of the search engines finds only 16% of the Web pages, not counting those behind firewalls.[3] These issues need to be understood when one is interpreting the results of a search and evaluating the overall usefulness of the Web.[4]

CREDIBILITY CHALLENGES POSED BY THE WEB

The immense body of information currently available through the Web coupled with its rapid, almost chaotic growth hold great promise, but raise serious issues about the legitimacy, veracity, relevance and timeliness of Web texts. Challenges to the credibility of sites on the Web come from many factors. Among these are the speed of change to Web-sites, the sheer quantity of information, commercialism, the distributed authority of Web authorship and the nature of hypertext.

Prior to the Web, the issue of speed was not often mentioned in discussions about the authority or credibility of texts. What has changed is that the Web combines in an interesting way the archival capacity of printed text with the real-time malleability of broadcast media. In some contexts, this means that the Web assumes a greater potential veracity. For example, Web-sites can include video segments produced in real-time. They can be updated as new information appears. On the other hand, the fluidity of the Web is one of its greatest defects. If the meaning of a site is defined in part by its relation to other sites, then one might say the meaning deteriorates rapidly, because links decay speedily over periods as short as a few months. Also, the fact that Web-sites can be produced quickly does little to increase the confidence of users that the sites have been thoughtfully constructed.

The Cable News Network Interactive Web-site is updated every few minutes. Other sites are created, posted on the Web, and never changed. Some sites, but not all, indicate when they were last updated, but it is usually difficult to determine whether the page you are viewing is the most recent in a series or just the one you happened upon. For an article about *Beowulf*, the timeliness issue may not appear severe, but for many domains, the question of timeliness is critical, yet unanswerable.

Beyond sheer speed, the enormous size of the Web is another dubious blessing. Hundreds of millions of pages hold forth the promise of presenting the text or images we seek, but the sheer volume of material gets in its own way. For example, a search for the US Department of Commerce's report, 'Falling through the net', about the racial and income inequities in access to new information and communication technologies, yields articles about World Cup soccer, and the performance of an accomplished goalie defending her team's net. Other searches find obsolete versions of material that exists elsewhere on the Web, while missing revised texts.

Given the number of Web pages, it is actually surprising that one can find anything at all, much less do so in a matter of seconds. Improved search engines make that possible, especially when the user understands how the search engines work and puts some effort into selecting a good set of keywords. There is so much material on the Web that the irrelevant far outweighs the relevant for any search. As Lawrence and Giles have pointed out, Web search engines are useful resources, but they lack comprehensiveness and timeliness. They compare the current state to a phone book which has most of the pages ripped out.

Commercialism is another issue for the Web as information resources. Most Web-sites are created to sell something, not to provide valid and useful information. A recent estimate is that 83% of sites have primarily commercial content (Guernsey, 1999). Even in cases where the information is useful, the commercial assault is something to be avoided in schools and other learning environments. Very often it is difficult to get past the many commercial sites, which have engineered their Web pages to appear first no matter how one specifies a search query.

Turning to the non-commercial sites provides no easy solution to the issue of quality. The beauty of the Web is that anyone can make a Web-site, for less than the cost of publishing a pamphlet. But a consequence of this is that there is no resort to any kind of recognised textual authority, no board of editors as for a respected encyclopaedia, who invite authors and vet articles for publication. And authority is a highly disputable term on the Web. When students, or anyone for that matter, actually do find relevant information on the Web, it is all too easy to copy that material without attribution.

Moreover, it is unfortunately the case that one cannot imagine any dark corner of human activity that is not now finding its representation on the Web. Sites promoting substance abuse, suicide, bomb-making, racial hatred, interleave with children's artwork, poetry, music and images from the Hubble telescope.

Finally, the hypertextual format of the Web is touted as one of its great virtues. Every Web page draws in part from its intertextual relations with other Web pages. But that makes it difficult to determine where meaning resides. The vast quantity of the Web pretends to a universality that it cannot support. It represents human knowledge, cultures and values very unevenly, yet the hypertext medium suggests that everything is really there and equitably represented somehow.

Moreover, to an extent not fully appreciated by most users, the meaning is constrained not only by the Web pages themselves, but by the search engines that navigate the hypertext, and by the interaction between the search engines and commercial and governmental interests. Most search engines are commercial enterprises designed to entice users by just good enough searches and thereby to expose them to advertisements. Web pages in turn are constructed to attain high positions in the search indices so that users will see those pages first. This means that searches that purportedly present information in some neutral way are actually strongly shaped by interests independent of, if not opposed to, the inquiry of the user.

THE WEB AS LIBRARY[5]

> The universe (which others call the Library) is composed of an indefinite, perhaps an infinite, number of hexagonal galleries, with enormous ventilation shafts in the middle, encircled by very low railings.

Thus begins the fantastic tale Jorge Luis Borges wrote in 1941, called 'La Biblioteca de Babel' or 'The Library of Babel'.[6] When Borges was fifty-eight, he became Director of the National Library of Argentina. In his fictional library he envisions a world populated by books. These books are held in a fantastic Library, whose architecture is like no existing library, but is nevertheless carefully and believably constructed. Each of the galleries within the Library is hexagon-shaped with bookcases on four sides. The free sides lead to hallways from which one can reach additional galleries:

> There are five shelves for each of the hexagon's walls; each shelf contains thirty-five books of uniform format; each book is of four

hundred and ten pages; each page, of forty lines, each line, of some eighty letters which are black in color.

These books contain all possible arrangements of the orthographic characters, punctuation, and spaces, leading some to assert 'the formless and chaotic nature of almost all the books'. It is assumed that:

> the Library is total...[it includes] the minutely detailed history of the future, the archangels' autobiographies, the faithful catalogues of the Library, thousands and thousands of false catalogues...the translation of every book in all languages.

This totality of texts means that one can find anything in the Library, beautiful writing in every conceivable genre, information for every purpose, and guidance for every problem:

> When it was proclaimed that the Library contained all books, the first impression was one of extravagant happiness...As was natural, this inordinate hope was followed by an excessive depression. The certitude that some shelf in some hexagon held precious books and that these precious books were inaccessible, seemed almost intolerable.

The Web today hides its treasures behind a greater mass of semiprecious and junk-grade texts. Moreover, it holds worse than useless works. As Borges would surely have surmised, it contains libelous portrayals, pornography, hate sites and simple falsehoods. This phenomenon of nonsense growing faster than sense has led many to seek ways to clean up the Web. So, in Borges's library:

> Others, inversely, believed that it was fundamental to eliminate useless works. They invaded the hexagons, showed credentials which were not always false, leafed through a volume with displeasure and condemned whole shelves: their hygienic, ascetic furor caused the senseless perdition of millions of books.

For better or worse, the attempts to limit the Web appear to be similarly futile. Restrictions of Web use in one country are quickly countered by the appearance of new Web-sites in another. Attempts to monitor Web use are defeated by tools that allow anonymous use. Replication and expansion of content proceeds much faster than any kind of control, whether rationalised by moral values or goals of content correctness. The Web remembers, because sites not only link to, but mirror,[7] each other by copying content:

> (since the Library is total) there are always several hundred thousand imperfect facsimiles: works which differ only in a letter or a comma.

What does all this incredible content mean? Are we moving toward some global encyclopaedia that accounts for everything or to an entropic doom of maximal disorder? Can we imagine that the Web itself holds the explanation of its own purpose and intrinsic worth?

> On some shelf in some hexagon (men reasoned) there must exist a book which is the formula and perfect compendium of all the rest.

Unlike an encyclopaedia, or a conventional library,[8] Borges's Library has no catalogue, no organisation, no board of reviewers, no content policies, no authoritative authors and no canon of established works. Or rather, it has all possible catalogues and so on. It contains every proposition and its negation, hence it is totally contradictory and incoherent. While stability over time is a goal for a conventional collection, stability has no meaning for the Library. It suffers none of the limits of time and space that define conventional collections. These attributes lead its users to both 'extravagant happiness' and 'excessive depression'.

Conventional libraries are rapidly being converted into digital libraries,[9] and the Web itself functions as a new medium for text creation. Thus, it is both as a repository for existing texts and as a global publishing house for new texts. By most accounts, the Web is now comparable to major university and national libraries, though it is still smaller than the US Library of Congress. However, many libraries are now rapidly entering their texts, photographs, movies and sound recordings on the Web. It is thus clear that the Web will soon surpass any conventional library in holdings. Given the size of the Web, and its rapid growth, it is not surprising that there is much work underway to build better search engines, search directories,[10] filters, jump sites, portals and other technologies to enable more productive use of the Web.

Though it does not have the unimaginable extent of Borges's Library, the Web compensates by its capacity to grow, to create a *de novo* response to every conceivable query. It is indefinite in extent rather than infinite, but its appearance to a reader is more like that of the Library than that of most conventional collections. The fact that new entries appear in the time of a single search is but one indication of its dynamic nature.

MODES OF READING THE WEB

The richness of the Web, and its corresponding unruliness, raise a fundamental question about the credibility of Web sources and accordingly about how one should read the Web. Various approaches to addressing this question recur in the plethora of writings about the Web. These range from seeing the Web as a great boon to seeing it as useless, or even dangerous.

A useful framework for addressing this question is Walter Kaufmann's essay (1977), 'The Art of Reading', in which he sets forth a taxonomy of modes of reading.[11] In that essay, Kaufmann concerns himself with characterising and promoting humanistic education, which he defines as including the preservation and appreciation of the great works of civilisation, the realisation of personal autonomy through reflection and the acquisition of a personal vision. His question then is whether it is possible to read the great works in different ways, and if so, which of these ways are most likely to advance that ideal of education.

If we see the Web as a massive text, we may then ask what are the different modes of reading it. For example, one prevalent view is that the Web offers great resources, and that our task is to understand how to use it so that we fully appreciate its bounty. This view is akin to Kaufmann's *exegetical* reader, for whom the text is definitive and the reader need only study it thoroughly to divine its true value. The exegetical reader of the Web assigns superior merit to the Web. Compared to print sources, the Web is seen to represent meaning through multimedia that gives richness and authenticity. The hypertext format allows copious interconnections of sources, providing meaning beyond that of any individual page. The rapid updating of Web-sites, including, in the limit, the use of live cameras, implies a freshness and verisimilitude that print cannot afford.

Just like readers of a sacred text, exegetical readers of the Web impose their own values on the text. They choose the elements that reflect their own preferences and then employ the text to legitimise those preferences. They typically select and appropriate specific Web resources to illustrate the excellence of the Web for a given purpose, conveniently ignoring the lesser sites that others bemoan. The danger here is obvious: the exegetical reader does not enter into the Web critically, and thus promotes a superficial understanding.

In contrast, other readers approach the Web in a *dogmatic* mode. They assume the superiority of print media, and look for confirming evidence in the Web or its typical uses. The rapidity with which Uniform Resource Locators become outdated, commercialisation, the ease of access to pornography and most of all the knowledge that anyone can make a Web-site, are all seen as reasons to be suspicious of the Web. Where the exegetical reader sees bounty in the multiple sites on a given topic, the dogmatic reader sees chaos and the inability to judge good from bad. The more the Web grows, the more the dogmatic reader sees its flaws.

Although the exegetical and the dogmatic reader are mirror opposites, they share some characteristics. Both selectively analyse the Web to suit their prior beliefs. Neither engages fully with questions such as how Web as media really differs from print, or with what confidence one can make encompassing assumptions about the quality of Web resources.

A third type of reading is what Kaufmann calls the *agnostic* mode, and which we might equally characterise as the standard mode for engaging the Web. In a fashion that is a priori appropriate in the information age, agnostic readers adopt a technical stance toward Web quality. They acknowledge that there are both good and bad resources, and so develop schemes for finding good sites and separating one from the other. The agnostic mode entails attention to developing and finding better tools for accessing the Web, to conducting effective Web searches and to evaluating the quality of Web-sites.

For example, the agnostic mode recognises that the choice of search engine or search directory is a major factor in how effective a search may be relative to some task; for example, to find information about a book it may be more effective to search the database of an online bookseller than to search the entire Web. There are now many Web-sites that provide evaluative information about the relative performance of different search tools. These sites rate search tools, but often say less than they might about how a particular tool works and what assumptions it makes, assumptions that directly shape the collection of documents a search produces, and ultimately, one's ability to find information on the Web.

In addition to seeking improved technologies for Web searches, the agnostic reader seeks to improve search practices. For example, one rule is to understand the language for searches. Each search engine has its own syntax for specifying Boolean expressions.[12] Usually, setting a phrase in quotes means to find that phrase exactly as written. Good searches depend upon expressing questions effectively in the appropriate search language. Another principle is to understand that search engines do not go out and look at every Web page in existence in order to answer a query. Many Web pages are hidden from the search engines behind organisational firewalls. Moreover, it would take far too long to examine every page as each query arises. Instead, the search engine builds a search index[13] that enables fairly rapid searches. A consequence of this is that the user is not searching the Web itself, but the index, and is thus dependent on the quality of the index, its organisational scheme and how recently it has been updated. Among other things, this means that recent additions to the Web may not appear as the result of a search.

Once a Web-site has been found the agnostic user applies a scheme for evaluating it, typically expressed as a series of questions, sometimes with point values to assign for each. The implication is that if a site scores well on the set of questions, it is trustworthy and useable, and if not is best passed over. Some of these issues are primarily syntactic, relating to formal properties of the Web-site. These include ease of navigation, accessibility to users with physical impairments or slow network connections, copy-editing or readability of the layout. Other issues are more at a semantic or content level, for example understandability and relevance of images, acknowledgement of biases, or indications of the source of information. Finally, yet other issues are pragmatic in nature, such as judgements about the reputation of the author, the site's primary purpose or the time of its writing. The agnostic reader of the Web thus sees a technocratic solution to the problem of Web variety: there are good sites, and there are bad sites. We just need to apply a formula to select our tools, find the sites and judge among them.

The agnostic mode does not prejudge the value of the Web, and it leads to some useful schemes for finding information. But in Heidegger's (1977) sense, it participates in or furthers the technological enframing. That is, the resources of the Web are interpreted as bits to be searched, retrieved and processed, rather than as an opportunity for a dialogical relationship with others. The agnostic mode is thus a technological framework that reduces the Web to a stockpile of resources.

There are two major problems with conceiving of Web searches as simply looking up information. The first is the practical one that we are often frustrated. The answers may be 'out there', but if we search inappropriately we get useless data back from the search. Interesting questions require some effort ahead of time to be formulated well. Moreover, good answers typically develop out of interaction with rich material and not as immediate prepared texts. All the general rules for searching suffer from the fact that the method of search depends on the problem being investigated.

This problem derives from a conception of searching the Web as a straightforward process of looking up information. For certain purposes, that conception is quite appropriate. For example, if I want to find some general information about *Beowulf*, the oldest epic in English, I type 'Beowulf' into my search engine and get 41,565 links to documents. There are complete texts of *Beowulf*, critical commentary, curriculum units and much more. But suppose I want to look deeper into these sites. I soon discover controversies regarding the Christian and pagan elements in *Beowulf*. For example,[14]

> She [Grendel's mother] was doomed to dwell in the dreary waters,
> cold sea-courses, since Cain cut down
> with edge of the sword his only brother,
> his father's offspring

There are disputes about the sources of these elements, the degree of integration and the implications for medieval history. If I want to enter into the critical debates I find many sources. Some are university sites, others from libraries. Some are from creation scientists and many have no clear attribution.

I come across the site of a professor of English, Jonathan Glenn. I am inclined to believe Glenn's modulated claim: 'The precise relationship between Grendel and the "kin of Cain" is unclear in the poem; that he is at least spiritually akin to Cain, however, is never in doubt'. The site is well-organised and has ample material, not only on *Beowulf*, but much of medieval literature. I am impressed by the care shown with the presentation, the detail of the documents, the citations of sources and the opportunities for feedback. I am further encouraged by the fact that the site links to several other sites that appear useful and well-constructed. Thus it serves as what has been called a 'hub' site. But as a novice in this area, I cannot be certain that this is the most credible starting point for my inquiry. Is this an authoritative site? Are there more credible sources, perhaps even espousing the same argument?

Despite these concerns, I am relieved in some ways. I do not see here troubling signs of the racism or pornography that percolate throughout the Web. My usual worry that the site may be superseded by a more recent one is partially allayed by the fact that the most recent update is less than one year old and the site appears to be well-maintained. Thus, although I do not know the author or much about the domain of study, I find the site to be worth further investigation. If I can believe what I read there, I have found a timely resource with all sorts of useful information and links for further study.

What I have discovered here is thus for my purposes a potentially useful source. But although I have spent some time examining it, I still have doubts about how to interpret what I read there. When I return to the massive list of documents that the search engine provided me, I feel a bit overwhelmed. Will I have to spend this much time on every document and still not know what to make of it all?

I have discovered something else. For certain kinds of queries, my search is far from a simple look-up. Instead, it appears to be part of the general process of inquiry, which is tentative and fallible. There is no absolute starting point, nor is there any sure way to reach the end, assuming such a point exists. I need to muster all my resources for critical thinking in order to navigate my way through the Web, but in the process may reap enormous benefits.

This leads us to the second problem with conceiving of Web searches as simply looking up information, that it obscures the Web's potential importance for education or other life activities. The true value of the Web lies in the way it can open up our questions. We ask one thing, but the Web leads us to ask more questions and to become aware of how much we do not know. A recognition of these problems leads us to move from a conception of searching the Web in order to find a piece of information to one in which a search is embedded in how we think. How can searching become not only 'looking up', but truly productive inquiry?

DIALECTICAL READING OF THE WEB

We now turn to Kaufmann's fourth mode of reading, the *dialectical*. Here, the word 'dialectical' is used in a specific sense not derived directly from Plato, Kant, Hegel or Marx. For Kaufmann, it is a way of capturing a 'deep experience' of reading. He says that dialectical reading is distinguished by the fusion of three crucial elements. The first is called *Socratic*, 'because it harks back to Socrates' dissatisfaction with the unexamined life' (1977, p. 61). This element asks the dialectical reader to be open to the different culture manifested in a text. The second element is *dialogical*, a 'deliberate exposure to alternatives' (*ibid.*, p. 64). And the third is *historical–philosophical*, attempting to understand the work in its larger contexts.

Kaufmann's use of the term 'dialectical' is perhaps closer to Dewey and Bentley's term *transaction*. As does Kaufmann, they reject both naive realism, which posits events independent of the perceiver, and subjectivism, which has no way of accounting for common knowledge. Instead, they adopt a constructivist theory of meaning. Knowing is then a process in which the individual learns through reflection on ordinary experience and through communication with others.

In both Kaufmann's dialectical mode and the transactional theory of knowing, each encounter with a phenomenon is a unique event, neither wholly determined by external processes nor independent of them. The meaning of a Web-site is then neither a superior representation, as it might be viewed in the exegetical mode, nor an opportunity for quick dismissal, as in the dogmatic mode. Nor is it simply a text to be selected, analysed, measured and categorised, as the agnostic mode would have it. Instead, the dialectical observer enters into a relationship with the text in which there is an openness to new values and ways of making meaning. The result is a process of accepting discomfort, examining alternatives, and searching for new understandings. Thus meaning is not static, but constructed out of the evolving activities of thinking and doing.

Furthermore, because no Web document stands alone, but is interlinked with the entire Web, the meaning of any Web page is ultimately dependent upon its relationships with other pages. For example, when I visited the Glenn site on *Beowulf*, I began to build my understanding of that site in terms of its relationship to other sites on *Beowulf*, medieval literature and in the final analysis all other sites on the Web. This implies a second-order transaction in which reading a Web page entails reading the matrix of texts in which it is embedded.

The dialectical reader must possess coding, semantic and pragmatic competence. But instead of just applying a set of rules for assessing Web-sites, the dialectical mode entails reading with a critical eye. This means engaging with the text in a way that goes beyond seeing it as an information resource, and instead permits a relationship with the text. That relationship can include reading what is not said and even reading against the text. On the Web, this means opening oneself up to different ways of interpreting the world and seeking to understand the political, social and historical dimensions of Web discourse.

Finally, the dialectical reader must see a specific Web page in relation to the Web as a whole. This means not only the other documents collected there, but the social practices associated with the Web—what genres and textual conventions are invoked, who controls the technologies and whose interests are served by particular communications. As Burbules and Callister (n.d.) point out, whether and how one has access to the Web is closely tied to one's ability to ascertain credibility. Critical understanding requires this level of reflection on the uses of the Web as well as its formal properties.

On the dialectical view, searching is the journey, not just the arrival. That is, one can never confidently say that the Web has been fully searched and the answer found. This suggests an alternative to the common practice of asking students to cite one library source and one online source for an essay. Activities such as that presuppose an order to the Web that simultaneously over- and under-states its value. Instead, we could turn the Web's unruliness into a virtue. We might say: 'Use the Web to find the answer to such-and-such a question. Now, report on three things you learned that you had never imagined before you did that search'. Alternatively, we might ask students to find some information on the Web, and then its opposite. That contradiction could then initiate an inquiry into the topic and the ways that authors write about it.

Although Kaufmann's analysis of reading is framed within a larger work on the future of the humanities, his taxonomy extends to the diverse genres of the Web, such as scientific texts, databases, news articles, images and interactive software. In fact, the need for dialectical reading may be even more critical for other genres. Consider the case of online encyclopaedias. Prior to the Web, one might have argued that a recognised encyclopaedia, with its selection of experts as authors, its review board, its wide readership and its unified approach was legitimately authoritative. Today, there are many digital encyclopaedias, including both traditional collections now in online or disk forms and new electronic-only encyclopaedias. Reading these competing online accounts of knowledge calls for both an openness to new ways of thinking and a concerted effort at Socratic, dialogical and historical–philosophical understanding.

CONCLUSION

The issues for reading posed by the Web are not new. Indeed, as I have argued, a useful construct for understanding the Web is Kaufmann's modes of reading from twenty years ago, which itself derives from a long tradition in hermeneutics and humanistic inquiry. There are direct parallels, for instance, between the dialectical mode and Gadamer's definition of the task of hermeneutics as 'the bridging of personal or historical distance between minds' (1976, p. 95).

Kaufmann (1977, p. 83) closes his essay with the warning that 'neither television nor computers can save the humanities if the art of reading texts is lost'. If anything, a close analysis of the processes of Web reading heightens the need for critical inquiry in its traditional senses. Multimedia, hypertext and the rapid change on the Web do not preclude the need for dialectical reading, but instead extend it in new directions. Viewed this way, the principles for search and evaluation that derive from the agnostic mode are useful tools. They acknowledge the particular features of the new discourse genre we call the Web, but they are only in service to the larger scope of dialectical inquiry.

NOTES

1. A search engine is a computer program that returns a list of the documents that satisfy a Boolean search expression; the term is usually used to refer to programs that search for Web documents.
2. A terabyte is a trillion bytes of information, enough to represent a trillion characters; about one hundred fairly large personal computer hard drives would be needed to hold this much information.
3. A firewall is a system that creates a partition between a private network and the larger Internet; it may restrict access both to and from the Internet.
4. Members of the Clever project (1999) estimate that roughly a million Web pages are added every day. This is one rationale for their effort to develop algorithms for more sophisticated searching. These algorithms are based on studies of the interconnectivity of the Web, on how Web pages have annotated connections to other pages. They estimate that there are more than a billion hyperlinks in the Web today, about one per page.
5. The following section is adapted from Bruce (1999).
6. The story was published in his collection, *Ficciones* (Borges, 1962).
7. A mirror site is a Web-site that maintains a copy of another site so that the access load is distributed more evenly across the Internet, or users in a distant part of the world can have faster connections.
8. My thanks to Paul Standish for suggesting expansions to this section.

9. Digital library—a concept with varying definitions; the Association of Research Libraries' definition suggests synonymy with 'electronic library' or 'virtual library'. Key elements are that the library uses new technologies to link diverse resources in a manner transparent to the user.

10. Search directory—a database that organises documents according to categories, and usually, subcategories; provides an alternative to general searching for finding particular items.

11. Ralph Smith (1989) applies Kaufmann's model in a similar way to the reading of other cultures.

12. Boolean expression—An expression that evaluates to *true* or *false*; for example, used in a Web search, the expression 'travel and France' is *true* for every Web page that contains both 'travel' and 'France'. Expressions that contain logical operators such as 'and', 'or', and 'not' are Boolean, but all Web searches implicitly involve Boolean expressions.

13. A search index is a large database of document locations based on the words contained in each document. The index facilitates efficient, meaningful searches and is created by a program within the search engine.

14. From *Beowulf* in *The Harvard Classics*, Volume 49. Copyright 1910 by P. F. Collier & Sons. This text is in the public domain, released July 1993. It is widely available on the Web.

7

Conjuring Notions of Place

JANE McKIE

> People who are constantly asking 'why' are like tourists, who stand in front of a building, reading Baedeker, & through reading about the history of the building's construction etc etc are prevented from *seeing* it. Wittgenstein, *Culture and Value*, 40e

To what extent does a guidebook 'map' a territory? At the very least it conditions decisions about where to go and where to stay: country, region, area, canton, county, town or city, hotel, gîte, houseboat, tent. Are there certain basic needs and standards that any traveller would require? How does one go about gathering information, and what criteria are used for inclusion and exclusion in a travel guide? An awareness of the diversity of travellers is required, but not every taste can be catered for within a single guidebook. Hence the proliferation of books, increasingly detailed and focused guides, not to mention the proliferation of Internet guides for travellers.

Consideration of 'the guidebook' has direct relevance to education, particularly as regards the tension between unique and shared proclivities, between autonomy and absorption in the crowd. Consider the following extract from an article in the travel section of *The Guardian*:

> People like to travel with a book nowadays. A guidebook. They prop it on their belly as they lie before the sea. They hunch over it at the top of mountains. They scrutinise it on slow, humid train journeys. The words on the page are used as captions: every moment of the journey can be compared with the earlier journeys of somebody else. Travel guides are ubiquitous now; they are always there to ensure that the going is never too rough, the planet never too lonely. They make it difficult to be in danger; they make it unlikely that you ever need to find anything out. You already know the local history, the price of the hotel. Your own experience is not your guide—the guide is the guide, and its wisdom is updated annually. (Andrew O'Hagan, 1999, p. 2)

The resonance with education is unmistakable. Students are autonomous beings. They should be encouraged to explore for themselves, to make and take responsibility for their own choices on the basis of their own interests and situation. Naturally, self-education can take a variety of forms. For example, we make decisions about what to read, listen to or look at, where to go, which conversations to participate in, all of which contribute, it is thought, to incidental learning. Autodidacts self-consciously gather knowledge through a variety of informal means. These modes of informal learning contrast with collective study under the guidance of a teacher. Curriculum and syllabus for the latter tends to be predetermined, usually by a course designer who takes responsibility for selection, although a syllabus may be negotiated to some degree. This negotiation raises a complex set of questions about the logic of progression, about compromise and consensus and, crucially, about what it is worthwhile to know.

The tension between personal autonomy within the context of the problem-based education advocated by Dewey, and the 'approved' forms of knowledge recognised by educational institutions, is one felt keenly in modern liberal societies. Furthermore, this tension is articulated when one turns to the modes of interaction made possible by the Internet. O'Hagan as a travel writer sceptical about the ubiquitous guidebook might well have followed Dewey: let experience be your guide. The following text of an advertisement for Microsoft software draws on the autonomy/guidance duality by suggesting that without direction it is impossible to 'locate' worthwhile information. Both the *amount* and *form* of the information available on the Internet can be bewildering. The text begins, 'Microsoft software is waterwings in a sea of information'. There is a darker side to immersion; without help, without 'waterwings', the novice Net-user could drown under a stifling weight of information. The smaller text of the advertisement is more explicit:

> Microsoft software makes the chaotic organised, the complicated simple. For example, with Microsoft Office, a benevolent Answer Wizard guides you gently through even the most challenging tasks . . .

Digital guides 'locate' order in chaos. Sometimes embodied through a playful personification, they offer the navigation skills of the expert. Navigation itself encompasses location and retrieval skills, and it is necessary to master both in the new information age (Buck, 1997). So also in academic work, location and retrieval skills have always been essential in terms of finding and accurately citing primary and secondary sources. With the Internet, however, 'navigation' aptly mixes the two concepts into an activity that is altogether more fluid. 'Navigation', like 'immersion', suggests searching for and finding items of knowledge, but also conveys the fluidity and connectivity of exploring this apparently seamless, information-rich domain. But how seamless this actually *feels* may depend upon what I described above as 'direction' to 'worthwhile' information. Neither are straightforward terms. 'Direction' can be task-orientated, or it can take a softer form as a synonym for 'guidance'. For example, distance-learning students may have to visit a specific Internet site to access a step-by-step learning programme. Other students may be given a list of specific sites to visit by a course tutor in order to complete an assignment. On the other hand, it is possible to detail the addresses of sites that provide *optional* sources of contextual information for a particular programme of study, and then to leave students to wander freely about there. A tutor may wish to encourage 'open' exploration around a topic and then discuss the results collectively or individually.

The charted and uncharted waters of the Internet accommodate planned sequential learning *and* chance and spontaneity. What follows focuses on two distinguishing features of the Internet—the unprecedented capacities for storage of information, and the flexibility of hyperlinks. Both have implications for choice: first, the sheer amount of information that can be recorded and modified expands choice for learners (as is implied in the advert for Microsoft Internet software); second, flexible hyperlinks respond to individual selection, presenting learners with experiential paths. There are dangerous extremes contained within the architecture of the Internet: that of over-determination versus too much information that fails to resolve into meaning. And it is this dialectic—the dialectic between structure and agency—that must form the backdrop for ongoing discussion of the educational potential of interactive technology.

GUIDANCE AND AUTONOMY IN LEARNING

Hypermedia or hypertext refers to any information that is structured in a nonlinear way so that any individual can choose their own path through that information with the use of navigational controls. It is this technology that is popularly believed to have the greatest impact upon the educational sphere as we shall see, and it can be broadly divided into the following two categories (it is also worth noting that *hypertext* need not necessarily employ more than one medium and is therefore not synonymous with 'multimedia'):

1.   *Hypermedia authoring packages*: Software that enables a user to create (that is, 'author') hypermedia applications by inputting text, scanning images and so on, and setting up the navigational links between 'pages'. Packages include HyperCard and SuperCard which

are compatible with Apple Macintosh hardware; and PictureBook, ToolBook, Authorware Professional and Macromind Director which are compatible with IBM PC hardware.

2. *Hypermedia Applications*: A popular example might be hypermedia encyclopaedias which combine multimedia (text, images and sound in most cases) with a nonlinear structure so one can choose which path to follow through the text—where 'text' is broadly defined to include a variety of different media—by clicking their mouse on the appropriate icon. Other hypermedia applications include, for example, the MicroGallery at the National Gallery in London (which was authored using HyperCard software); the interactive touchscreen systems in the main hall at the Natural History Museum in London (which was authored using SuperCard software); even the ubiquitous cash machine can be thought of as a hypertext system, although it is fairly simple in structure, with little scope for exploration.

Criticisms of hypermedia have been voiced with reference to the relationship between canon, curriculum and the potentially competitive autonomy of the user. That the student—who, with the advent of hypermedia, could also adopt an editorial or authorial role—is able to determine the learning path that best fits their own agenda rather than that of the tutor is a challenge to those who are engaged in contemporary computer-mediated instructional design. Henrietta Shirk (1994, p. 81) gives voice to some central questions: how do learners know what they do not know? Should discovery be allowed to happen by chance? If structure is written into the system, what characteristics should this structure have?

What seems compelling about the Internet is the way that its structures are amenable to deconstruction. Patricia Carlson (1994, p. 74) contrasts the ossification of traditional course content with hypermedia's potential for liberating domain knowledge. Taking the higher education sector as an example, one can imagine the syllabi of both face-to-face higher education institutions and distance learning institutions such as the UK Open University benefiting enormously from online provision in which the 'connections' to pages of relevant material are updated regularly. In addition to the course tutor's searches, enterprising students electing to search independently might volunteer online resources and initiate links between them. The advantages would be twofold. First, when a course is designed and resource material gathered it usually has a finite life span. Although core material, in some subjects at least, may retain its centrality for decades or longer, supplementary scholarship is continually being produced, new works and commentaries written, new paintings painted and so on. In many cases these supplementary activities take on an importance that begins to unravel what was central to the curriculum. Maintaining sensitivity to new production depends on effective networks for the dissemination and discussion of ideas. In addition to conventional research, online resources could provide the key to keeping up to date. This raises a number of questions about the means and rights of access to information, the quantity and quality of information and, indeed, about what is deemed to be core and supplementary in the first place.

The integrity of a subject area, always provisional, is further destabilised by the proliferation of interdisciplinary links. Some have read this as a postmodern change, indeed, as a postmodern opportunity: there can be greater plurality in the realm of ideas than was the case previously. In an essay in honour of Paul Hirst, Jane Roland Martin asserts that a curriculum can sustain many and varied voices without becoming detrimentally fragmented:

> After denying that knowledge is a unity, Hirst made a point of saying, 'Neither is it a chaos' (Hirst, 1974, p. 137). Our elders have embraced the false dichotomy he was so careful to avoid. Is the equation of curricular inclusiveness with chaos valid? To make the curriculum of our schools and colleges receptive to voices and perspectives that have been excluded is no more a prescription for disorder than any step towards democracy. The 'democratisation' of the curriculum undoubtedly introduces a degree of complexity. But complexity does not entail chaos. (Roland Martin, 1993, p. 125)

The association of the Internet with democratic processes is well documented. It has been called an *agora*, a space for democratic global exchange. At the same time as idealisations of the democratic potential of the Internet abound, so do criticisms that focus on dystopian aspects such as the cultural dominance of the USA (Boshier, Wilson and Qayyum, 1999), surveillance (Poster, 1990) and information capitalism (Castells, 1998). Chernaik, Deegan and Gibson (1996) suggest modern and postmodern readings for generic digital development. Thus:

> Ours becomes an age of the triumph of modernity in techno-science. In the 'modern' account of it, the new technology becomes a means to greater *transparency*: improved understanding, better and more extensive knowledge, clearer and more plausible representations. The new technology therefore does not usher in a transformation of knowledge or thought. It is rather another stage in our emancipation or, at least, in the growth of our power over our world. (*ibid.*, p. 7)

In contrast, in the 'alternative' postmodern reading of technological advance the new media break down 'unilinear structures' and 'centralized perspectives'. The foundation of established knowledge is undermined. The same phenomenon can indeed be read in different ways. Take the example of the anonymity that the Internet offers. Not only can new identities be created for oneself (or a real identity disguised), one can read conversations posted to Internet bulletin boards or discussion groups without having to declare oneself or take part in dialogue. Some might see this as a real opportunity for people who are reserved in the context of face-to-face interaction. Perhaps they can find a voice previously undiscovered, or participate vicariously without the perceived risks of speaking out. Others might suggest that there is a *special* immediacy to the face-to-face, and that the alternative immediacy of a surrogate life in cyberspace encourages an emotional distance tantamount to digital voyeurism. People are enabled to sit in on conversations without the 'real-life' responsibility to make any sort of contribution, even if that contribution is simply the barest acknowledgement. Further, the emotional distance permitted in virtual exchanges is of a very different character to the 'distances and hidden horizons' of the fleshly world which render it worth knowing (see Michael Heim, 1993b and 1995).

These differing interpretations can be grafted onto the aforementioned dialectic between modern and postmodern meta-theory: anonymity creates space for multiple selves; anonymity creates specific moral entailments for the relationship between self and others. That the same phenomenon can have such radically different readings is telling. Neither reading is exclusive; rather both have an explanatory power because of the ambiguity of technological advancement.

CHANGING PERCEPTIONS OF TIME

Given this ambiguity, it is not surprising that the tension between autonomy and guidance has application in the context of interactive technologies. A postmodern reading might focus on the process of browsing for its own sake, viewing a diversity of sites and forging one's own personal and intellectual links. In this reading, hyperlinks are explored to their fullest potential: one follows nodes of interest, one pauses, one loses the point of origin. With the loss of the point of origin, does one's sense of linear time become distorted? Does the lack of a discernible 'shape' to the search at hand encourage a greater feeling of immersion? The contrasting, modernist, interpretation of a search would be a more instrumental one: the Internet is a learning *tool*, and there are clear objectives at stake when one engages in a Web search. The suggestion that there is a danger of becoming overwhelmed when using the Internet expresses a distinction between centre and periphery in terms of relevance of information. It suggests that there is a 'best fit' for any given objective, and this in turn presupposes a particular educational 'agenda'. Incidental learning is arguably devalued in this interpretation. It is precisely the devaluing of incidental learning that is colourfully critiqued by O'Hagan. There is an immediate qualification to the opening paragraph of his article, however:

> Travel writing is meant to be something else, and the better part of it might encourage you to wander the modern roads in the company of the dead. Travelling with long out-of-date travel books is better fun than going with a contemporary guide: it helps you notice changes, to make contrasts, to conjure with previous notions of the place. (O'Hagan, 1999, p. 2)

Guides are not, therefore, jettisoned altogether in favour of the primacy of firsthand experience. Rather, past descriptions of place are favoured over contemporary ones. With the invocation of the dead lies the invitation to imaginatively engage with the perceptions of those who walked before us. With this temporal dimension the experience of travel is deepened. This is relevant to thinking about the Internet in a variety of ways.

Considerations of place cannot be easily divorced from considerations of time in any context. When one decides to travel is reciprocally influenced by where to go, how long it will take to get there, how easy it is to get to and so on. Not everyone will favour the shortest route. Nor is it clear that more information always helps in the finding of a meaningful path. These considerations are also germane in the context of the Internet. Different individuals feel differently about Web browsing or surfing because of personality, learning style or interest in the activity. By tracing nonlinear connections on the Internet might it be possible to forge a worthwhile sensitivity to different temporal modes such as chronology and synopsis, to compression and flow? Mihaly Csikszentmihalyi and Rick Robinson describe a phenomenon they term 'the flow experience':

> [P]eople play chess, climb mountains, compose music, and do a hundred other nonproductive activities not because they expect a result or reward after the activity is concluded, but because they enjoy what they are doing to the extent that experiencing the activity becomes its own reward. This autotelic experience, that is, one that contains its goal in itself, was called flow because respondents used that term frequently to describe the deep involvement in and effortless progression of the activity. (Csikszentmihalyi and Robinson, 1990, p. 7)

Learning from a flow experience often coincides with a leisure activity (typically one that is pursued in the individual's 'own' time). There is a distortion of perception of time that is associated with the flow experience, most usually a loss of the conditioning awareness of linear time. A flow experience can be contrasted with the notion of reward on completion which is inextricably entwined with a structured, goal-oriented activity. While a radical separation between the qualitative experience of time during productive and non-productive activities can be contested, the thrust of the above definition is that absorption engenders a distinct time-sense. If the term 'immersion' is not a misnomer, then browsing the Internet partakes of the particular suspension associated with flow, though this response may be a more or less individual affair. An individual browsing the Web may experience time differently within a single time-banded session. Similarly, they may be undirected, may be directed by their personal goals or may be directed by some externally imposed goal that they have adopted as their own. These different 'attitudes' to the activity reciprocally affect perception of time.

MOVING FROM PLACE TO SPACE

As well as changing perception of time, attitudes towards an activity can also affect sense of *place*. One can approach a Web search as a process of locating a series of discrete 'sites' to be seen, with an emphasis on the visual 'product' of each path taken. On the other hand, one can focus on the process of navigation, a process that opens up *spaces* in which to act and interact. Both characterisations can be found in the discourse of leisure, particularly in descriptions of tourist activity.

John Urry (1990) uses the term 'gaze' to describe a mode of seeing, rather than a mode of actively engaging in, specific to the leisure experience in which travellers passively look at what they encounter. Drawing on Walter Benjamin's (1973) concept of the male *flâneur* (one who has the leisure to wander a city watching the urban spectacle), Urry suggests that this strolling *flâneur* was the forerunner of modern tourists. One can easily see how the tourist 'gaze' evolved as a descriptive tool. The tourist experience as a mode of (sight-)seeing, as a fundamentally visual experience, seems on one level to correspond with our experience of the interface as visual spectacle. 'Spectacular culture' has been described in terms of power over appearance, a power whereby the engineering of a visual effect is rendered invisible to the viewer (Slater, 1995). Slater identifies this power as successful magic—specifically, the ability to transform reality. As well as involving an assertion of imagination (a suspension of disbelief), imagination is *captured*, an experience that induces a feeling of wonder (the feeling of being transported to a fully realised unreal world (*ibid.*, p. 219)). (This unreal world could be a computer game with highly coloured, spectacular graphics; it could be the Internet; it could be a television programme such as the BBC's 1999 series *Walking with Dinosaurs* which films the lives of digitally generated dinosaurs in natural history format, a clear example of engagement through mimesis.)

Wonder at the unreal has a second dimension: appreciation of the incomprehensible, hidden technology which makes it all possible (*ibid.*, p. 219). The less visible the technology, the greater our appreciation of the technological artistry. Thus, through concealment —for example, the use of icons as shorthand for sequences of code— the individual is more able to suspend disbelief and participate in spectacle in a digital context.

These ways of interpreting interaction with the modern machine are clearly focused on the screen. Alternative interpretations of online cultures relate to narrative and the hermeneutic process. Sherry Turkle (1996, p. 263) describes processing the online encounter in terms of 'an anthropologist returning home from a foreign culture'. This attention to the *interactions* that take place in cyberspace is at odds with a privileging of the visual metaphor, and arguably balances it. Betsy and Stephen Wearing (1996) suggest that the imbalance arose from a too sharply delineated subject/object distinction. Instead they substitute what they describe as a more 'feminized' notion of leisure as a space for interaction, implicitly treating the screen itself as a place to be looked at, like a tourist 'site' to be seen:

> By examining a feminized reconceptualization of the tourist destination as a space in which dynamic social interactions occur, rather than as a static and bounded place, we have linked tourist experiences to possibilities for extending the self beyond the limitations of culturally specific discourses. In so doing we have challenged the concept of the universalizing gaze of the tourist or 'flâneur' on the image of the tourist destination. Instead we have posited a feminized conceptualization of the tourist as a 'choraster' interacting in a creative way with the 'chora' of tourist space so that the self is involved. (*ibid.*, p. 240)

In Plato's *Timaeus*, *chora* signifies the inchoate space in which the Forms gestate:

> In the same way that which is going to receive properly and uniformly all the likenesses of the intelligible and eternal things must itself be devoid of all character. Therefore we must not call the mother and receptacle of visible and sensible things either earth or air or fire or water, nor yet any of their compounds or components; but we shall not be wrong if we describe it as invisible and formless, all-embracing, possessed in a most puzzling way of intelligibility, yet very hard to grasp. (Plato, *Timaeus*, 51)

The Platonic *chora* is not a template. It is without form, indeed, without ontology, and as such can be re-inscribed with new meanings, re-conceptualised in terms of different configurations between figure and ground, form and function, ornament and structure, theory and practice—the oppositions that have rendered traditional architecture hegemonic. Moreover, these oppositions are gendered. Elizabeth Grosz (1995a and 1995b) develops Derrida's reading of the Platonic *chora*: nursemaid to the divine, immutable Forms and feminine and neutral receptacle that supports the Forms without itself receiving support. One can see how the idea of *chora*— the mutable, invisible, formless screen—can be reappropriated to describe the relational space to which we travel and in which we converse.

LET EXPERIENCE BE YOUR GUIDE

Travels in space, and cyberspace, can no doubt result in superficial descriptions of things, as well as a desultory engagement with things: engrossed in Baedeker, do we miss the building itself? Rather than jettison the visual metaphor altogether, perhaps one can use it in a different sense. In order to really 'see' the building, or person, the tourist needs to do more than look. For Wearing and Wearing, an encounter in the context of different or alternative space is an opportunity for the development of self-understanding and self-growth. Because, in their view, *chora* encourages us to engage in meaningful interactions, whether or not 'the space offers an authentic representation of the host culture, then becomes irrelevant. It is the actual experience that is the reality' (Wearing and Wearing, 1996, p. 235). In other words, the product—for example, a Web page—cannot be emphatically divorced from the process, in this example the act of forging connections between hyperlinked sites and viewing text and graphics. Furthermore, O'Hagan suggests that awareness of different time-frames, specifically an engagement with the past, can enrich experience. In both descriptions, the traveller's experience is qualitatively altered: first, by a heightened awareness of the process of interaction; second, by a heightened awareness of the inextricable relationship between time and place.

The intention of a guidebook is clarification, but the end result can be obfuscation. Through mediation, an experience can lose its edge, its focus and definition. Guidance can come in a pre-digested form that blunts the development of critical awareness. O'Hagan suggests that an authentic journey might entail both provocation and evocation. This claim has also been made for authentic *learning*. Similarly, in navigating the Internet, too much direction may impoverish the experience. To play with some of the associations that are revealed by a Web search may be both evocative and provoking—eliciting responses that encourage reflection on the process, the product at hand and, potentially, oneself. These responses are in danger of becoming lost in prescriptive approaches. On the other hand, imprecision in a search could mean that checking sources is a Herculean feat, one that potentially engenders feelings of failure. In order to locate specific information one needs to have domain knowledge to be able to judge 'relevance'. Time spent immersed in a Web search becomes problematic in the following cases: when hundreds of 'hits' are generated, pages are difficult to locate or graphics are slow to emerge on screen. These factors are compounded by the lack of editorial control over information posted on the Web. Readers must themselves judge both the salience and the quality of the information found. To some extent this presupposes a highly developed critical faculty, though the process of searching could itself be harnessed in the ongoing development of just such a faculty, as the individual searcher becomes more adept at screening, selecting and reading.

In conclusion, the nature of a learning activity is conditioned by considerations of autonomy and guidance. Furthermore, the nature of this activity affects perception of time and space. This has relevance to modes of learning from the Internet. Navigation can be a more or less individual affair, more or less goal-directed, with varying levels of support—all factors which, in turn, affect awareness of time and define the spatial architecture for any given search. Deconstructing what it means for the guide, rather than experience, to 'be the guide' is salutary. Sometimes it can be rewarding to ditch the guide, go off the beaten track, take risks, take more time. The guide is not an incontestable source. Rather it is a form of secondary text, one that can sometimes obscure awareness of the benefits of experiencing the terrain first-hand.

8

Learning Places: Building Dwelling Thinking Online

DAVID KOLB

Lack of information is hardly our problem. Information comes at us in waves, sloshing out of the magazine rack, lapping at our computer monitors. It repeats and repeats on all-day news shows. It comes neatly packaged as sound bites, or little nuggets ready for trivia games. We have plenty of information, but it is not often the information we need. Even if it is, we need to learn how to deal with it. It is not just the amount, but the speed. Too much happens everywhere that may be important anywhere. Too much comes for us to think it over.

A serious enemy of education is a life of quick immediate intensities. Little intense bits of information delivered by sincere talking heads. Isolated serial intensities, one show or one song after another, one simplified role after another. Moments of intense experience, branded and labelled. Neither the information nor the experiences are abstract in the usual sense of the word, but they are abstract in another sense, taken from Hegel and Marx, where to call something abstract means that it has been pulled out of its constitutive relations and contexts, and so is not encountered in its full reality. Education should restore those relations and contexts. It should dispel that illusory immediacy and completeness.

ONLINE ISSUES

We are all familiar with the liberal arts rant about specialised education and the need for critical thinking and a wide background in an age of mediased superficiality. Few would disagree about the danger. But what do we do?

At Bates College, the library was redesigning its Web-site, and they asked me to participate in a usability study of the new pages. They presented several trial versions of the pages and asked me to locate certain information using each version. While I clicked and searched they timed me with a stopwatch and noted the sequence in which I visited the pages. I was told later, however, that when they tried the same procedure with some students, the library staff were not able to do the timing and sequencing because the students clicked, scanned, clicked and changed pages so rapidly that the observers could not keep up. If what the students were looking for did not jump out at them they were on to another page, and another.[1]

As an educator perhaps I should find this discouraging, since it shows that the students are scanning for bits of information instead of going for context, structure and critical evaluation. Part of the answer to increasing the critical and evaluative component of online education has to involve slowing down the inhabitation of the Net to provide time for thought and evaluation.

That is true, but it would be a mistake to conclude that we should teach people to read all Web pages more slowly. We scan in print too. Watch how experts leaf through a series of periodical issues in their field. A deeper inhabitation is not achieved just by going slowly and analytically. Readers do that when they get near to what they are looking for. We have to teach that what to look for is not always quick bits of information. The expert relies on an already built-up structure of categories and priorities in which to relate what is taken from the pages. The educational worry is that the Web-scanning student has little such background cognitive structure, or, perhaps worse, has only the uncritically accepted background forced at us by the interests trying to control the media.

The best way to have someone develop a more sophisticated cognitive and evaluative background is to help them develop it themselves in contact with the material in question. If the media glut is online, education ought to be there too. The learners have to spend aware time there, and try new concepts, make mistakes and get feedback. They have to stay there a while. But is there any 'there' there?

THE SENSE OF PLACE

Part of what is needed online is more sense of place. If an online educational site is more than a series of pages I flip through, if it is a place where I am willing to linger, then I may have space and time to re-examine and reconstruct how I construe and evaluate information, and re-examine my values. I still would not treat every single Web page or piece of email as a teacher might want me to treat a page of Shakespeare or Nietzsche. It would be the site or the location, not the individual screen-full, that would be a place I could linger in. If I did, then I might be disposed to spend a lot of time on important screen-fulls, once I could tell which were the important ones.

In my writing I use some non-standard (read: not Microsoft) software: Nisus Writer for word processing, Storyspace for hypertext, Mailsmith for email. These come from small companies (Nisus Software, Eastgate Systems, Bare Bones Software) that each probably have between five and twenty employees. Two of the companies are supplemented by mailing lists where users share tips, observations, hopes and complaints with one another and with company people. Software-oriented mailing lists are quite common, but the lists associated with small companies develop a greater sense of belonging and ownership. Perhaps it is the shared feeling of vulnerability, or the feeling that one is part of a select few; perhaps it is a sense of connection when the president of the company answers your email; in any case you occasionally find on such lists self-congratulatory messages about the list itself and how much people enjoy its personality. That kind of self-reflexive belonging is one component of 'a sense of place' even in the limited text-only environment of email. There is a small community where I fit in, where I am at home with the conversation and feel that the horizon and the people are familiar enough that I can expose my vulnerabilities and ignorance with a little humour and confidence.

I have created mailing lists in connection with my classes, but they have never attained this level of at-home-ness. They have had questions and answers, and occasional enthusiasms and a few flame wars, but they have never had the sense of community I have noted and felt on the software lists.

Email is a restricted medium compared to what can be done on the Web, and the Web is restricted compared to what will be coming down the fibre in a few years. But if even email can create a sense of community, we should be able to make online educational environments more like places where someone would want to linger, with time to reflect and to shape and be shaped by the atmosphere of the place. Such online places would need to have some amplitude, some room to wander and hang out and those internal differentiations that allow for place creation.

THE PLACE DEBATES

What does it mean to inhabit a place? Is it important to have a sense of being at home or rooted in a place? Can inhabitation be self-critical? There is a rich architectural and planning literature about place and inhabitation.[2] Much of that discussion involves the relation of architectural objects to the natural environment, and worries about the destruction of traditional towns and the banalities of modern planning. There are ways to transfer that debate to considerations about the Net and online places. For instance, within that literature there is serious dispute about whether effective places need architectural centring devices and hierarchical structure. Traditionalists and modernists both urge centrality and hierarchy as a means to clear legible places, with many modernists wanting a more univocal legibility. Various kinds of deconstructionists favour labyrinthine constructions and unexpected topological connections. Most Web-sites opt for hierarchical organisation around a few central pages, but some have experimented with more complex kinds of connectivity. There is also dispute in the architectural literature about whether or not we should strive to amplify the sense of being at home in a place, with modernists and deconstructionists urging that such a sense is ideologically dangerous and defeats attempts to live with full awareness of the precarious nature of our interpretative frameworks. The underlying issue is the degree to which inhabitation can be or should be mediated by critical reflection. This is a relevant issue for educational places, and especially for those participatory online places that are experienced as entirely deliberate constructions, such as MOOs and MUDs. If these are put to educational use, it seems appropriate to build so as to encourage critical inhabitation, helping the user confront and reflect on the local conventions and rules as such, especially if the user has some means of influencing the content and structure of the site.

Much recent debate about place refers to Heidegger's ideas, especially those in his 1950s essays 'The Thing' and 'Building Dwelling Thinking'. Heidegger wants to show how places and things open up for us the meaningful structure of our world. Being at home is not just a nice feeling; it tells us when we are in a place that 'gathers' our world together.

Heidegger describes true places and things as events in which four aspects or dimensions come together. These include fruitful yet retiring support ('earth'), cycles of time and changing mood and atmosphere ('sky'), vocation and aspiration ('gods') and self-aware finitude as the place of revelation ('mortals'). These dimensions are not particular beings such as rocks or clouds, although his descriptions rely on our familiarity with them. The four are aspects involved in every authentic encounter with things and places. Things and places are not fixed beings but ongoing events in which each of the dimensions comes into its own by being brought together with the others, and their particular mode of togetherness is both the place and our encounter with it. Cycles of time and atmosphere, for example, are what they are and have their meaning through their interpenetration by aspiration, surrounded by ongoing supportive presences in the open intensity that comes from awareness of oncoming death. That awareness, in turn, is what it is through its sense of vocation to be worked out amid generous yet self-retiring things revealed in a particular temporal and mood atmosphere.

This could be translated into the language of the social sciences— the four dimensions would become: objects, times and moods, values, and individual subjects. Heidegger would object that such a translation would be yet another example of redescribing experience in a vocabulary that reduces the revelation of things to a process going on among already revealed items. This blocks our under- standing of the more basic ways in which things and places locate and define us, rather than being merely our tools or products.

Heidegger's four dimensions do suggest ways in which truer places might be constructed online. For an online site to be a place, it needs to be more than a static block of data. It needs 'earth', objects to interact with that have some independence and thickness of their own; it needs 'sky', times and changes, so that it is not always the same but varies according to its own rhythms; it needs 'gods', ideals and aspirations and calls to what we might become; it needs 'mortals', a sense that choices are meaningful in finite careers, that time makes demands and is not unlimited in amount. This sense of opening possibilities and an identity being offered and forwarded puts more 'there' there.

However, Heidegger's four dimensions are often read so as to block from the outset any attempt to create technologically mediated places. Heidegger has many negative things to say about technology, and his examples favour rural life. The four dimensions can be read as describing a deeper mode of being in the world than technology allows. This deeper dwelling would be more open to the interplay of our mortality and the rich presence of things. We can get in touch with that deeper dwelling only if we stop building technological places and renew our relations with time and nature. We are dominated by an understanding of being as raw material for manipulation. We need to change our way of thinking and living. This romantic reading of Heidegger forecloses any discussion of how we might make liveable and learning places within the online world, which can only be seen as part of the problem.

There is another reading, however, which sees Heidegger's fourfold play as a description not of a specific primal dwelling but of the process by which any world, including the technological world, is revealed. Earth and sky can gather and we as mortals be open to the gods whether we are with jet airliners and computers, or the wine jug that Heidegger describes. In technological items a different constella- tion of possibilities and roles reveals a different time and new aspirations. They are in some ways less rich, and in other ways more free, than the traditional world of the wine jug. But there is no other, deeper dwelling available to us underneath the technological world. We need to learn how to live in this world more attuned to the process of its revelation. We need to grasp more authentically our groundless dwelling in the play that is a meaningful world.

In philosophical jargon, this second reading of Heidegger takes his discussion of the dimensions of our living as anti-foundational. This seems to me a better interpretation of Heidegger's ideas. It encourages us to make our places richer in those dimensions that all places share. It also warns how our inhabitation can be unduly narrowed (in the case of online sites: overly information-oriented).

This other reading can also encourage us to add to the play of the four dimensions gestures and creations that foreground our process of dwelling. With this we return to the issue of self-critical inhabitation. In creating a learning place we want to help people to be aware and critical not just of facts and arguments, but of the process by which they inhabit and learn. If our online places are more than just collections of facts, and have something of those four dimensions, there is then room for becoming more aware of how we dwell there. This awareness can be aided by writing, artworks and architecture, on or off line, that work to question the naturalness of received structures of place and urge a deeper and more self-aware inhabitation. In the context of this discussion these can all be seen as educational gestures.

Such gestures and works are often called deconstructive, but deconstruction is not un-building. It is an attempt to show how dwelling within familiar meanings, such as a sense of enclosure and at-home-ness, arises and is supported within a play of dimensions or processes that goes beyond our ordinary conceptions of stable meanings and objects. Educational places online need to learn how to incorporate such gestures in order to help learners deal with the immersive and seductive qualities of the new media.

Heidegger's fourfold play offers a privileged vocabulary and an essential description of what it means to be in a place. Much debate around the notion of place fights about what is the best vocabulary for describing places. Theorists hope to find in a privileged vocabulary guidelines for designing places. While I do not think that we should be limited to one privileged vocabulary, we do need a way of thinking about places that will suggest what we might do to improve the place-quality of online sites. Above, I tried to show how Heidegger's fourfold play could help in this regard, but I do not think that it gives us enough guidance. To discuss the sense of place online, we need a description of place that is general enough to include online places and give us guidance about what we could do to improve their place and character. We need a way of characterising places that does not reduce them to collections of data, nor claim they must resemble our most familiar and homey dwellings.

To this end I suggest the general description of a place as an extended location where a perceived (physical or virtual) expanse is linked to norms and expectations for appropriate or inappropriate actions. For example, if you and I are conversing as we walk along the street, there may be no particular relation between the character of the area we walk through and the moves we make in our conversation. Our conversation takes place in an area but that area does not function as a special place, only as a background. But if we stop and continue the conversation in a café or on a park bench, we may soon set up norms and expectations that create a special place for our talk. When we were walking along the pavement, the distance between us varied but these variations were irrelevant, at least within some culturally defined limits, but now that we are seated, when I lean forward or move away on the bench, this signals a new phase in the conversation, or changes in my attitude. The width of the bench, or the table between us, now become sites of our activity in a stronger sense than was the pavement or the trees we passed while walking. Highly ritualised places such as courtrooms, or concert halls, or fast food emporia, have their own normative sub-locations and behaviours: here we socialise and there we all look in one direction; here we talk and there we are silent; here we stand in line and there we sit.[3]

Places—including virtual places—are loci of 'our' actions and expectations and norms. Some email lists may have a sense of belonging that includes local expectations for how one writes or presents one's self, but for a thicker sense of place, we need a more perceptible locale, which could range from the coloured backgrounds and designs of some Web pages, to the engrossing graphics in a game of Myst or Riven, to some future apparatus that you plug into and find yourself re-located into a virtual world that has all the perceptible marks of daily reality, such as William Gibson imagines in some of his novels. In this last case, the virtual world would probably be larger than the various places contained within it. It is not their virtual design that would make them places, but the way we use them and associate them with norms and expectations and meanings for action.

If there are no such appropriate ways of acting, and no 'we' correlated with local features, then a physical or virtual locale offers only a background. This is hardly trivial, for a background may influence us strongly by its shape or architectural features, as the weather influences us, but if the region does not offer significant sub-regions with differential appropriatenesses for our action, it is not yet our place. The four dimensions Heidegger speaks of do not come together specifically there. This is the case for most current online sites.

Places are not the result of a dominant creativity simply imposing on passive space. There is a mutual interpretation of features of the space and features of our action, each enticing the other. Qualitatively different regions and textures invite the assignment of possible actions, as we build and reinterpret ways of acting linked to features of the locale. Such place-making, however, becomes more complex with online places, since their background regions and textures are in fact our creations. We have to learn how to use the revisability of online locales to solicit mutual creation of the place, the community and the norms of action in that place. Too many online locales provide only a background, often quite literally a background graphic on a Web page. To make these into places where we can be and change together, the locale needs to invite more possible trajectories of action. It needs differentiated sub-places with differentiated norms and expectations.

On simple sites this might be as straightforward as indicating: read here, comment here, post notes here, chat here. But this is not enough; we need to design to suggest an appropriate style and trajectory of actions, and provide a sense of the community people can join by sharing here. For the kind of education we are speaking about, the norms need to encourage and the place permit pauses for self-reflection and change. Such environments need a user interface that does not get in the way, while still capable of a large-enough range of possible actions and responses. The environment, whether it is a perceived virtual space or just a sequence of Web pages, also needs a memory. It needs to record traces of our interactions, so that we can make it ours. What is the electronic equivalent of carving one's initials in a tree, or putting a book on a special shelf?

THE OPEN SPACE

Inhabiting a place involves more than learning the rules; it also involves playing around with them. Online places of learning need to provide openings for departing from the script. This goes against the teacher's fantasy of the totally controlled classroom. Imagine a virtual classroom where the students were in effect chained to their desks and where they could not be distracted by what was happening outside the windows during the discussion. Many online learning locales try for such commanded attention, thus reproducing the worst of the old programmed learning machines and memory drills. This is the wrong way to build a learning place.

There is space in a real place to push the rules, to try out behaviours that do not quite fit, to look out the window, to pass notes to your friends. This is distracting in a classroom, but the urge can be used to help group learning activities. The same is true online.

I 'spoke' (from Maine) at a virtual conference session hosted at IATH-MOO (in Virginia). The other panellists and I wrote introductory statements, which were posted in advance. We then made live comments on each other's remarks, and carried on a discussion with the audience. We panellists attended on line, but the audience was mostly assembled physically at a university (in Florida), where they sat at terminals in a large room together. While they asked us questions and contributed to the official conversation they were also holding side conversations with one another on the local Net. The final transcript of the panel included both the official and the side conversations. Those side comments were irreverent, impatient, sometimes irrelevant, but also showed a lively engagement with the topics and with one another.

My own and other teachers' experience with real-time computer conferencing is that such side conversations always develop. If the technology allows, side conversations develop on the Net; if the technology does not allow that, the side conversations happen as vocal comments. In a classroom online discussion led by Michael Joyce at Vassar I saw his students simultaneously carrying on a central conversation on the top of their screens, plus several smaller conversations on the bottom of the screens, plus comments made aloud to the persons sitting around them. Students multitask such sessions. For instance, in several course I have invited outside speakers to 'talk' from a distance with students who had read their articles in advance. On the earlier occasions I used an amplified telephone conversation, with students coming one at a time to a microphone to ask questions. Side conversations developed in whispered comments among the students away from the microphone. On later occasions I had students and speaker gather together in a room at a convenient MOO. Students did not wait their turn, so there was more of a jumble of questions and comments that the speaker chose from in framing remarks. The software also allowed the students to send private remarks to one another. I recorded what I thought was the public conversation but the log turned out to include all the private remarks as well. I was surprised at how successfully the students were carrying on several parallel conversations.

Movie theatres now have to post notices requesting the audience not to talk, since the active audience and side-conversation has spread from home TV to film. Maybe educators should not view this noisy participation as a bad trend, since we are trying to get people to respond critically. We need to encourage informal communication and side conversations into a learning mode, to be analytical or reflective about the ongoing central conversation or about contexts, attitudes, frameworks, values. Such official side conversations would undoubtedly generate yet another layer of unofficial side talk, but the point would be to enlist this tendency of the online medium, in order to heighten the participant's sense of reflection and critical thinking.

At the Florida conference and in my classes it was important for the side comments that the participants had been with one another for meals and for face-to-face talks and discussions, and so had developed ongoing relationships. We panellists had no such connection among ourselves. One of the best recipes discovered for online education has turned out to be a mix of face-to-face sessions and online communication. In already mixed physical/online settings such as a residential college these opportunities already exist. Some online business degree programmes require that participants come together for summer workshops or other communal activities. When distance or finances make that impossible, a similar effect might be achievable purely online by special requirements for shared formal and informal online time together, but designing places that encourage that kind of sociality would be a major challenge.[4]

THE DISNEY MOVE

So far I have discussed education online largely as an extension of traditional read-and-discuss seminars or group projects. Perhaps something like required readings are available online, perhaps these are being jointly composed by the students, and the discussion component becomes more prominent. One tries to build an environment where people feel at home, a place where they can accept norms for this small community, risk some self-exposure and be willing to challenge their own preconceptions and learn new modes of critical inhabitation. But if we are going to talk about education online we have to consider a very different model than the seminar. You can build a Web-site, but Disney can build a world. What about computer games, virtual-reality rides, theme parks, simulations, immersive worlds? Is there a way to make them more available for learning?

The usual suggestion here is the use of simulation. There are many kinds of simulation with different educational effects. Dissecting a simulated frog or practising a skill in a simulated setting make for good training. However, the more complete the simulation becomes, the more some critics fear that it may lead learners into solving fantasy issues that avoid real world problems. However, virtual experience can rehearse dealings with real situations. Virtual experience can increase our sensitivities. A virtual world can hold real events. Shared simulations can become real group activity. In a MOO that is having policy debates about the rules of the game, democracy is not being simulated, it is happening.

Simulation does not have to be online. For instance, on one of the several islands in the Caribbean where cruise lines have manufactured a protected vacation experience, there are artificial fossil whale bones buried on the beach so that children can uncover them as part of a palaeontology programme (Patron, 1998, p. 67). Whether in a crafted physical environment or in a computerised virtual reality, similar educational issues arise. For instance, how do we balance the educational benefits of a carefully planned simulation that carefully guides learners into the complexities of a situation or a subject matter, as opposed to the different educational benefits of surprise and working together on difficulties unexpected even by the teacher or planner?

There is also the issue of helping learners discover how to use simulations as tools. We give children toys that simulate adult activities. We encourage them to watch highly produced educational TV shows full of fictionalised history and far too convenient nature. We do not want them to think that these simulations are just like the real world; we want them to learn how to project from the simulation, how to read the analogies. We need to find ways that people can be *in* the fantasy but not *of* it. This is another role for side conversations and simultaneous reflection. We get immersed in the movie or the Disney ride, and yet at the same time we are wondering how they produce the effects, or perhaps whether the effects are altogether salutary. Education wants to increase the internal complexity of experience. We should not reject virtual edutainment experiences just on the basis of their preplanned artificiality. The educational issue is content and complexity, and whether meta-level acknowledgement and reflection is encouraged.

A good example of how to encourage reflective participation is the simulated phone-in conversations that occur at the end of the children's TV show *The Magic School Bus*. The show presents a teacher and her class travelling in a magic bus that can, for instance, become very small in order to show them the inside of a machine or an animal. Each show is devoted to some topic such as sound, the chemistry of cooking, astronomy, spiders, together with some examples of interactions and tensions among the members of the class. At the end of the show, the animation switches to the office of the show's producer, and fictional child callers criticise the show's characters, correct the facts presented and give viewers the sense of belonging to a community that uses, rather than is captured by, the fantasy. There are printed books derived from the show, and they also contain texts of such phone-calls.

THE THOREAU STRATEGY

I have been suggesting that we can take on some of the features of the new media that seem potentially destructive, and use them for educational purposes. Side conversations, simulation and immersion, rapidity of interaction, excitement and stimulation can all be turned to learning. But there is another approach, what we might call the Thoreau strategy of withdrawal, to achieve perspective and get in touch with deeper values.

In the debates about architectural place this has been strongly championed by Michael Benedikt, who writes about what it would take to create 'real' places that are outside the bustle of style and image.

> The urge is strong to make a building complete in itself and finished, a totally encompassing, dazzling, climate-controlled and conditioned experience. But totality and completeness are too often achieved at the expense of reality . . . much contemporary architecture lacks emptiness, by being quite literally full. Full, if not of people and goods and pushy displays, then of Design. (Benedikt, 1987, p. 60)

Benedikt wants us to get away from places that try to mean too much, so we can locate ourselves in the encounter with rock and wood, ordinary human needs and the dimensions of our own mortality. This is a salutary admonition. Does it then follow that education online is doomed to such cloying fullness of design? Current crowded Web pages certainly make it seem so. Should we then escape from the online buzz, or let it be at most a tool but never a place for us? While the grounding in built solidity and quietude that Benedikt talks about is surely valuable, and can give people more space to be, will it manage to give learners the critical edge and skills we need in the media storm?

Ann Cline writes about creating places where we can get away and into ourselves into temporary communities formed around basic needs. She suggests building simple primitive huts in backyards and interstitial places:

> In societies like ours, where architecture and history make meaning out of vast and shifting complexities, the primitive hut is a search and attempt to pare away what is given and apparent, to find something else to satisfy our deepest emotions. (Cline, 1998, p. 109)

Cline imagines a utopia where such huts are common healing refuges:

> Many of the early huts were created for tea making, or for coffee making . . . soon, however, there appeared huts with masters who told stories or provoked poetry or discourse, who practised magic or seance, who explored fable or fetish—who, in short, encapsulated the rich opportunity for moments of engagement brought about by existence as a human being. By these moments, increasing numbers of people saw as miraculous and whimsical the temporary forms of energy in the universe and engaged in an appreciation of them so long as life and breath held together body, mind, and spirit. (*ibid.*, p. xiii)

Could this happen online? Maybe it already is? Cline and Benedikt would probably deny the possibility, because the online world epitomises that bustle and hurry and meaning that we need to escape. But while I think that their strategy has a vital role, we should not cede the online world to the marketers.

Cline speaks about the need to provide, 'free from aggressively righteous agendas . . . a contingent community, a sangha of silence' (*ibid.*, p. 130). It sounds almost blasphemous to suggest an online community of silence. In a physical hut you can share silent presence as you serve tea, or watch the moon rise. Online, you can not do that, at least until virtual reality becomes infinitely better. But do not essentialise the technology; it may be used in more than busy ways. Imagine quietly composing a jointly written poem together, or listening to haiku. Imagine an online place where works of art are shared peacefully but intensely, where discussion evolves slowly. The technology and methods currently used do not favour such places, but they are not impossible.

One characteristic of such a 'hut' online would be a weakening of the distinction I urged above between central and side conversations. Such a place would be both less focused on a central topic and more focused on the present moment. The technological challenge would be to create an environment with tools for interaction that encouraged a slowed-down contemplative encounter. Such places should not be too full of in-your-face design, even though the whole environment is designed. We should not assume that this could not be done. Computers are meta-tools. The computer and the Internet can morph into different forms and different kinds of interactions. They do not all have to be fast and furious, and all of their modes have educational and spiritual potential. There are never guarantees, but we can try.

It is too easy to define life and education online in opposition to 'real' life. As technology changes that contrast will change too. Pencils are technology, as are shoes. A generation that has grown up with computers and media will not isolate them in opposition to the real stuff they had as children. I have been arguing that we can have real and educational life online. The primitive huts Cline writes about involve older technologies—carpentry, candles, lanterns, tea. Those move at a slower pace. But—aside from using the current slowness of Web connections to encourage contemplative or thoughtful pauses— we could design in ways that push the needed speed of calculation and implementation down into the computers, leaving us free to create more tranquil spaces for learning at whatever pace we find best.

Quiet places online are possible, and would be very valuable. But we also need busy yet educational places, and places that encourage deconstructive moves that foreground the process of inhabiting and being online, making this available for critical awareness and revision.

Socrates would have cautionary things to say about edutainment and much of today's online education. As Plato pointed out, one of the problems with the training offered by the Sophists was that it demanded nothing from you except your cash. They offered to teach you skills to achieve your goals, without ever questioning your goals or desires. Socrates would also equip you with skills, but he would challenge you to change and question yourself. I have tried to suggest some strategies for building online places that might renew those challenges.

NOTES

1. Such rapid skip and scan reading tallies with Jakob Nielsen's studies of the dynamics of Web use. See his 'Alertbox' essays at http://www.useit.com/alertbox/

2. For recent debates about place see phenomenological discussions such as Casey (1993, 1997), Harries (1997), Norbert-Schulz (1984, 1985). There are as well discussions more dependent on deconstruction and critical theory, such as Boyer (1994), Deleuze and Guattari (1986), Lippard (1997) and Tschumi (1994). Some other discussions emphasise town and city planning in a contemporary or historical context, such as Kelbaugh (1997) and Sennett (1990).

3. In speaking of places as 'our' construction I may seem to be going against Heidegger's desire for a sense in which places locate us rather than are something we manipulate in a sovereign fashion. But with the intertwining and mutual constitution of individual and social identity with each other and with context and history, place creation is no simple sovereign act on our part.

4. Some features of physical togetherness would be very difficult to recreate online in anything short of the ultimate virtual reality. Bodily togetherness includes getting tired together, taking comfort breaks, dealing with a sick colleague, sharing food and weather and common noise levels, all of which create a sense of connection and obligation to one another. (I owe this insight to comments by Paul Standish.) The disembodied quality of online communities is one reason for the inappropriate behaviour that can develop. If the community had a shared place that had more 'body' to it, standards of appropriate behaviour might be easier to develop. Such thicker places online might seem to await new technology, but it may be more important to make the place (for instance a shared Web-site or simulation) sufficiently complex to reward exploration, and able to change so as to record the gradually developing shared history of the community of users/learners. We might learn methods for this by examining shared unofficial Web-sites that develop around celebrities or films, or examining the interaction of home pages in a shared environment such as Geocities.

9

Electronic Writing and the Wrapping of Language

JAMES D. MARSHALL

INTRODUCTION

In Victor Hugo's novel, *Notre-Dame de Paris, 1482*, the priest says that, alas, 'this will destroy that', meaning that the book upon which his hand was placed would destroy the building opposite. He is looking out of a window at the immense Cathedral of Notre-Dame (Hugo, 1967, p. 197). If the cathedral is a library to be read by the religious, and if the church is the symbol of authority and the repository of medieval knowledge, then the priest means not only that the book, printing and new literacy would undermine the church's authority, but that human thought will undermine the church's expression of its authority (Bolter, 1991). The priest continues:

> the principal idea of each generation would no longer write itself with the same material and in the same way, that the book of stone, so solid and durable, would give place to the book made of paper, yet made more solid and durable. (Hugo, 1967, p. 199; Bolter's 1991 translation)

Following Hugo's challenge, Bolter says that we must look up from our laptops to the books on our bookshelves and ask ourselves, in similar fashion, whether one will destroy the other. But that may be to make an unwarranted jump, for the printed book destroyed neither the cathedral nor handwriting. Nor did it *replace* them. Whilst it did not destroy or replace the cathedral's authority, it *displaced* it. Printing replaced the handwriting of the scribes, but it did not replace handwriting per se. Will electronic writing destroy, replace or displace the printed page? As books and journals are now computerised before being printed in traditional forms, for ease of publishing, it is but a short step to distributing them electronically, and another short step to distributing them *only* electronically. Will electronic writing destroy, replace or displace books and texts in learning and teaching? These are important philosophical questions because they impinge not merely upon language, and how the configuration of language affects notions of knowledge and authority, but also upon how language impinges upon the self, others and the world.

In trying to answer this question the first point to note is that neither the cathedrals nor handwriting have vanished totally. But are cathedrals visited for readings of the 'books' of authority, and the refurbishing of people's spirits, or are they visited for historical and cultural reasons: to admire such things as the stained glass, the architecture and the art treasures? Are they becoming more a part of a refined culture than a church? And whilst handwriting has not entirely disappeared, even here the fountain pen has become a luxury item—a Rolls Royce—which is perhaps employed by the elderly, or used by some as a snobbish affectation. Will this be the fate of the book and print literacy?

A second point is that if print literacy were to be lost in the move to electronic writing it is not obvious that literacy itself would be lost. But even so literacy would take on a new form in electronic writing as electronic writing is *wrapped* differently from that of print (Poster, 1990; Bolter, 1991). A new form of literacy would affect how we process electronic writing and hence how we learn. What is required however is more than the equivalent of functional literacy. It must involve more than being able to understand technical aspects of how to use technology, as if it is a neutral tool, which unfortunately seems a common educational aim of technology curricula (see, for example, Marshall, 1999). There will be a new form for the expression of authority, as there was for the church in the early production of Gutenberg's Bible, though the bible hardly differed from those versions compiled by good scribes. It did not seem, therefore, to be an example of a radical change in technology (Bolter, 1991, p. 3). For many people electronic text does not seem radically different from print on the printed page but, it will be argued, it is in fact quite different.

By 'wrapping' Poster means essentially the configuration of language, the way it is composed and presented, and the ways in which meaning can be processed. Consider the wrapping of oral language: it is spoken and must be listened to, as there is no automatic possibility of hearing what is said a second time, as in the case of a second reading of a sentence or phrase on a page, to obtain meaning; it varies in volume and tone and emphases; it is continuously shifting in a social context; and so on. Thus it clearly differs from print, and print differs from electronic language (Poster, 1990, p. 11). Different wrappings of language not only alter the ways in which the subject processes signs into meanings, and hence how she or he learns, but also reconstitute the notions of the subject, and restructure the subject's relation to the world (*ibid.*).

Bolter is quite adamant that whilst print literacy may continue, it will be in a changed form. Perhaps it will become like the tourist's conception of Notre-Dame. The Church for many is no longer the privileged 'book', the authority and repository of knowledge. Similarly, it would seem, the book and print literacy will no longer be the authority in defining the organisation and production of knowledge, as they have been since Gutenberg. But where will authority rest, especially in the approach upon us of the knowledge society? If it is to rest anywhere it might seem that it will be in a computer disk, or on a Web page. But perhaps the presentation of this question on authority is the wrong way to pose such a question. Presupposed in that wording of the question is a continuation of certain notions from print to electronic writing as if electronic writing were an extension of print technology, or a neutral tool to assist the compilation and dissemination of text.

In this chapter I wish to raise a number of philosophical issues about conceiving literacy in electronic writing as but an extension of print literacy, and about conceiving this new technology in a neutral manner. Technology is often seen as neutral, as something which can be mastered and used by humans with full and proper regard for social and environmental factors. In addressing these issues I will draw upon the work of Mark Poster (1990) and Jay David Bolter (1991) on the wrapping of language, and Martin Heidegger (1977) on the value-laden nature of technology. But I will not draw upon these thinkers uncritically as I believe that their positions should be taken more as indicative of dangers and possible changes, rather than as predictions of inevitable changes for notions of literacy and the self.

WRITING SPACE

The early printers took fine manuscripts as their model and used the same layout on the printed page. It was some generations before they realised that they were working in a different writing space. But it was the new technology that made this apparent, for they could now make print more readable and use less ink if the space was conceived differently (Bolter, 1991, p. 3). The technology permitted a better ordering of the writing space and a better ordering of the ideas, but did it affect those ideas?

According to Victor Hugo's priest (1967, p. 199) it is the principal ideas of a new generation that need a different medium, for there is something about the earlier medium that is inadequate for the presentation of these new ideas. It seems, if the priest is correct, that there *must* be a new medium to present new ideas. Perhaps, more strongly, new ideas *demand* a different medium for their proper presentation and dissemination. Is there an interdependence between technology and new ideas so that one affects the other and vice versa?

If we return to the advent of print and Hugo's example of the church, it is quite clear that the ideas of religious dissidence and independence from the church could not be expressed authoritatively through the monuments of the church. That was not the right medium. Thus Martin Luther claimed that truth could be found in the Bible. Bolstered by the 'truths' of the Bible the dissenters of the Reformation denied both the authority and the knowledge claims of the established Roman church. Given the control of scribes and resources by the established church, clearly a new medium was required. But it could not be a medium based upon establishing monuments like Notre-Dame or upon redeploying the mainly church-controlled scribes to the compiling of different types of texts. (Ironically the early printed Bibles could scarcely be distinguished from the work of a good scribe). It took several generations of printers to improve the technology of printing, to make print cheaper and more legible, and thus to produce a new writing space (Bolter, 1991, p. 3).

A possible analysis of this change would be that the Gutenberg Bible can be seen as a mere extension of the work of the scribe so that it takes changes in technology to provide the new writing space. However within this new space, the printed page, more quickly and cheaply disseminated, eventually displaces the authority of the Roman church and becomes a repository of new knowledge (Luther's first conflict with the church was in 1517, some sixty years after the appearance of the Gutenberg Bible). It should be noted here that the technology of the printed page seems to have been seen initially as neutral, as a tool that could be used by either side in the religious debate. But in the way that it organised previously existing knowledge as saleable resources it was not neutral, as it placed new organisational demands upon that knowledge. This was a knowledge that was no longer *revealed* by the priest but was *demanded* by the new technology to be organised in such a way that it could come forth in print. The distinction here between the notions of demanding and revealing is to mark, for Martin Heidegger (1977), a difference between ancient and modern technology (see below). Hugo's priest was right then, as these new ideas did need a new writing space.

Arguably it has taken time to produce a new writing space with electronic writing, and we may yet be in an interim stage. Initially word-processing was seen as an extension of typing, though with certain advantages in the correction and ordering of texts. And it has been seen as neutral—as an extension of these activities in the production of what were pages of print as 'pages' of electronic text.

There appeared to be no new writing space. But now it is clear that the page of text on the electronic screen is not the writing space of the printed page of the book. On the contrary in electronic writing the page is not a meaningful unit. Instead the electronic book's meaningful unit is determined by technology. It is the capacity of the computer to structure and process text that determines the appropriateness of an electronic book (Bolter, 1991).

How do we understand this new writing space? First, the configurations of pixels on the screen are not similar to the symbols on the printed page. Configurations of pixels can be altered by shape, size and figure–ground relationships. The text can be made easier or harder to read and converted into sound. The surface of the text has become malleable in ways in which the printed page clearly is not. But it has also become self-conscious as tensions arise in the production of text between the demands of presenting information and those of presentation itself. Thus authorial and production decisions run together producing a text that may not be so transparent as the traditional page of print. According to Lanham (1993, p. 5) the textual surface becomes bi-stable as we both look *at* it and *through* it. If we look through it we see facts as facts in the real world. When we look *at the text* however we have deconstructed this real world so that questions of style and stylistic patterns take over at the command of the electronic keyboard and the text can be read aesthetically. This is different from the stable transparency of the printed page. Electronic writing can be mechanical and precise like print, flowing and ever-changing like handwriting and visibly eclectic like a picture. Language is no longer to be restricted and understood simply as a medium of expression.

Nor is the electronic text's reproduction of a printed page the unit of writing on the screen. The electronically produced printed page can be expanded almost indefinitely, depending upon the capacity of the computer to structure and present text. But if we can expand the page and the configurations of printed pixels on the page indefinitely then any meaning and authorial control of meaning as exists on the former printed page becomes lost in this potential infinite expansion. *If* this is the case then the reproduction of a printed page cannot be taken as a meaningful unit for electronic writing. The writing space in electronic writing is then different from the writing space of print technology (see comments below on Derrida and notions of expansion of meaning).

Another element of the new space is in the arrangement of ideas. Printed pages are arranged hierarchically in a book to represent the logical plan of the argument, and paragraphs and sentences reflect at a lower level the arrangement and progression of ideas in a hierarchical order preconceived by the author. But suppose the reader wished to physically order the text by similar topics or by topics which shared certain relationships. Given a conventional book there would be need for scissors and paste and the book could be reduced to a series of slips of paper attached in various ways. But such ordering—hypertext—is not only possible in electronic writing (Bolter, 1991, pp. 23–25) but is realised in practice. Whereas conventional writing attempts to impose an order on verbal ideas through a hierarchy of structure (given in a table of contents) it essentially ignores a different order of associations and relationships that underlie the traditional order of chapters, pages and paragraphs. At best it permits the reader to make such associations without reading the whole text through an index which transforms a linear transmission of ideas into something more like a tree. Given that there is a variety of possible readers there may be no privileged form that the tree should take.

But what is the relationship between this new technology of electronic writing and ideas? What effects does it have upon people? What effects does it have upon society and its institutions? Are these effects the result of ideas or does the technology, in turn, elicit ideas and help constitute the new generations to which Victor Hugo referred? Here we will turn to the work of Mark Poster.

THE MODE OF INFORMATION

Historian of ideas Mark Poster sees us as entering a new phase of production of information as a result of electronic media. As he says:

> The prospect of instant universal information, introduced by electronic media, clearly has profound effects upon society, the extents of which are still to be determined. But the conquest of space and time by electronic media augurs more for institutions and for theory than a mere returning of practices and ideas to new communicational frequencies. (Poster, 1990, p. 3)

By the mode of information he means a form of symbolic exchange in which there is a unique mode of production of electronic language but also one in which the subject is not constituted as an agent centred in rational autonomy, but as a self which is 'decentred, dispersed, and multiplied in continuous instability' (*ibid.*, p. 6). Poster takes from post-structuralist philosophy the ideas that subjects are constituted in discourse and that changes in the wrapping of language must reconfigure the subject's relation to the world (*ibid.*, p. 11). Thus he devotes chapters to Jean Baudrillard and TV advertisements, Michel Foucault and databases, Jacques Derrida and electronic writing, and to Jean-François Lyotard and computer science.

Poster's claims that language is being wrapped differently by new configurations in electronic communications have several aspects. First, there is the distance between addressor and addressee which imposes different social relations from, say, face-to-face oral communication, or between reader and print on a page. Second, there are changes in the traditional notion of the authority of the author. There are new relations between message and context, as there is no real context in which the 'truth' of information can be assessed (in Wittgenstein's terms there is a break between a form of life and everyday language). Finally there are differences in the ways in which senders and receivers may represent themselves. This new wrapping of language, Poster argues, imposes in turn new relations between science and power, between the individual and both society and the state, between authority and the law, between consumer and retailer, and between family members.

There are several related issues of concern here. These are: a concern with the fragility of social networks; with the potential breakdown of traditional authority structures associated with oral and written communication; with new ways of exercising power relationships through these different forms of 'knowledge'; and with new ways of constituting the self, in the new realm of electronic communication. Finally there is the element of control and/or dissemination of information. While, for example, information is readily available on a scale never previously envisaged, it seems that it is not being freely disseminated. There is a politics of control which may deny access to those who do not have the technology and the assets to *purchase* information. In principle information is available to anyone, with traditional barriers of space and time obliterated by electronic communication. Why restrict access (see Burbules, 1998)?

If Poster is correct then the mode of information has a marked effect upon the constitutions of selves and society. In particular there are parallels between the dispersal of meaning and truth in the new writing spaces and the notion of the self as decentred, dispersed and non-permanent. Again it seems that the electronic text (like discourse) constitutes the subject (see here the writings of Michel Foucault) but is it perhaps that decentred individuals, the new individuals, are those writing their ideas in the new writing spaces? The relationship seems to be in two directions and not mono-directional as in the priest's prediction of the destruction of the church by print. Clearly there are major implications for how we need to conceptualise learning through electronic media.

But before turning to Heidegger and technology we look at three of these issues in more detail, albeit briefly. These will be, and in this order: the work of Derrida and the deferral of meaning; the notion of language which underlies electronic writing; and Foucault and the effects upon the self.

When we looked at the notion of the new writing space above it seemed that meaning in electronic text was capable of almost infinite deferral, because of the possibility of infinite expansion of the writing space. Jacques Derrida talks of how meaning is deferred and of the advent of electronic writing. In *Of Grammatology* Derrida sees the present age as one in 'suspense between two ages of writing', namely electronic writing and the printed page of the book (Derrida, 1974, pp. 86–87). This suspense Derrida saw as arising from upheavals in forms of communication, the ways in which new structures were emerging in formal practices and the treatment of information, which heralded the reduction of the role of speech, and linear writing (the book). But it is not clear that if his work heralds a new age of writing it also seriously grappled with the philosophical issues. Ulmer has argued that Derrida's work needs therefore to be supplemented (Ulmer, 1985a).

Derrida's coined term was '*différance*' which suggests not only that which is different but also that which is deferred or even that which is absent. Because meaning, as we normally understand it, only emerges in a field where what has been excluded is absent, when we examine a text we cannot be sure of the essential stability of signs. We must defer meaning so that we can ascertain what has been excluded. Thus texts must be examined for what is left out as well as for what is included or inscribed in the text. This represents an attack upon meaning as representation and notions of the authority on meaning of the author. Now Derrida is not arguing that an established meaning given to a text must be replaced by another meaning but that meaning is indeterminate, ambiguous and metaphorical. Of course this must be self-reflexive upon Derrida's own texts.

Ulmer's major criticism is that Derrida does not investigate the mode of writing appropriate to electronic writing. Poster appears to build upon this criticism and claims that where Derrida considers electronic writing he must hedge his bets (Poster, 1990, p. 101). On the one hand he considers that electronic writing is a destabilising influence, but on the other hand he believes it may reinforce notions of stability inherent in the printed-page technology. This is different from the infinite and destabilising extension of the writing space countenanced by Bolter above. For these sorts of reasons then Poster suggests that electronic writing is a minor though not insignificant theme in Derrida's works.

Wittgenstein talked of meaning as use (Wittgenstein, 1953) and the close relationship between language and the world, or a form of life. As he does not separate language from the world it is more proper to talk about language-in-the-world. But the notion that configurations of pixels no longer have 'reference' to a real world, but that they are self-reflexive and refer to themselves as simulacra plays havoc with Wittgenstein's close relationship between a public language and a form of life. Indeed he argued that not everything in a form of life could be put into language and that certain things could only be shown: for example why do we follow one direction 'suggested' by a pointing arrow? Wittgenstein says that we cannot explain this but only that (*ibid.*, #87): 'the sign is in order—if, under normal circumstances, it fulfils its purposes'. Texts on particular electronic screens with configurations of pixels that do not refer to any form of human life seem rather like Wittgenstein's notion of a private language. A private language is not a language because it lacks the notions of a rule and rule-following which, in turn, depend upon regularities perceived in the real world. If such a language displaces traditional languages in electronic writing then, from a Wittgensteinian position, serious questions would be raised about the stability and continuation of our forms of life.

The problems identified above have arisen because configurations of pixels are not the same as print on a page. But earlier the printing machine stabilised style, presentation, meaning and spelling. Print itself had to be controlled, for example to curb the stylistic flourishes of scribes, and for a variety of reasons print was to become more or less uniform. But what has become hidden, lost or forgotten, is that thought, as represented in print, was therefore *mediated*. As Lanham says:

> . . . once all this was done, unintermediated thought, or at least what seemed like unintermediated thought, was both possible and democratizable. And this unselfconcious transparency has become a stylistic, one might almost say a cultural, ideal for Western civilization. The best style is the style not noticed; the best manners, the most unobtrusive; convincing behaviour, spontaneous and unselfconscious. (Lanham, 1993, p. 4)

It would seem then that from a Wittgensteinean position configurations of pixels and electronic writing will require some form of mediation.

Discourses and practices affect human beings and constitute the self. This has been discussed in considerable detail by Michel Foucault. Foucault has discussed how we become normalised and subjected individuals through the practices of public institutions like prisons, the army and the school (Foucault, 1979). These can be termed techniques of domination. But his later writing was concerned with technologies of the self: first, how we aid and abet in constituting our selves (Foucault, 1980); second, how we can do this to ourselves (Foucault, 1985). Later again he was to talk of care for the self (Foucault, 1984; 1990).

Poster concentrates on databases, or Superpanopticons, in his chapter on Foucault, because they are a means of 'controlling masses in the postmodern, postindustrial mode of information' (Poster, 1990, p. 97). He sees us as both being controlled by databases and also acquiescing in the constitution of ourselves as *subjects* (who are subjected). But there are other interesting aspects to electronic writing that Foucault may have wished to consider. These are inherent in the new notions of writing space discussed above.

First the surface of a writing space has become more malleable between the demands of presentation of facts and demands of production, between description and rhetoric. No doubt if we are to become more interested in useful and saleable knowledge (Lyotard, 1984) how we present knowledge may become very important. But in the outcome we may care less for the importance of truth. Second, the reader can interact with the text, by changing the configurations of the pixels, by changing a text's linear narrative (Hamlet lives!), and by changing from a linear and hierarchical order to an order (or orders) based upon ideas, or the reader's interests. Thus the reader may be less concerned about the authority of authorship on the one hand and become more creative on the other hand. Foucault would see this freedom which the reader has to deal with text as providing new forms of liberty, and liberty for him was a precondition of the exercise of freedom and hence of an ethics of the self (Foucault, 1984). Foucault then would see electronic writing as changing the self away from subjection by authorities. If databases are Superpanopticons and subject people (Poster, 1990) then according to Foucault, electronic writing would seem to provide a subversive space for resistance to authorities.

Heidegger was also concerned with technology (in general), and its effects upon human beings in particular. If Foucault would seem to be optimistic about interactions between technology and humans, at least in the case of electronic writing, Heidegger would seem to be pessimistic given that electronic writing is itself an example of modern technology. However, his pessimism arises not so much from technology itself, but from humans believing that technology is essentially neutral. If they were to understand the essence of technology then they would be able to respond to it in ways which did not reduce us to the state, as he calls it, of being merely clever animals.

HEIDEGGER ON TECHNOLOGY

Martin Heidegger (1977) believed that technology was not neutral, and that conceiving it in that manner prevented understanding the *essence* of technology. Indeed he considered that modern technology had turned human beings into clever animals unaware that they too had become part of the ordering of resources in the world into a standing reserve. Humans as clever animals act with *gross hubris* towards the environment and other human beings. In this section I briefly outline Heidegger's account of technology and apply it to electronic writing.

In his essay, 'The Question Concerning Technology', Heidegger says 'we shall be questioning concerning technology' (Heidegger, 1977, p. 3). The continuous present tense of the verb 'question' does not imply a *static* question, 'what is it now?,' and a closed-off answer, but rather a continuous ongoing way or path, of questioning concerning the essence of technology. By 'essence' then Heidegger does not mean simply what something is now but, also, the way in which it pursues its course, the way in which it endures through time, the manner of its 'coming to presence', or the way in which it 'reveals' itself to us, and hence the ways in which we can respond to it. Heidegger's question then is not the *static* question which might evoke a mere temporal and situated, here and now, type of answer.

According to Heidegger the way forward is a way of thinking which will lead us through language 'in a manner that is extraordinary'. We should like, he says, to prepare 'a free relationship' with technology, and in our questioning the relationship will be free if 'it opens our human existence to the essence of technology' (*ibid.*). To have a free relationship with technology we cannot come to it with any presuppositions—for example, that it is neutral—and we must be prepared to follow where thinking takes us through language, because our ordinary thinking stultifies, or ossifies or fixes language in accordance with 'ordinary' thinking. This involves an initial response to technology, *before* any decision is made as to what it is and, then, how we are to respond to it. For to respond to it we must have grasped certain things about ourselves, about human being, so that we can 'open' ourselves to the essences of both human being and of technology. This must be a simultaneous and mutual opening up or recognition, and not a temporal response, for human being and technology are in a mutual interrelationship. This is difficult to understand, given traditional philosophical logicist, positivist and Anglo-Saxon understandings of language and logic and a traditional overt antipathy to metaphysics. But, phrased in more traditional terminology and divested of his metaphysics, Heidegger is offering us a prescriptive account of the concept of technology, one which does not accord with present use of the terms.

Heidegger opens by stating that the essence of a tree cannot itself be a tree which we could encounter, for we are seeking something which pervades all trees and not merely what is obvious or given in a particular tree. By analogy, the essence of technology cannot be something technological, but something which pervades or dwells in all forms of technology. Nor should we seek something which is neutral for, common and persuasive as this view might be, it 'makes us utterly blind to the essence of technology' (*ibid.*, p. 5).

Traditional accounts claim that technology is a means to an end and that technology is a human activity. But these two accounts belong together, for to posit ends and also to procure the means to achieve those ends is a typical human activity. Heidegger says that whilst this *instrumental* view is uncannily correct about technology (*ibid.*), it is not the (whole) *truth* about technology. Instead it conditions every attempt 'to bring man into the right relation to technology', because we tend to see that relation as one of mastery over instrumental technology, of not letting it get out of hand. Instead, he says, we must ask: 'What is the instrumental itself? Within what do such things as means and end belong?' (*ibid.*, p. 6).

Heidegger's criticism of the notion that the instrumental is the essence of technology commences by drawing a distinction between ancient (hand technology, or handcraft) and modern technology. The difference is that in ancient technology what is in nature is (merely?) revealed by a bringing forth, whereas in modern technology there is a *challenging* or *demanding* of nature. This involves a demand placed upon nature by modern man, who tries not merely to *reveal* nature, but to *demand* of nature that it be ordered as standing reserve. Heidegger uses the notion of enframing (*ge-stell*) to refer to this demanding of nature. His claim is that *enframing* is the essence of modern technology; it is 'that challenging claim which gathers man thither to order the self-revealing as standing-reserve' (*ibid.*, p. 19). To see the essence of technology as instrumental is to see it as being neutral, as being neither good nor bad, as only the ends to which it is put have value.

Heidegger says that enframing means the gathering together of that setting upon which sets upon man, that is, challenges him forth, to reveal the real, in the mode of ordering, as standing reserve. Enframing means the way of revealing which holds sway in the essence of modern technology and which is itself nothing technological. On the other hand, all those things that are so familiar to us and are standard parts of an assembly, such as rods, pistons and chassis, belong to the technological. The assembly itself, however, together with the aforementioned stock-parts, falls within the sphere of technological activity; and this activity always merely responds to the challenge of enframing, but it never comprises enframing itself or brings it about (*ibid.*, p. 20).

How can we take up or enter into a relationship with technology when it reveals itself to us as standing reserve? Heidegger says that the questions asked about man's relationship to technology and about the essence of technology come too late if we think that we can enter into any such relationship *subsequently*. This would presuppose a revealing of the essence of technology as standing reserve independently of and prior to any human relationship with it. But the revealing and the relationship must be simultaneous; we must enter into such relationships for the essence to be revealed, for our very experiences and our experiences of ourselves have to be challenged by the essence of technology as standing reserve, for this enframing to 'come to presence' (*ibid.*, p. 24).

According to Heidegger, modern technology reduces humanity to the state of a clever animal, with no obligation to shelter things or to protect their being, as everything including humanity is turned into a standing reserve. If modern humanity is aware of problems in modern technology, it tends to focus on issues such as loss and destruction as the result of the applications of technology. But this is itself part of the modern technological stance. Exposing the nature of modern technology shows us that we act, unknown to ourselves, with gross hubris, not only to things and nature, but also towards other human beings, as humans themselves become part of the standing reserve. It is not just that humans cause social and ecological change, as well as destruction, but that humans are changed and, in this ordering and controlling of standing reserve, in turn change other human beings.

These are clearly important issues that affect human beings and their intertwined relationships with the total environment. Do we merely act with gross hubris? Are we merely clever animals? Unfortunately these issues cannot be pursued further here (for a discussion of curriculum and technology as neutral, see for example, Marshall, 1999).

Heidegger's point here, generalised to cover electronic writing, is that unless we understand the essence of electronic writing, then we may come to see it as neutral. If we understand and apply technology as if it were neutral then it affects us as human beings in certain ways. Thus we may enter into relationships with the environment and with other human beings so that we ourselves become part of standing reserve. Thus we would be ordered and subjected in ways which are not only inimical to the environment but also to human beings.

CONCLUSIONS

The priest's question

How are we to answer the priest's question, rephrased and posed by Bolter, in the Introduction: will electronic writing destroy the book? But the jury is not yet out and scarcely even called. Like the time lapse with the advent of the printed page, it is not clear yet whether electronic writing will substantially replace the printed page. Enthusiasts, including some philosophers, seem to see replacement as more or less inevitable. But if there is already a displacement then that is something other than replacement, and this is far from being destruction. Nor is it yet clear why the jury should even be called. There is therefore, I believe, an important role for philosophers, and philosophers of education, as we seem already to have entered a stage of displacement. In other words philosophers have a role here to shape the way in which this displacement proceeds, rather than waiting to act like *post-facto* Lockean underlabourers. Hence we should be able to lay before 'the jury', first the philosophical issues which need to be tackled and, second, the educational issues which stem from them. It might be claimed the latter discussion can hardly wait as we rush headlong into more and more electronic writing and technology in education.

Prior to some clarification of the philosophical issues and of what is at stake by adopting one position rather than another, what might be said about education is unclear. It could be premature: it could be highly speculative in a mixture of logical and empirical possibilities; or it might just be vague and indecisive (or both). With those provisos I will list a number of the philosophical problems identified above. These include:

- The new writing spaces of electronic writing.
- Problems of meaning in electronic writing space.
- Problems of authorship and authority.
- What literacy means in relation to electronic writing.
- Issues related to the notion of the self, in particular the decentred self.
- The relationship between the ideas of the new generation of decentred selves and electronic writing.
- Wider questions concerning technology and the technological society.

Identifying the problems is one thing: disseminating them to others who are not philosophically trained is another. Not only does it take time, effort and patience to understand notions such as writing space (Bolter, 1991; Lanham, 1993), and Heidegger's (1977) argument that technology is not neutral, but it is extremely difficult to describe these notions in everyday terms. Understanding the philosophical issues is one thing, and understanding how they are to be disseminated pedagogically is another. Therefore any answer to the priest's question must be deferred.

Nor is it possible to deal here with each and every issue identified above, and introduced in the text. Instead I will concentrate upon one topic only—the decentred self—and outline very briefly what it means and how it might be made sense of educationally.

The decentred self

Normally a self is seen as at least a centre of consciousness, with a capacity for self-consciousness and experience, and able to engage in thought and deliberative action. As the self is seen as self-conscious it is also seen as capable of knowledge about the self, in particular that its thoughts are its own. The notion of the decentred self would deny many of these assumptions. Whilst it is seen as self-conscious, the knowledge of the self which it has is not its own, but instead is the result of certain historical and social discourses and practices which have constituted it in various ways. If its thoughts are not its own, any actions chosen as the result of what is seen as autonomous (and normally rational) deliberation cannot be the self's own either, beyond the sense of that self being an originator of the action.

Michel Foucault is quite comfortable with a notion of the decentred self. For him, there is no one self or subject, but several, for the subject is not conceived as an *individuated* substance but as a form ' . . . and this form is not primarily or always identical to itself' (Foucault, 1984, p. 290). A number of questions then arise. Which self am I at any one particular time? Which self do I want to be? Which self *ought* I to take up? Which of these selves *owns* a text as *the* author? In answer to the last question: if it seems that one of Foucault's selves owns *The Order of Things*, then that self seems different from the self who wrote *The History of Sexuality*. If the selves are different, how is the authorship of these two books credited to Foucault? However it is not only in post-structuralism but also in electronic writing that ownership and authority seem to have been dispersed.

Bolter and Lanham see the self in writing space as being decentred and Poster sees this writing space as affecting the self. If the decentred self is thereby becoming an increasingly prevalent idea, in part 'caused' by the technology, then there is a further series of psychological and pedagogical issues for education. The sorts of social education which we have traditionally pursued would seem to be at odds with the implications of a decentred self. For how confusing would this be for young people searching (desperately?) for just one stable notion of a self? Which self should we encourage? Where go notions of responsibility for deliberative actions when some other self can be blamed? What happens now for the learner working with electronic script to accepted notions of authorship, individual work, responsibility, truth-telling, plagiarism and so on? If the self really is decentred, then there is a number of knotty issues for us as parents and educators. These problems would seem to be immense and almost intractable, were all of this talk of the self as being decentred *valid*.

Foucault does, however, offer us a way forward in his talk of care of the self (Foucault, 1984, 1990). Very briefly, for Foucault, the self is decentred in the sense outlined. Nevertheless without taking any narcissistic turn we can *care* for the self, and thereby care for others. So not anything goes for Foucault on the self. Liberty is said by him to be a presupposition of freedom and ethics is seen by him as the exercise of freedom. To be ethical then we must have learned how to care for the self. This, he argues, we must learn in a *pedagogical* relationship with an elder mentor, one who will tell the truth to us and not manipulate us through the power which a mentor must possess. We not only have the model of the mentor, but there are countless models in society which we can fashion ourselves upon. As learning to care for the self requires entering into human relationships where the concept of care is an integral part, so also will we care for others because of what we have learned in learning to care for ourselves about care and others in the right pedagogical relationship.

If I understand Foucault correctly such decentred selves would not manipulate others, would not misrepresent themselves, would not plagiarise other authors and would exercise their freedom ethically. This ethical position on the decentred self is compatible with Foucault's earlier discussion of the disciplinary society (Foucault, 1979) and its problems (Foucault, 1983), and of governmentality in his later writings.

Learning through electronic technology then becomes from this position a selection of the right mentors (texts, Web-sites and so on) which permit the learner to care for the self. Again not anything goes but the criteria for judgement (again in Foucault) remain unclear, if one is to avoid subjection and a position of tutelage. Indeed, those readers who are familiar with the later work of Michel Foucault (for example, 1983) and Heidegger's (1977) brief suggestions as to how to avoid becoming standing reserve will recognise Foucault's indebtedness here to Martin Heidegger. In general, those familiar with post-structuralist emphases on the politics of difference, the politics of resistance, its anti-colonialism and its anti-globalisation thrusts, may discern some way forward from Foucault's notion of ethics as care for the self.

The pedagogical implications for education *systems* in modern Western democracies would seem to be immense, if not intractable also. But Foucault's and Lyotard's (1984) point would be that modern state-education systems have lost sight of their liberal notions of emancipation and enlightenment in the call of performativity, as education has been subsumed under demands for the efficient functioning of social and national systems. Of course one does not need to go down a post-structuralist path to share such concerns. However, a major question which both Foucault and traditional liberals share is whether it is possible to return to those liberal values.

Would a reincarnation of Victor Hugo's priest look out upon such 'edifices' and see electronic writing as a way forward to enlightenment and emancipation, and not to performativity? Could electronic writing destroy those edifices? Certainly Mark Poster (1990) sees the possibilities inherent in the mode of information in that way.

10

Fetish for Effect

PAUL STANDISH

'Do you have a computer at home? Are you online?' When such questions are asked today, various things are taken for granted. It is likely that most people reading this chapter will answer yes to the first question. What is understood by 'computer' here is probably the desktop; typically this will incorporate the box housing the processor and drives, a keyboard and a screen.

But computers do not need to be like this, and, as we have recently been reminded, our homes are alive with a host of miniature computing devices that the millennium bug might have infested. The fact that we do habitually think of the computer in terms of this particular configuration of box, keyboard and screen reflects, quite naturally, the way in which the technology has developed and the part that it plays in our lives. It is not difficult to imagine a different machine without screen or keyboard, one that relied primarily on a combination of number key-pads, microphones and loudspeakers, and yet that used more or less the same microchips. The home computer that we in fact have has developed in the context of particular social activities and cultural meanings. It cannot be understood merely in terms of an inevitable technological evolution, a kind of inhuman force that increasingly determines our lives.

'Are you online?', as this is typically understood, presupposes precisely the kind of configuration of box, keyboard and screen that is taken for granted here. Of course, some day things will surely be different. But this present situation is sufficient to illustrate the way that earlier developments, not only of a purely technical but of a socio-cultural kind, are embedded in the growth of the Internet.

In what follows I make no apology for considering technologies other than the Internet. This reveals the ways that instrumentalism and a preoccupation with presentation (presentational allure, metaphysics of presence) have their bearing on the context in which online education is being developed.

ESSENTIALISING TECHNOLOGY

The embedding of the socio-cultural in any technological development, its sedimentation and stabilisation with use, have the effect of a
naturalisation. At the same time there is a tendency, in Western
culture at least, towards a reification of technology in terms of its
function: the functional is the real. In his recent *Questioning
Technology*, Andrew Feenberg explains this as follows: 'What
differentiates technology and tools in general from other types of
objects is the fact that they appear always already split into
"primary" and "secondary" qualities, i.e. functional qualities and
others' (Feenberg, 1999a, p. 211). Secondary qualities are then seen as
inessential in a way that both reinforces our tendency to lose sight of
the socio-cultural factors incorporated in those artefacts and inclines
us to essentialise the functional:

> Thus an initial abstraction is built into our immediate perception of
> technologies. That abstraction seems to set us on the path toward an
> understanding of the nature of technology as such. However, it is
> important to note that this is an assumption based on the form of
> objectivity of technology in *our* society. Function is not necessarily so
> privileged in other societies. The functional point of view may coexist
> peacefully with other points of view—religious, aesthetic, etc.—none
> of which are essentialized. To the Western observer this eclecticism
> appears as mere confusion but it has its rationale, as we will see. (*ibid.*)

The broad thrust of Feenberg's argument in this book is to the effect
that the tendency to essentialise is found not only in common ways of
thinking about technology, but also in the work of such thinkers as
Martin Heidegger, Jürgen Habermas, Jacques Ellul and Albert
Borgmann. It is beyond the scope of this chapter to consider how far
such a characterisation of the work of these philosophers is fair.
More germane to a discussion of online education is the significance
of any general tendency to essentialise the technological, and
accordingly this will be my concern.

To illustrate the ways in which a technological artefact always has
already incorporated into it certain meanings and values and a
certain know-how, Feenberg draws on the celebrated account of the
development of the bicycle offered by Trevor Pinch and Wiebe Bijker
(*ibid.*, pp. 79 ff.; Pinch and Bijker, 1987). This shows how an initial
ambivalence of potential came to be resolved, with ensuing effects on
the bicycle's progressive design and development. Initially it was not
clear whether the bicycle was to be a kind of toy for sporting
purposes, where speed would be of the essence, or a means of
transport, where ease of use would be the priority. Because of the
development of certain types of demand—that is, a confluence of
certain socio-cultural factors with the elements of the hardware—the

latter role came to the fore. This was gradually fed into the design of the machine and led to the familiar form of the bicycle that we know today. (Racers, mountain bikes and other variations are relatively minor divergencies in style, but they have similar explanations. It is not difficult to trace the combination of environmental and life-style factors that have contributed to the development of the mountain bike. It is interesting to note, however, that for many young people today, this may be the archetypal bicycle, rather than the sleek racers that were common a generation ago when the mountain bike was unknown.)

As was said above, it now seems natural to Western eyes to see the artefact in terms of primary and secondary qualities. This may be fairly readily apparent in terms of a machine such as a bicycle, though not all products of technology are like this. The 'failure' of some societies to separate the functional and the aesthetic or religious aspects of a thing is generally taken in the West to be a kind of confusion. But this perception begins to be dispelled when more culturally complex things are considered. Thus:

> even Westerners are capable of falling into the same 'confusion' with respect to certain richly signified technical artefacts, such as houses, which we must strain to perceive as 'machines for living', in Le Corbusier's phrase. In cases like this, it is obvious that a fuller picture of technology is conveyed by studying the social role of the technical object and the lifestyles it makes possible. That picture places the abstract notion of 'function' in its concrete social context. Thus it becomes clear that what we describe in functional language as an artefact is equally describable in social language as the objectification of a norm or of a symbolic content. (Feenberg, 1999a, pp. 211–212)

The example of the house helps to extend the idea of the technological, away from such relatively simple tools as hammers and such relatively straightforward machines as bicycles towards vastly complex constructions—constructions, it should be noted, where function is increasingly difficult to specify fully. The example of the house is significant, moreover, because this is less an artefact or machine than an *environment*. As such it provides the *site* for an infinite range of activities and things. If the language of tools and instruments resonates with some aspects of computer use, this vocabulary of these more complex things is plainly more proximate to that of the Internet. The tendency to see technology in terms of primary and secondary functions is then even more inadequate when it comes to something as complex as the use of the Internet in education.

There is no shortage of evangelism about the potential of the Internet to transform education today. In part such evangelism is motivated by an understandable conviction that many teachers and parents are unbelievers and have yet to hear the word. The transformative power of the Internet for education should not be in doubt. But neither is it doubted by many of those who fear its effects. Their hostility relates to the potential of the Internet to reduce knowledge to information, to displace the immediacy of classroom interaction, or to fragment and depersonalise learning; some fear also the almost inevitable increase in commercial involvement in education.

Technophiles and technophobes alike are inclined to essentialise. Technology, they say, cannot be resisted: it will work itself out for good or ill. If Feenberg is right, such views amount to a kind of bad faith, a failure to acknowledge the centrality of socio-cultural values within which and through which technology's development takes place. Of course, many people are neither technophiles nor technophobes but rather express a level-headed scepticism: technology in itself is neutral and its value depends on the uses to which it is put. But this does not get things quite right either. Seeing design and function as something separable from the pure machine, these assumptions fail adequately to acknowledge the extent to which the technological incorporates values that have already been espoused.

Ultimately this manner of thinking of the technological artefact is driven by a belief in the thing-in-itself: there is an essential thing there, independent of the various uses to which it might be put. To deny this is not so much to say that it is impossible to isolate the object and to hold it up for scrutiny, as it were. Rather it is to assert that when this is done, the abstraction alters the thing; in short it ceases to be the technological artefact, the very thing at issue. In contrast a correct understanding of that artefact acknowledges its location in a network of practices in a way that defies both a subject–object dichotomy and a spectatorial stance. The argument for this is most persuasive in connection with relatively simple craft tools such as the hammer, which blends inconspicuously and unselfconsciously into the carpenter's craft activity. But the point can be extended to our ordinary being with things. For example, we operate smoothly and seamlessly with any number of tools around the home—light switches, door handles, cutlery, ballpoint pens. We normally encounter these things in 'equipmental-wholes', where they occur in a nexus of related things, and where they are not thematically apprehended for deliberate thinking but disappear in our practical orientation, whatever it is at the time—say, to go into the study to write the letter (see Heidegger, 1988, pp. 162 ff.).

Thinking of technology as something other and objectified, on this view, not only misunderstands the machine: it misconceives human being. From the most primitive tool use, this being-with-things in equipmental-wholes is a defining feature of human existence. The kind of experience evoked here cannot be captured in terms of a mental consciousness directed towards non-mental objects. Yet it is not automatic and far from mindless. As the example of the carpenter indicates, it is very much the realm of skilled behaviour, which adapts and refines itself on the strength of a vast accumulation of experience, acquired in the course of purposeful activity. We might at any time hold an artefact up for inspection, but it is normally only when something goes wrong—the light switch fails to work—that the smooth flow of this being-with-things is broken: then we think about the thing deliberately and we are repositioned in a subject–object orientation.

Just as simple tools that we commonly use disappear in ordinary activity, so too do complex things fade into the background. The house is a place where an infinite variety of activities can go on, and as these different activities preoccupy us the bricks and mortar, indeed almost all aspects of the house, disappear from view. In similar fashion, the Web-site provides a kind of shell in which an infinite variety of material can be located. This infinity is not a matter of the range of types of material—text, graphics, video and so on—that can be included but rather to do with the substantive variety that these media can contain: the variety extends to whatever can be presented. Sites are nodal points in Web space but they become locales as they are given substance and links. It is this substance that gives us reason to visit them—to explore, to spend time, to revisit, perhaps to interact. We revisit the locale to pick up the same conversations or to play the same games. But the extent of what can fall into the background here seems remarkably limited in relation to the ordinary experience of living in a house. The relation between what is the immediate object of our attention and what fades into the background is of a different order. (For a detailed discussion of these matters that takes a different line, see David Kolb's chapter in this volume.)

It was Heidegger's insight that technology is one way in which the world is made manifest to us but that it alone has the power to displace all other modes of revealing. His later remarks on cybernetics make more explicit the significance of this with regard to information technology. Industrialisation is characterised by factory production geared primarily towards the satisfaction of needs, and the reduction of the human being to the labouring animal. In later phases, however, production is controlled and shaped by information technology and hence is conceived increasingly in terms of systems theory. Needs satisfaction is supplemented by the exploitative creation of desire, especially desires relating to the simulacra of experience and to the celebration of cybernetic systems themselves. Modern electronics hides in black boxes to make possible an ergonomic design and an ease of use that in certain respects are reminiscent of pre-industrial work activity. The use of the home computer itself in some ways expands this realm of the ready-to-hand (*Zuhandenheit*)—witness the unselfconscious fluency that children so readily acquire in the use of keyboard, mouse, links and so on. The centrality of the screen itself to this experience raises troubling questions about what else is changed.

A starting point for addressing these concerns is provided by the question of the relationship between personal computers and television. Some critics have endorsed the intuitive assumption that computer usage is similar to television watching (see, for example, Postman, 1990). The fact that primitive home computers were often designed to be used through the television set, and that many games still are, has certainly reinforced this assumption. But a number of factors weigh against this, as Paul Levinson has argued (Levinson, 1997, p. 163 ff.). First, television, with the exception of home video recorders, is programmed by television professionals while computers, with the exception of underlying programs, are programmed by the proximate user. Channel-hopping is quite unlike mouse-clicking, it might be added, in that different channels are more or less unrelated whereas links operate only where a connection has been identified (idiosyncratic though these may sometimes be). Second, and notwithstanding the dramatic proliferation of channels, television in a sense broadcasts the same thing to everyone. Although perhaps physically alone, a person watching is one of 'the viewers', the intended audience for the programme. The computer, on the other hand, permits the display of 'the pinpoint, specially tailored decision of each user: to word-process, and if so, what to write; to browse the Web, and if so, where; to discuss a topic, asynchronously or synchronously, in whatever online forum; etc.' (*ibid.*, p. 164). A third consideration is that television is to a significant degree an 'incidental' medium. That is, one can watch television while doing something else, or attend to it intermittently, or more or less ignore it while it is nevertheless on; and one can be a 'couch potato'. In contrast, the computer typically involves the user in interactive communication; computer users are more likely to be alert and focused on what they are doing, and perhaps partially oblivious of what is otherwise going on around them. Fourth, television screens traffic in images and sounds, with occasional written words, whereas computer screens present text, perhaps adorned with graphics, and with occasional images and sounds (though Levinson acknowledges that this is changing) (*ibid.*, pp. 164–165).

Already, however, these observations look dated. Perhaps the most important point here is that with the advent of digital television there is the likelihood of the convergence of the home computer and television. Moreover, the suggestion that computer screens primarily present text scarcely does justice to the range of messages—video images, graphics, games—that Web-sites can contain, nor does it adequately reflect the larger and more complex non-textual messages that increased computing power progressively makes more feasible. What is possible in principle should not, however, cloud our judgement about what the resourcing of education is likely to make possible in practice in the short and medium term. It is not difficult to imagine school children frustrated at the slowness of machines that the school cannot afford to replace. It may also be the case that Levinson underestimates the significance for education of children's usage of games, where, in the case of arcade games at least, there is a saturation of images, movement and sound, with highly circum- scribed and limited forms of text. Can the child's quick and sophisticated reading of the lurid imagery and sensational subject matter of computer games, it might be asked, be channelled towards more educational ends, or is it merely obstructive of those ends? How far indeed does it desensitise? It is Levinson's fourth point, however, that is perhaps most salient in the context of the present discussion. Most pages of the Web are heavily text based, as more generally is use of the Internet for other purposes (for example, email): most usage involves reading or composing words on screen. The significance of this for education is a central concern in the final section of this chapter.

In order to clarify what is at stake here it will be helpful to look more closely at the phenomenology of this use. The user of the Internet is typically someone who is alone, seated at a desk in front of a monitor with her hands on a keyboard and mouse. Of course, in the cybercafé or the learning centre she may be with others but, for the most part, she is in effect operating in a capsule alone. Her input is via keyboard and mouse, and the data she receives are in the form of on-screen text, graphics or pictures. As with the instantly 'refreshable' television or cinema screen, there is the expectation that the pages that present these will appear instantaneously on the screen. It is, of course, necessary to scroll down to see more of any page that exceeds the screen, and in practice graphical or coloured images especially can take time to 'fill in'. Although the speed of links will vary with, amongst other things, the power of the computer, the experience of this will be rather unlike an ordinary searching for things: the user simply has to wait passively, and then the page suddenly arrives. Apart from the computer's occasional beeps and the soft clatter of the keyboard, most of this activity takes place in silence. As with watching television, the user looks at the screen.

Technological artefacts vary enormously, but a common characteristic is to be found in the way that they amplify some aspects of perception while subduing others. The telescope, for example, amplifies sight while limiting smell and touch. As the foregoing account shows, the computer emphasises the visual with its particular concentration within the field framed by the screen. In contrast to the experiences of, say, playing football or driving a car, computer usage involves a concentration of visual attention on the immediate object placed directly in front of the user. This effects a stark separation of that immediate object from the background awareness that must inevitably accompany any perception. Concentration on this kind of presentation—here in front of me now—has further implications in terms of our relation to what is hidden and to what cannot be made present. This perhaps helps to explain the experience of absorption in working on a computer.

It is a further distinctive feature of this concentration that its object is presented on a screen that is instantly refreshable, at the click of a mouse. Hence the loss of peripheral awareness tends to coincide with an orientation or mood of strange ambivalence, poised between an absorption that tends towards the obsessive—addiction to arcade games or Free Cell, the emailer's compulsive response to the beep of in-coming messages—and a restless flitting from link to link.

Ergonomic design and relative ease of access further release attention to concentrate on the visual. What is seen is framed, as with the television screen, and opens onto a world. In the case of Internet use, this world is defined in the terms of a kind of pastiche of the environments, sites and domains of the everyday world. Of course, there is interactivity, and of course virtual reality may become more rich as the hardware—of gloves, suits, and so on—develops. But at present the fact that the user sits directly facing the flat screen concentrates experience in the gaze. That what is seen depends on intricate hidden codes and that it appears from this darkness on the refreshable screen intensifies the sense in which this gaze is voyeuristic. And this is complemented by a further factor to do with the very scale of the Web. Web-sites for bomb-making and sexual perversion there may be, but the fact that these are *presentations* within this structure means that in many respects the worlds that the technology opens onto are neutralised in advance (compare with confessional television).

In some respects the prominence of the visual in the technology may be a contingent thing, readily superseded as Web-sites become richer and hardware develops. But the fact that this is how the technology has to date developed reveals the extent to which this voyeurism is embedded. In many respects this is the outcome of the spectatorial stance characteristic of the modern world.

The metaphysical implications here are profound. For something to be virtually real it must be able to be presented. Hence in virtual reality presentation has no other. Ironically though, even as the technology has its *raison d'être* in what can be made virtually present, even though it is the logic of presentation that determines how this world is experienced and understood, the user is tacitly aware of the causal relation between this and the hidden wizardry of programming. If the medieval world can be seen as semiological, as Charles Taylor suggests, understood as the word of God, so also is this virtual world, its encryption constituting the apotheosis of a certain kind of rationality. Everyday reliance upon that virtual world entails a forgetting of that encoding. It is not the layperson's ignorance of the technology that makes this puzzling—this predates the growth of cybernetics. It is the hidden yet decisive nature of that coding. In this particular machine, the ghost is in the crypt.

FETISH FOR TECHNOLOGY

In the preface to *Questioning Technology* Feenberg suggests that the essentialising attitude to technology is reminiscent of an earlier attitude to capital:

> The same kind of ignorance that bound men to the gold standard for centuries maintains the illusion that technology is an alien force intruding on our social life from a coldly rational beyond. The forces of the market were believed to transcend the will of peoples and nations. The economy was treated as a kind of quasi-natural system with laws as rigid as the movements of the planets. The social nature of exchange had to be discovered against tremendous ideological resistance. Today it seems absurd that modern societies renounced control of their own economic life to a second nature they had themselves created. Yet where technology is concerned we remain in wilful submission to a second nature just as contingent on human action as the economy. Liberation from technological fetishism will follow the course of liberation from economic fetishism. The same story will some day be told about machines that we tell today about markets. (Feenberg, 1999a, p. viii)

It may be difficult to share Feenberg's sanguine confidence that belief in the transcendence of the market has been outgrown, but the general point is plausible enough: we are today confronted with a fetishisation of technology.

In an earlier account, Mark Poster speaks in similar terms, suggesting that 'history may be periodized by variations in the structure...of symbolic exchange, but also that the current culture gives a certain fetishistic importance to "information"' (Poster, 1990, p. 8). The contemporary prominence of information has tended to encourage a reductive conception of knowledge and understanding. Moreover, its more or less technical sense in Information and Communications Technology (ICT) parts company with the epistemologically normative implications that ordinarily attach to the term, referring instead simply to sets of electronic impulses (see Graham, 1999, p. 89 ff.). The glut of information and the ease of its accessibility reinforce the tendency to think of the communication of information as the epitome of language, and of information as the substance upon which our thinking skills are exercised. Heidegger explicitly links the reduction of language to an instrument of information with the foundationalist demand for security (associated especially with Leibniz) and with the suppression of risk; this engenders a calculative thinking geared to the 'objectification' of all things and to the establishment of human domination over the whole earth (Heidegger, 1991, p. 124). The growth of cybernetic systems then constitutes a crucial stage in technology's domination.

Just as the economy has been treated as a quasi-natural system, so electronic texts involve deep shifts in the sense of what is most real. While the conventional technological device amplifies perception of an aspect of the real, the surrogate reality of the formal system entices us away from the stubborn messiness of everyday life (see Albert Borgmann, 1992, p. 68 ff.). This seems like an ideal extension of the epistemology of 'what works', and leads to a fetishisation of instrumentality itself. The significance of such arguments becomes all the more apparent in the light of the phenomenology of watching ideally manipulable virtual objects on an instantly refreshable screen.

The fetishisation of instrumentality needs to be understood against the background of the mystical character of commodification. This does not originate in the use-value of things that are produced but in their exchange. In the *locus classicus*, in *Capital*, Marx writes:

> It is as clear as noon-day, that man, by his industry, changes the forms of the materials furnished by nature, in such a way as to make them useful to him. The form of wood, for instance, is altered, by making a table out of it. Yet, for all that the table continues to be that common, every-day thing, wood. But, so soon as it steps forth as a commodity, it is changed into something transcendent. It not only stands with its feet on the ground, but, in relation to all other commodities, it stands on its head, and evolves out of its wooden brain grotesque ideas, far more wonderful than 'table-turning' ever was. (Marx, 1886, pp. 41–42)

The fetishism of commodities arises out of the fact that a social relation between producers assumes a fantastic form as a relation between things: this social character acquires an objective character— turns into a thing—and becomes stamped on the product of the labourer's work:

whenever, by an exchange, we equate as values our different products, by that very act, we also equate, as human labour, the different kinds of labour expended upon them. We are not aware of this, nevertheless we do it. Value, therefore, does not stalk about with a label describing what it is. It is value, rather, that converts every product into a social hieroglyphic. Later on, we try to decipher the hieroglyphic, to get behind the secret of our own social products; for to stamp an object of utility as a value, is just as much a social product as language. (*ibid.*, p. 45)

Marx speaks of the crystallisation of commodities in money (*ibid.*, p. 59). With the loss of the backing of money by gold, and with the progressive replacement of coins and notes by electronic records, the referent for money disappears, enabling a kind of ideal circulation of currency.

What is seen in the market place, what is presented for exchange, masquerades as simple and hides what is truly at stake. Marx enjoins us to recognise what is hidden, and the true worth of the thing (seen in terms of its use-value). In *Specters of Marx* at one point Derrida offers a reading of this on Marx's own terms:

One must see, at first sight, what does not let itself be seen. And this is invisibility itself. For what first sight misses is the invisible. The flaw, the error of first sight is to see, and not to notice the invisible. If one does not give oneself up to this invisibility, the table-commodity, immediately perceived, remains what it is not, a simple thing deemed to be trivial and too obvious. This trivial thing seems to comprehend itself (*ein selbstverständliches, triviales Ding*): the thing itself in the phenomenality of its phenomenon, a quite simple wooden table. So as to prepare us to see this invisibility, to see without seeing, thus to think the body without body of this invisibility—the ghost is already taking shape—Marx declares that the thing in question, namely, the commodity, *is not so simple* (a warning that will elicit snickers from all the imbeciles, until the end of time, who never believe anything, of course, because they are so sure that they see what is seen, everything that is seen, only what is seen). (Derrida, 1994, pp. 149–150)

The demand for evidence, for ocular proof, is complicit with this inability to acknowledge the invisible, and with this snickering. We shall shortly see the price of this credulity—the error of first sight, the failure to see the invisible—as this is exacted in education. But, first, let us note that Marx's lament at the commodification conveys a sense of loss or occlusion of the thing-in-itself (in its use-value). Derrida points to the elusiveness of what is at stake by showing ways in which Marx's critique is itself partially compromised. How does Marx lead us to see, and present, the commodification? It is quite different when the table becomes a commodity,

> when the curtain goes up on the market and the table plays actor and
> character at the same time, when the commodity-table, says Marx,
> comes on stage (*auftritt*), begins to walk around and to put itself
> forward as a market value. *Coup de théâtre*: the ordinary sensuous
> thing is transfigured (*verwandelt sich*), it becomes someone, it assumes
> a figure. (*ibid.*, p. 150)

When Marx reaches for the simple sensuous phenomenality of the
thing, the table already takes on a role. His description, directed at the
contortions the simple table is forced through as it submits to market
exchange, *animates* the table as it sets it on the stage: the wooden table
is set on the stage of his drama at the very point where the table is
required to become an *exemplum*. Marx repeatedly exposes conjuring
tricks, the calling up of spirits. This animation of the exemplum,
Derrida suggests, is the phenomenological conjuring trick.

The commodity is such a tangled thing that Marx must have
recourse to the religious: 'Precisely in order to analyze the
metaphysical and the theological that constructed the phenomenological good sense of the thing itself, of the immediately invisible
commodity, in flesh and blood: of what it is "at first sight" (*auf den
ersten Blick*)' (*ibid.*). The 'metaphysical subtleties and theological
niceties' at the very start of 'The Fetishism of Commodities and the
Secret Thereof' reflect an irreducibility of the religious in Marx's
materialism (Marx, 1886, p. 41). Marx wants to have done with the
revenant, to set the wooden table firmly on its legs, but his
elaboration of the metaphor of the spectre betrays a real and
inevitable haunting: the phenomenological setting on stage is
inescapably implicated with what cannot appear. The table
becomes 'a tableau of the becoming-immaterial of matter' (Derrida,
1994, p. 152). Marx's 'table-turning' turns also on itself.

TABLE-TURNING

> Dr Budgell found that, with small variations, he could take the table
> which ranked the poverty of the intake of Sheffield's schools, turn it
> upside down and find himself looking at the table which ranked
> academic success. (Nick Davies, 'Schools in crisis, part 2', *The
> Guardian*, 15 September 1999, p. 4)

Tables can turn the fate of a school. In England and Wales the series
of changes led by the 1988 Act created the elements of a market in
state schooling. The power of local education authorities to allocate
children to schools was weakened in favour of choice on the part of
parents. Children's test results would be published in league tables,
and these in turn would have a powerful influence on parental choice.
Schools attracting the most children would be awarded extra funds,

the vast bulk of the budget being determined by the number of pupils on a school's roll. The school with the best results would then have the pick of the pupils for the future: league-table rankings become self-fulfilling.

But turn the table on its head and a different story is told, one that undermines the very thing the tables purported to demonstrate: it is poverty that is the main cause of failure in schools. The series of articles by Nick Davies that *The Guardian* ran on its front pages had its impact because of its stark exposure of the effects of poverty. It pointed also to the strange power that such tables have come to acquire. In a climate of performativity league-tables circulate, with their characteristic heads and tails. There is a perverse energy here of the kind that money generates in bullish stock markets, and a strange animation too: the tables fascinate and excite. They do not, of course, stand alone but belong to a genre of writing significantly shaped by ICT. With its characteristic hieroglyphics this sets itself up as presenting exactly what we need to know: numbered paragraphs and bullet-pointed lists, spread-sheets, flow-charts, appendices, summary reports. All is explicit, all made present. Anything interior or hidden is *incorporated* in the phantoms of learning, the presentation of learning outcomes.

Consider David Reynolds, Government Advisor for Numeracy, as representative of the genre. Reynolds advocates that schools be run as Highly Reliable Organisations—organisations, that is, such as nuclear power stations and air-traffic control, where mistakes must be avoided at all costs. The goal, the laudable one, is to raise the floor of achievement, and for Reynolds at least the solution is clear. We now have a research base that shows clearly how schools can become highly reliable, and the price of failing to implement this is dire: 'The more recent estimates of the cost of avoidable school failure within the United States (and I know these beg serious questions) estimate that cost as the equivalent of a plane crash every week, yet historically little has been done to prevent school failure by comparison with that done to prevent air traffic control failure' (Reynolds, 1997b, p. 106).

Of course, the need for such cutting-edge research may be lost on those who imagine, as Reynolds anticipates, that teaching is an art and not a science. Elsewhere the technological orientation of education, the possibility that it may deliver more, is celebrated: teachers in Taiwan are 'proud to be applied technologists, not philosophers' (Reynolds, 1997a, p. 21). It is, in fact, a peculiarly British parochialism, a hostility to grubby empiricism, that has prevented this from being realised sooner:

the continued concern about 'ends' not 'means' that has characterised much educational research, over the last twenty years has been a particularly British one, and is not paralleled in any other country that I know. In its essential Britishness, it has reflected a national culture that gives more status to the pure than the applied, to the useless more than the useful and to the educational philosopher more than the educational engineer, that dirty-handed and overall-clothed school effectiveness researcher. (Reynolds, 1997b, p. 99)

Now that major questions concerning educational aims have been settled, what more do we need but a straightforward listing of the facts of the matter, with the tabulation of results? What indeed could be plainer? The tables that are presented to us in education, four-square on their wooden legs, are as sturdily reliable as can be. Hence the no-nonsense straightforwardness of the technological approach:

> Not for us in school effectiveness the celebration of new policies because they are new or because practitioners like them, or the opposition to new policies because they potentially damage the interests of educational producers. For us, our 'touchstone criteria' to be applied to all educational matters concern whether children learn more or less because of the policy or practice. (*ibid.*, p. 97)

Reynolds is plainly putting his cards on the table here. What the cards tell is a rather different story, for what purports here to be an account of a technology, what casts itself as rigorous empirical research, has its effect not so much because of the reliability of its data or the cogency of its argument as because of a certain rhetorical style. Reynolds' texts are replete with an imagery that is elaborate, emotive and picturesque, with humorous slurs at the expense of his critics (in which the reader is invited to collude), and hence with a self-conscious positioning of author and audience in the inner circle of the initiated. The honest and self-effacing educational engineer is clad then in designer dirt, the 'touchstone criteria' dressed up in inverted commas (what could be more palpably secure?).[1] This, a context in danger of being taken for granted, is the epistemology of 'what works' in education. Its technology is less science than séance.

There is a strange calling forth of phantoms that hides what is really at stake. For Marx, 'the height of the conjuring trick here', so Derrida claims, 'consists in causing to disappear while producing "apparitions," which is only contradictory in appearance, precisely, since one causes to disappear by provoking hallucinations or by inducing visions' (Derrida, 1994, p. 128). And these apparitions have deadening effects: the allure that attaches to the smooth-running system drains education of its unpredictability and real life. The dance that Marx sometimes sees in exchange-value is arrested in this reification. While exchange-value is congealed in money (Marx, 1886, p. 106), the digitalised knowledge economy tranquillises us against the deadening effects of information overload. Exuberance of the dance is replaced by necromancy of effect ('The whole mystery of commodities, all the magic and necromancy that surrounds the products of labour so long as they take the form of commodities . . .' (*ibid.*, p. 47)).

But, contrary to Marx, this is not to say that there is a way of simply dispensing with these spectral effects. Return to traditional values, learn from direct experience—these different calls towards authenticity borrow something of their power from the mystique of the 'real thing'. As soon as this very move is made, this reclamation of authenticity, a theatricalisation is inevitable: the real ligneous matter is set self-consciously on the stage. Just as there is no pure use-value to the table—free from the contamination of exchange, free, in effect, from iterability—so there is no pure authenticity of teaching and learning.

Far worse, however, is the denial of the invisible. Necromancers of the curriculum are transfixed by apparitions that cause to disappear whatever cannot be accounted for. But we are inevitably affected by what is not to be made present, even where this is most strongly denied. We must acknowledge the real ghosts that can vivify teaching and learning. Critical for education is the quality of our engagement with this non-present. This is the concern of the final section.

CONVERSING WITH THE DEAD

Technophiles make much of the extraordinary range of information that the Internet can make readily available to the learner but also of its potential for providing rich sensuous virtual experience: the virtual classroom will take forms that we can as yet only dimly imagine. Whether or not such promise is fulfilled, however, two factors suggest that the emphasis on development should be elsewhere. The first relates to practicability and cost, the second to the quality of the learning that is promoted.

In his recent 'My Adventures in Distance Learning' Feenberg has drawn attention to the relative scarcity in computer networks of the bandwidth that such enriched experience requires. Hence such developments will only be made widely available at great cost. But this should not be a cause of consternation:

> we have a well established method of communicating in a narrow bandwidth. It's called writing. And we have a rich experience of using writing to overcome the limitations of bandwidth. Writing is thus not a poor substitute for physical presence and speech, but another fundamental medium of expression with its own properties and powers. It is not impersonal, as is sometimes supposed. We know how to present ourselves as persons through writing; this is what correspondence is all about. Nor is it harder to write about ideas

than to talk about them; most people can formulate difficult ideas more easily in written form than in speech in front of an audience. (Feenberg, 1999b)

Writing is not always prominent in the use of the Web. Of course, the Web user can be seen to be busy enough, but it is the quality of that activity that is important for education. The probing and clicking of the mouse may seem active enough but these are movements along paths determined by hypertext designers. They may encourage, in fact, an inflated sense of control and an illusion of objectivity on the part of users. In contrast, there are aspects of Internet use where writing is the paradigm form of expression and communication.

In an interesting recent discussion, Michael Margolis and David Resnick draw a distinction between the 'old Internet', which centred around conversations, and the Web-based Internet, which centres around presentations (Margolis and Resnick, 1999). The crux of their concern is with the way that the latter uses texts (of whatever form) that can be repeated without losing their essential qualities, that—most importantly—are intended for an audience, and that require special talents or expertise in their construction. Presentations in these respects are not egalitarian. In contrast, while there may be brilliant conversationalists, conversations are fundamentally egalitarian and are the basis of community. The crucial difference is between activity and passivity. The Web, they argue, is so structured and used as to encourage predominantly passive behaviour on the part of audiences. Movement within a site appears to be free but it is manifestly structured by the links that are provided. Sites may have space for users to communicate with each other, but content may be censored or removed by the designer or owner. Those who log onto sites are (typically) sold to, entertained, informed, influenced, or persuaded. 'Despite all the hype about interactivity,' they claim

> Web browsers are also largely responsible for transforming the Net into a relatively passive medium, considerably less active than claimed by those who celebrate the Web as a spectacular breakthrough in interactivity. Users need only point and click their mice, much like the proverbial couch potatoes point and click their television remotes . . . It takes less effort to flit from presentation to presentation as the spirit moves you than to engage in a conversation. Participating in a conversation often requires initiative and attentiveness, whether on the Internet or in the real world. (*ibid.*)

The authors draw attention to a debate between Internet advertisers about how people experience the Web:

> One group argues that they are 'passive', and the Web experience is really a variant of television viewing. The other contends that they are 'active'. This group insists that they don't watch the Net, rather

they use it. While the debate has implications for advertising and the structuring of commercial Web-sites, whichever side is right—and there is no reason to believe that only one side must be right—the Web experience for the overwhelming majority of users is not genuinely interactive, nor do they want it to be . . . The future of the Internet does not lie in recovering its more egalitarian and participatory past. It has become a mass medium and as such major content providers will dominate it. (*ibid.*)

The context of these remarks here is the introduction in May 1999 of Third Voice, a free browser enhancement service, the purpose of which is to enable users to place annotations on any Web page that they visit. Subsequent readers equipped with Third Voice can access these annotations and follow through particular series of them systematically. Its introduction has generated a heated debate. Some have seen the 'inline discussions' that Third Voice makes possible as an extension of the democratic potential of the Web. But others point to the fact that much of the usage of this service so far has taken the form of graffiti, hyperlinks to pornographic sites, flame wars and commercial advertisement.

If the reality so far has been disappointing, there are various reasons why this may be so. The scale and anonymity of the potential audience discourages the kind of personal engagement that might be found in a conversation. Predominantly passive experience of the Web may have reduced in users the capacity for a dialogical response—in spite of the constant emphasis on the ostensible interactivity of Web use. These considerations make all the more persuasive Feenberg's suggestion that electronic networks should be appropriated by educational institutions in full recognition of the fact that written interaction is both a limitation of online environments in their present form but also their potential. The online environment can never be anything but a poor copy of the face-to-face classroom. But it can and does promote writing, with all the richness that that implies—something those in education should be especially ready to recognise.

The prevailing concern with efficiency and effectiveness, however, militates against this recognition. The technological approach to education looks for success in the form of clearly identifiable outcomes, and it seeks the most efficient means to their realisation. Writing, in contrast—including the writing of chat-rooms and email discussions—is anything but this. Its qualities are rarely to be understood in terms of discrete end products, nor are its exchanges normally instrumental in this way. They may be crucial for critical and creative thought but they remain opaque to the educational engineer. What are the qualities of this writing online?

First, there is a certain rhythm. The ease and speed of writing and replying, without the paraphernalia of letter writing, without the intermediary of secretary or typist, help to generate series of exchanges and the familiar intimacy that is a feature of the medium. It has come to seem natural to tolerate typos, lack of case differentiation and free punctuation. Of course, many messages involve exchanges of information, but this is often couched in a language and mode of address that encourages good wishes, repartee, cryptic one-liners, the sharing of jokes. Indeed, in spite of the absence of handwriting (and perhaps partly because of the presence of typos), there is a sense of directness and signature to the words on screen. The absence of the more rigid conventions of letter writing may release a kind of spontaneity. Attentive and with the freedom to innovate, you become absorbed in the writing, which elaborates, becomes discursive and picks up speed. Of course, people can become cosily insulated in groups. Of course, addictive online chat can distract you from your 'real work'. But in certain respects this is a development of literacy. This rhythm helps to show how far the writing is not instrumental. Over letter writing it has a speed that keeps communication fresh. And the loss of immediacy that distinguishes it from speech allows the space for rumination.

A second factor is the nonlinear nature of the thinking that writing promotes. Much has been made of the rhizomatic nature of the Web, where links make possible multiple paths and lateral connections. In using the Web the learner can find out things by chance, valuable things perhaps, though they were not the point of the original search. Yet Web-browsing is different from leafing through the books in a library. The eye does not rove about nor the hand flick through pages: the hand points and clicks the mouse, with the eye fixed on the screen. That there are hidden goods that the Web user may come across indeed suggests the limitations of a curriculum that tries to plan too much in advance. But the case of writing makes this point all the more radical: if the constructed links on the Web take the learner to unknown sites that are then presented, the 'natural' links that are provided by words, to diverse histories and potential contexts of use, always exceed anything that could be made present. The activity of Web use remains channelled and commercially compromised, and this contrasts with the rich engagement that writing promotes.

A third factor, and one that again generally differentiates Internet writing from Web use, is the way that the appearance of the screen fades from consciousness as one becomes absorbed in what one is writing. This absorption owes little to the presentational allure that is otherwise a feature of the Web. Essentially preoccupied with words, it is a form of Internet activity that separates itself readily from the spectatorial orientation. As such it makes possible a kind of activity that is not so readily characterised by the manipulative control of things—with symptomatic pointing and probing of the mouse—but by a more humble relation to the possibilities of words.

It is not the democratic or egalitarian implications of these different uses of the Internet that are the central point in the present discussion: it is the quality of learning that they make possible. A programmed curriculum dedicated to learning outcomes drains the life out of what is to be learned, yet there are many well-intentioned educators who would develop online education in just this way. Instrumentalism and the preoccupation with presentation are prevailing features of the socio-cultural context in which such practice is embedded, and they are in danger of becoming beyond question. The alternative is not a kind of reclamation of authenticity, with all the problems of nostalgia and theatricalisation that that entails. Rather it is a recognition of the centrality of writing to education and of its possible development in rich conversation.

It is not difficult to find examples of the forms this might take: the use of pen-pals in the geography class; a pairing of students in remote places as 'buddies' to compare notes and collaborate on course materials provided through the Net; a noticeboard for children in a class to express their reflections on a story or poem; or for students to follow up a lecture (given conventionally or online) by sharing their responses and subsequent research; not to mention the shared ease of access to classic texts and secondary sources, and—why not?—archives of information, to which such conversations can so easily relate. There are social gains here whose importance has less to do with extrinsic motivation than with what is integral to the study in question. And if these suggestions seem unremarkable, that should merely direct us to the piecemeal ways whereby online practices can fruitfully be incorporated into teaching and learning.

The reduction of knowledge to information (with its concomitant skills) erodes education and crucially this concerns a relation to the past. 'We do not yet', Michael Oakeshott writes, 'live in the ashes of a great adventure that has burnt itself out' (Oakeshott, 1989, p. 30), though it is clear that he sees the encroachments of contemporary 'socialisation' (including utopian predictions for ICT) as threatening education's death. His recurrent invocation of the inheritance into which we must be initiated calls on us to rekindle the words of the dead.

We are at a stage where the conventions, manners and registers of language online remain fluid, unstable and poorly understood. How these develop in education will depend to a large extent on the kinds of curriculum decision that are taken. Such tips and techniques as are suggested above scarcely begin to realise the rich significance of the idea of conversation as this runs through Oakeshott's thought. Yet the possibilities of sustaining conversation of that kind will depend very much on the kinds of discursive practice that are promoted through education online. There is no uniform recipe for how this should be done. Much will depend on the sensitive exploration of precisely the kinds of opportunities suggested above. But what is to be remembered is that the point of such activity is not to be found in some end product but rather in the quality of the conversation itself. The 'conversation of mankind' reconvenes the words of the dead, in reading and in writing, and in so doing draws a kind of vitality from what cannot be made present. There are rich possibilities of online education here, and they are altogether different from the fetishism of effect.

NOTE

1. Elsewhere Derrida writes of the theatricalisation of inverted commas, the stage curtains they create (Derrida, 1989, p. 31 ff.).

11

Electronic Texts are Computations are Electronic Texts

HERBERT HRACHOVEC

The notion of 'electronic texts' has gained universal currency. What, exactly, does this phrase refer to? Most authors answer by describing a set of surface characteristics resulting from the application of computer technology to traditional texts. Such depictions, I want to argue, can be seriously misleading. They presuppose a conventional understanding of 'text' in order to make sense of the phenomenon of digitised inscriptions. The simple choice of the phrase 'electronic text' suppresses the radical challenge raised by the new medium. Its impact is supposedly captured by modification of an existing concept, so it is hardly surprising that most accounts end up with a typical ambivalence. Electronic texts, we are told, are quite different from—but, at the same time, comparable to—their traditional precursors. Some things that could not be done in the entire history of literacy have become possible nowadays. Yet, it is this very history that provides the background for the understanding of digital processes. Describing something previously unknown by means of well-known categories is bound to lead to these kinds of mildly schizophrenic pronouncements. This chapter discusses their initial plausibility and probes their underlying logic.

A more sophisticated methodological approach to the present issue is the following one: drop the implicit assumption that there is a general notion of 'text' which can be qualified by adding a new adjective, namely 'electronic'. It is, on reflection, by no means obvious that digitally manipulated 'texts' retain their distinctive properties. Scanning a book page, to pick an easy case, turns texts into pictures. Typing letters on a keyboard produces so-called 'scan-codes' which are, in turn, translated into key-codes by the operating system. (We will come back to this.) Conceptualising texts as inputs of computations eliminates many of their intuitive features. And since it is this technical metamorphosis that triggers interest in 'electronic texts' in the first place, a suspension of familiarity with the components involved seems more appropriate. Calling the output of typing at a keyboard 'code sequences' is one way to cut through the ambivalence of ground-breaking novelty explained by well-known categories.

This cannot be a satisfactory conclusion, though. Texts do not simply 'get lost' in code sequences. Provisions are made to reconstruct them from such sequences. The emphasis is on 'to reconstruct them from such sequences'. There is an *a priori* framework enabling us to recover significant features of the original input. Some computational processes are modelled along the lines of the conceptual tool-set of writing and reading. Referring to its standards those digital transactions are declared to be the implementation of text processing. Since this is a proposal to enlarge the common use of the respective concepts we have considerable control over what we ought to say on such occasions.

One available option is the immediate phenomenology of word processing. Taking the appearances on a monitor at face value such descriptions try to delineate the most important features of the 'electronic word'. But this very appearance is manufactured in order to appeal to intuitions acquired in literal societies. Technology underlies phenomenology. Software designers are responsible for what appears to the users of computer programs. The situation calls for analytical scrutiny.

The following three sections will elaborate these remarks, starting with an example of the phenomenological use of 'electronic text' and its ensuing problems. The technological arrangements underlying those 'phenomena' are usually passed over. The second section calls attention to some basic facts concerning digital encoding and asks whether texts can be regarded as 'texts' in such environments. We do, actually, call them texts—a fact that has to be emphasised against the background of naive phenomenology as well as jargon from computer science. This is the concern of the third section

The procedure to be followed is circular in an important sense: in judging some computations to be 'electronic texts' one refers back to an understanding of texts rooted in a pre-electronic world. The final section of this chapter attempts to allay suspicions involving vicious circularity. One has to be grounded in some established conceptual practice in order to be able to change the meaning of the words employed. We can, of course, dismiss those conventions and start a new set of linguistic activities, including expressions much like the ones used in a prior context. This dissolves the circle—only to lose the problem at hand. What is the price to pay for the amenities at our disposal once we call the results of computations texts? Trying to answer this question will involve us in an investigation of the reinterpretative logic of conceptual change.

ELECTRONIC TEXTS ARE . . .

There is no shortage of suggestive descriptions in the literature. The electronic word is fragile, variable and malleable, it has become permanently bi-stable. Being simultaneously transitory and potentially available (in many different versions) on a global scale it radically changes the conditions of writing, publishing and reading. Digital writing subverts hierarchical settings, strengthens participatory democracy and allows for an ever-increasing amount of shared knowledge to be distributed around the world. None of this, we are told, could be achieved by traditional means of inscription which, by comparison, seem fixed, permanent and unresponsive to interactive manipulation. To focus the argument I shall consider George Landow's well known treatise on hypertext:[1]

> Electronic linking shifts the boundaries between one text and another as well as between the author and the reader and between the teacher and the student. As we shall observe below, it also has radical effects upon our experience of author, text, and work, redefining each. (Landow, 1992, p. 33)

Notice the internal tension within this remark. Landow assumes an understanding of 'text', 'author' and so on which is to be submitted to 'radical effects'. How incisive are they supposed to be? Advocates of the digital revolution are not content with simply adding features to the traditional notions of a literal society. The following sentence reveals a more experimental attitude: 'Changing the ease with which one can orient oneself within such a context and pursue individual references radically changes both the experience of reading and ultimately the nature of what is read' (*ibid.*, p. 5). Redefinition is to work by leaping from quantity to quality, changing 'nature' by changing circumstances. This claim can be read as an important anti-metaphysical position:

> The evidence of hypertext, in other words, historicises many of our most commonplace assumptions, thereby forcing them to descend from the ether-reality of abstraction and appear as corollaries to a particular technology rooted in specific times and places. (*ibid.*, p. 33)

There is, however, a second, more problematic reading. Pretending to know about 'nature' is, after all, a standard metaphysical move. Radical novelty, one might argue, is only comprehensible given insights into the essence of things. Eidetic intuition of the 'evidence of hypertext' does not mix easily with the mastery of 'particular technologies'. This sort of ambivalence arises from attempting to understand unprecedented change. Let us take a broader look at the strategy involved. Landow is juxtaposing traditional and electronic textuality. He is comparing two kinds of text. Bracketing, for the moment, the 'deep' methodological question, a preparatory question is, surely, what kind of juxtaposition Landow envisages.

As the subtitle of his book indicates, Landow's working hypothesis assumes a 'convergence of contemporary critical theory and technology'. Picking out two prominent cases, namely Jacques Derrida's 'emphasis on de-centring' and Roland Barthes' 'conception of the readerly versus the writerly text', Landow remarks: 'In fact, hypertext creates an almost embarrassingly literal embodiment of both concepts, one that in turn raises questions about them and their interesting combination of prescience and historical relations (or embeddedness)' (*ibid.*, p. 34).

Jacques Derrida and Roland Barthes, according to this account, occupy avant-garde positions within traditional literary criticism, poised to tip over into digital practice. Landow's hypothesis presupposes familiarity with traditional writing as well as hypertext and tries to 'redefine' text by elaborating on the forces operative within their convergence. There is a problem, though. Knowledge of books can reasonably be expected—but what is hypertext?

Hypertext, as the term will be used in the following pages, denotes text composed of blocks of text—what Barthes terms a lexia—and the electronic links that join them (*ibid.*, p. 4). A somewhat simple-minded way to read this would be to understand Landow as proposing the following thesis: contemporary avant-garde criticism is to converge upon blocks of texts joined by occasional digital switches. Hypertext = traditional text + electricity? That is obviously not Landow's point. There is a wide array of technologies and practical abilities ordinarily understood as constituting 'hypertext'. Can we make sense of the claim that those are the points of convergence?

There is a certain *prima facie* plausibility in Landow's thesis, relating Derrida's and Barthes' use of terms like 'node', 'link' and 'network' to their obvious counterparts in hyper-fiction and on the World Wide Web (WWW). Derrida's intricate cross-references within the corpus of the written tradition as well as Barthes' artful synthesis of fragments of texts can profitably be rendered in hypertext format. But networked computing is just another set of practices and it does not *per se* exert a force of convergence on critical theory. For Landow's hypothesis to carry conviction it has to be shown that talk about 'network' in some printed environment is more or less the same as reference to digital constructions like those supported by the http protocol (to name the most prominent candidate). The suggestion is that the terms mentioned above 'cry out for hypertextuality' and that Derrida 'gropes towards a new kind of text: he describes it, praises it, but he can present it only in terms of devices . . . associated with a particular kind of writing' (*ibid.*, p. 9). Had he used hypertext, the story goes, he could have avoided being stuck within an antiquated medium in order to develop ground-breaking insights into the nature of text. Landow's suggestion is, as I indicated, intuitively appealing. But it does not bear closer scrutiny.

Consider decentring, a prominent issue in arguments purporting to demonstrate that electronic textuality will definitely break the hierarchical pattern of active authorship and more or less passive readers. There is, undoubtedly, a lot of (playful) deconstruction of 'the author' in postmodern writing—in books and papers which clearly indicate their provenance. This is quite different from writing on the Net, which allows for multiple identities, uninhibited plagiarism and automatic generation of preformated textual design. Those features are, admittedly, also available in print media. But it is one thing to use the traditional prerogatives of an auctorial role to cast doubts upon them and something else to work within a framework that lacks the most basic provisions to mark and protect individual work.[2] Decentring can be done from the carefully constructed position of an actual writer or one can find oneself within a situation lacking any centre. The first option need by no means converge with the second one. (It is, in fact, more likely that it will strongly oppose attempts to push authorship towards anonymity.)

This is not to deny that the experience of Web publishing strengthens the theoretical case for diffusion without origins. It is just to point out that there is no indication at all that (pre-)hypertext theory converges with the gigantic bric-a-brac of current networked communication and that bridge-words like 'hyper-text' can easily bear the burden of mediating between 'texts' as we know them and 'texts' as they figure in largely unexplored (digital) circumstances. The Web offers nothing like the authority enjoyed by the international 'stars' of the academic circuit while, on the other hand, it consists of innumerable definite locations that must be identified uniquely for the whole setup to work properly. The source code of 'interactive fiction' or the Internet's name space do not allow for ambivalent signifiers. A program's bugs and crashes are, first of all, a matter of complaint.[3]

Whereas nobody can control the content of the WWW it is crucial to ensure that each of its documents obeys one rigid naming convention. Those discrepancies between different instances of 'authorship' clearly show that—in changing the environment—one has to change a whole set of attributes and inferences. It is by no means obvious in what sense authorship is to be understood in a wider digital context. Landow's hypothesis, in short, only seems plausible as long as one disregards most of the technological apparatus operative to produce existing hypertext. It is bridge-building which simply assumes that the distant shore will exhibit the same terrain the proximate one offers.

Some of traditional writing's characteristics do not carry over to the digital domain. The consumer's power over the visual appearance of electronic texts challenges what used to be once-and-for-all decisions made by authors and printers. Or take the following subtle architectural feature of Roland Barthes' book *S/Z* (Barthes, 1970). The reader is initially kept in the dark about the meaning of this unusual title. Only in the forty-seventh of the ninety-three sections is its meaning explained. Barthes' exegesis of Honoré de Balzac's novel about the Italian opera singer Sarrasine puts special emphasis on his castration, which is figuratively repeated by the forward slash in Barthes' title. The author wilfully avoids having ninety-four sections[4] which would have divided the book in two parts right at the end of the crucial Section 47. The effect is echoed with respect to pagination: Section 47 starts on page 103 of Barthes' original text which runs for 205 pages. These are just clever and amusing details, to be sure. Still, they can very well illustrate the general point. Printed text is bound to unique physical implementations. Its content cannot be entirely abstracted from the palpable, tangible pages onto which it is printed. Books are objects, sharing certain properties with tables, bricks and ropes. Some textual strategies well established within print media are not therefore available in the digital format (and vice versa). There is no harm in letting both coexist side by side, but if one wants to offer a consistent teleological story ('convergence', 'progress', 'overcoming' and so on) more than episodic observations are needed. One has to offer an account involving a general notion of text that can be shown to underly progressive development and qualitative change.

Even though I have only indicated some problems in Landow's approach to electronic textuality and not touched upon the rest of the literature it seems, at this point, safe to point towards a typical impasse with respect to comparisons between traditional and electronic texts. One option is to take 'text' as an overarching notion, qualified by some new epithet ('blocks of texts joined by electronic links'). This is no help in clarifying digital textuality, since it simply assumes that texts can feature as electronic processes. Alternatively one might wonder how to describe operations performed on texts once they are cast in digital form. There is no guarantee for such operations to preserve textuality. Turning all the letters of a play by Shakespeare into tiny pieces of dough and putting them into a soup does not count as a promising enlargement of the scope of textuality. We have to spell out in which particular way the introduction of digital technology impinges upon our habitual use of 'text'. As long as media philosophy skips over the details of code encryption its propositions and prognoses are largely empty.

... COMPUTATIONS ...

There seems to be consensus that attaining 'computer literacy' is an important educational goal. Its most prominent features include the ability to interact with an operating system, use word-processing as well as accounting software and search the Internet. These abilities can be considered as practical skills, demanding a certain amount of training and dexterity and very little reflection. Once the initial strangeness of the digital environment is overcome, 'old acquaintances' reappear: pictures, texts, sounds. Initially puzzling, almost random events on an unfamiliar surface turn out to be rationally controllable sequences of letters and images. One has, for example, learned to put a recent memorandum on disk. Given this kind of pedagogical approach it seems natural to add one further step and consider the implications of such changes: electronic texts surely open up some previously unavailable possibilities. This seems to be a natural move but its presuppositions are not at all transparent. In teaching the layman 'how to use the computer in order to write a paper' a crucial step is passed over in silence. The practice of computer writing is built upon conceptual and technological arrangements that deserve closer inspection. These presuppositions determine what gets called 'electronic text' and philosophy is ill-advised to disregard those formative factors.

This amounts to an obligation to look closer at the details of how traditional inscriptions are handled in computer systems. It might be objected that questions concerning the implementation of information technologies should be discussed by engineers and do not fall into the area of competence of philosophers. Familiarity with the mechanism of combustion engines is unnecessary in order to drive a car. It would, indeed, be a category mistake to expect philosophical ideas to apply directly to questions of computer science or electronics. Writing source code or establishing a local-area network connection is quite external to theoretical reflection. But this is not the point under discussion. As the previous section has shown, we are confronted with *philosophical* claims concerning essential change, that is, in textuality. (Compare discussions about the new age of electricity and automatic transportation in the twentieth century.) Such claims can, admittedly, be put forward without the slightest reference to any particular technological development or apparatus. Martin Heidegger's talk about technology as 'framing' (*Ge-Stell*) (Heidegger, 1962) is a case in point. But it should be noticed that even Heidegger's distinctively speculative enterprise must take a stance towards actually existing technology, even if only in denying its philosophical relevance. ('Technology does not think.') Heidegger's is one possible move within the general framework of thinking about change induced by technology, that is, turning to the 'history of Being'. This option is derived from Heidegger's (negative) stance towards the issue under discussion, namely whether technological expertise has to be taken into account in developing philosophical arguments. Invoking the revelations of Being is an extreme case of philosophical self-assurance, directly opposite to an absorption of philosophy into the sciences in a Quinean spirit. Steering clear of both doctrines, some account of how, for example, software design is in itself accessible to a philosophical treatment is called for.

Consider the sequence of developments and regulations that brought about 'word processing'. The digital system of numbers and its physical implementation in an electro-magnetic medium allow any kind of information—given its numerical represent-ability—to be stored and manipulated. In the early days of computing 128 digital numbers were available to represent letters. (This encoding is known as pure ASCII and has since been supplemented by enlarged sets of mappings using 256 numbers and covering all existing Western alphabets, the so-called ISO-entities.) Once a correlation between symbols used within alpha-numeric civilisations and their counterparts in the realm of numbers is set up machines can perform remarkable transactions. Computers auto-matically map keyboard inputs into a digital encoding which can in turn be visualised on a monitor, changed by interactive manipula-tion, transferred over the network or piped into further digital code. The effects of traditional typing thus become visible on a screen, malleable, transmissible and even instrumental for real-life changes within the machinery. Is this another form of text? From the point of view of the operating system it is simply numbers. Keyboard inputs can just as well be channelled into a program computing random primes or shooting down what look to be foreign invaders on some high-tech display.

Digital code is heavily under-determined by the ASCII and ISO/IEC standards. It is just 'alpha-numeric chauvinism' that makes it appear as if the specificity of literal signs is without further ado mirrored into the digital domain. There are a number of mappings, to be sure, but the realm conventional signs are mapped onto is—on the whole—governed by rules entirely different from rules applying to written inscriptions. Digitally stored numbers are input and output for computations, regardless of whether they encode letters, pictorial information, sound or check sums. There is a dramatic incongruence between the concatenation of alpha-numeric signs and computations involving their digital correlates. It is important to get one's priorities right here. The decisive switch is not from one kind of instrument to another, more 'modern' one, as standard educational practice leads one to believe. The momentous change occurs when letters-qua-digits acquire a potential completely foreign to letters in the traditional sense. The basic mechanism is, of course, unmysterious. Something very similar happens when financial transactions are conducted via bank accounts instead of cash payments. A certain coding between items of everyday conduct and some innovative technical apparatus turns out to open up a new range of applicability for established concepts. The mapping *per se* is not at all difficult to understand. The challenge is to assess the consequences of matching two distinctly different domains. The isomorphism, to put it in formal terms, between letters and digital numbers imposed by the ASCII regulations, tends to obscure the fact that numbers follow their own set of rules which by no means coincide with the customs of the alphabet. This seems an appropriate focus for philosophical investigations.

What used to be inscriptions or printed patterns is translated into a vastly more flexible, mathematically enriched, technologically accessible environment. The shape of the current discussion on the educational importance of the digital revolution is usually determined by two conflicting attitudes. One is to make the most of the new context, relishing the multimedia boom, exploring ways to break down previous barriers between expressive modes. The opposite attitude is scepticism against this kind of panglossian bonanza. It is pointed out that—in order to distinguish information from noise— one has, in the end, to stick to quite determinate translation rules, clearly distinguishing between letters, pixels and acoustic events. Multimedia presentations—according to this view—presuppose the separation of the various sensual channels they are synthesising on the basis of their—mutually disjunct—numerical representations. Common to both positions is a scenario of conceptual change familiar within analytical philosophy. According to a standard account conceptual content is defined by the inferential practices of a language community at some given time (see Brandom, 1994). With the advent of unforseen contexts and experimental application of established notions a set of rational discursive practices is disturbed and tested against as yet unfamiliar circumstances. The 'meaning' of the terms a community uses is put into question, forcing speakers to re-orient themselves within altered circumstances. Encoding letters into numbers that can be digitally processed is a striking example of such conceptual rearrangements. The common wisdom is that computers force us to revise our understanding of 'text' and this is quite correct, but it fails to indicate how this revision is to be accomplished and which criteria should be employed to judge the outcome. Phenomenological comparisons just scratch the surface. A given 'electronic text' is, from the point of view defended here, first and foremost an innovative, disturbing mapping.

One should, therefore, regard the present problem as a special case within a theory of translation. Many correlations between alpha-numeric systems and target domains have been proposed, from kabbalistic speculations to social security cards. How to describe the particular translation at hand? Three distinct types of activity can profitably be regarded as at issue in digital encoding. A *technical reaction* is to take the isomorphism at face value and to explore the implications available in the target domain. A second, more *common attitude* is to take advantage of some of the technical advances while preserving the basic structure of the traditional mindset. Testing the inferential power of the concepts involved, drawing the boundaries between mere propaganda and genuine assertions, is a third option, frequently taken up by *philosophers*. It is often assumed, for practical as well as polemical reasons, that one or the other of those activities is autonomous, but it is easy to see that all of them—technical, commonsensical and philosophical attitudes—are usually present when scientific or technological change comes under scrutiny. This is where the argument to determine future meanings is joined and one of philosophy's contributions can be to monitor the changing patterns of discourse into which certain terms are embedded. This is, admittedly, an analytical position, undercutting reference to metaphysically or phenomenologically given 'meanings'. The emphasis on creative, counterfactual conceptual design can be enlightening and liberating. But given the fact that the issue is the impact of very prosaic machines it seems fair to assign second place to speculative ingeniousness here.

The following section will offer some ideas on the issues that arise from the mapping described. One point concerning the attitudes listed above should be added to avoid a certain misunderstanding. The scenario of conceptual change has been described as if the forces impinging on a given tradition could be kept neatly distinct. Computer scientists and philosophers could, in this case, after all, operate in splendid isolation and it would hardly matter whether critical analysis turns towards clickable buttons or the ASCII rules. It has to be stressed, against this impression, that in the event of genuine conceptual change those boundaries are constantly shifting. This is where philosophy truly meets its contemporary challenge. The cognitive advances implied by certain technical achievements are much more interesting than the invention of a new philosophical jargon. The engineers are, in some sense, philosophical innovators, while the task of monitoring changes is a matter of—indispensable—accounting closer to the maintenance of standards usually associated with administrative and technical departments. Ordinary language, furthermore, turns out to include highly contested areas when its users confront the terminological shift, quite often mixing the technological, pragmatic and philosophical stances. Teaching 'computer literacy' should be geared towards those ongoing adaptive processes. Making people familiar with this year's brand names is grossly insufficient. The meaning of the phrase 'electronic text' is yet to be settled upon within a reasonably worked out cognitive equilibrium.

... ARE ELECTRONIC TEXTS

We have been discussing the conceptual ramifications of adding a simple adjective ('electronic') to the well-entrenched notion of text in order to capture its role within information processing. Given the pressure to re-adjust some of the core concepts of literacy in the information age this seems to be an urgent question facing educational institutions. It has been argued that a straightforward concatenation of terms is not up to the problem posed by computer writing. Mapped onto the digital domain, erstwhile texts enter a largely unexplored neighbourhood which does not allow an easy transfer of many familiar features of text into the new setting. At the same time claims of radical change should be approached cautiously since they tend to elide the continuity at work in the move from a concept well embedded in history and actual social practice to its innovative application within information technology. One reason for this elision is that technical progress has overwhelmed us with such rearrangements. Most people easily accommodated the term 'electric guitar' even though it triggered dramatic changes in musical production. One technique available to philosophy is to run such conceptual shifts in slow motion, closely looking at their micro-structure in order to get a grip on the logic under consideration.

Computer equipment is not just another way to materialise inscriptions. Its potential is vastly superior to anything stones, parchment or paper could provide. Recall that digital processing provides instant interactivity, revisability, global transmission and computability of any suitable input. But also keep in mind that texts can be recognised in electronic settings. They do not vanish like, to pick a nostalgic example, the smell of old manuscripts. It is at this point that the conceptual change under discussion can, as it were, be regarded in close-up. Its dynamic is generated by two opposite moves that have to be brought into some sort of equilibrium: the unprecedented projection described in the previous section and the countervailing move to widen the scope of a given understanding of texts so as to include features available by means of the former projection. Textuality is imposed onto the digital domain and textuality's meaning is revised in unforseen ways as a consequence of this imposition. The character of texts changes because of the application the concept is shown to be capable of. Putting it in these philosophical terms suggests an arcane procedure. But there is nothing mysterious about it. When engineers and software designers approach computer resources they cannot help but operate on the basis of the established concept. And their achievements reflect back onto this conceptual base.

All too often philosophy has concerned itself with delineating the shape of given patterns of thinking, disregarding conceptual shifts and the pitfalls of using familiar words in unfamiliar environments. For such crossover-phenomena to be discussed seriously it is important not to let one or the other side slip out of the equation. Otherwise an unmediated juxtaposition of text and technology threatens, just the caricature of 'humanism' that media theorists like to make fun of. Those 'thoroughly modern' approaches are, it has to be added immediately, just the flip side of the coin. Where the 'conservatives' refuse to consider far-reaching conceptual change, the 'radicals' simply assume that digital gadgets provide the necessary intuitions. But an understanding of 'electronic text' does not come for free once we are able to master the basic steps of a WYSIWYG word-processor. Given the audacious projection of an established concept onto mathematics, computer science and mechanical engineering, the outstanding philosophical and educational task is to reassess the impact of this projection upon the original notion. This in turn demands a certain amount of knowledge of technical details. Otherwise hermeneutic accounts get stuck in platitudes.

There is no quick and easy way to pinpoint the crucial spot where 'text' acquires 'a new meaning'. Rather, a tentative philosophical strategy to deal with the issues of computer literacy is to call special attention to those technical processes which force us to rearrange our conceptual economy. Quite modest remarks can, under those circumstances, bring considerable enlightenment. Returning to the issue of encoding used as an example throughout this chapter, consider the actual arrangement which translates alpha-numeric symbols into digital signals. If you press and then release a key, two 'scan-codes' are sent to the 'kernel keyboard driver', that is, the program managing the information exchange between the keyboard and the operating system. The stream of scan-codes is examined by the driver and translated into key-codes. Typing 'a' on an ordinary PC keyboard, for example, produces scan-codes 0x1e and 0x9e which get converted into key-codes 30 and 158 respectively. Key-codes, in turn, are the input to a further mapping, associating them with characters according to a 'key-map'. This is how a single keyboard can be made to produce a considerable variety of alphabets: different key-maps define different translations for given key-codes. The standard (PC version) ASCII map correlates key-code 30 with the letter 'a' whereas the Hebrew map sets it to 'aleph'. Alternatively, key-code 30 corresponds to 'right bracket' on a Macintosh. (Most inter-platform mistranslations of digital documents are caused by inconsistencies between the encoding sequences.)

Once in a while when working with a digital document, one is confronted with strange graphemes that do not seem to obey the common rules. The usual reaction is to attempt normalisation or else call for expert help. Such incidents are ordinarily taken as a nuisance concomitant to digitalisation. But, as the example demonstrates, more than meets the eye is at issue here. Knowledge of the rules of the transitive mappings not only removes some puzzlement from computer use, it opens up a new perspective on textuality. 'The results of typing into a keyboard show up on a monitor and are recognised as strings of letters'—this description hides a momentous leap. Enough has been said to indicate the technical details, but this is, obviously, just the beginning. In concluding here are some glimpses of the larger picture. The century has been shaped by unparalleled achievements in tele-communications: phone, radio, TV. None of these are literal media. Books, journals and newspapers have occupied a different segment of knowledge production up to very recently. Nowadays alpha-numerical symbols, on their way from computer keyboards to the monitor, enter into the realm of increasingly homogeneous information exchange. The written word has become just as ubiquitous and malleable as TV images and soundbites.

It would take another paper to elaborate on the consequences of this development. But consider, briefly, the matchless novelty of mailing lists or Internet Relay Chats (IRC). A mailing list is a globally distributed, virtually simultaneous, symmetrical, literal communication facility; a person's writing is more or less instantaneously available to a selected group of people regardless of any intermediary printout and with minimal transportation cost. IRCs are real-time meetings on the Internet, employing the written word in lieu of voices, producing a continuous, collaborative flow of text strangely blending characteristically oral and literal features. Descriptions of such phenomena are almost inescapably forced to juxtapose established customs with procedures that have—quite simply—never existed in history. Small wonder that those accounts are often marked by a certain pomposity. The sense of awe is quite understandable, but it does not preclude an analytical assessment. Compared to the conventions established to link the spoken and the written word at the beginning of literacy, digitalisation is a second-level encoding, encompassing both speech and print, removing customary distinctions between spontaneity and protocol, local and global availability, discourse and authorship.

There is a telling similarity between these assessments and the standard elaborations of the 'electronic word' mentioned at the beginning of the first section. The line of argument developed here has indeed turned full circle. A first look at the entanglement of texts and digital technology produces apprehension, freely floating intuitions, certain behavioural obligations and a lot of hype. One way to resolve the ensuing conceptual confusion is to take a closer look at the encoding underlying these developments. This shows the problem, basically, to be one of translation. Learning a foreign language one is confronted with unexplored associative and inferential patterns, exhibiting a different set of values and practices. Something very similar holds for meeting the challenge of computational technology. Some catch-phrases may translate easily and establish a certain elementary, pragmatic hold on the new terrain. But there is not yet a working dictionary that could provide safe guidance between the realms. From a philosophical point of view such a dictionary should not simply define meanings and correlate words. A more demanding task is for a 'translation manual' to document the inferential shifts and cross-dependencies that begin to operate when two 'cultures' confront each other. Top-down approaches are of little use here. One needs to be aware of the type of problem and know something about both sides involved. The rest is teaching oneself— and others—a new language which, confusingly, sounds very much like English.

NOTES

1. For a critical account of the most prominent theories of hypertext see Grusin (1996).
2. The most popular program designed to remedy this deficit is Phil Zimmerman's 'Pretty Good Privacy' (PGP) which allows users to encrypt texts with their 'private key' which—in order to be resolved—has to be supplemented with a 'public key' which the author may choose to make publicly available. The program can also produce digital signatures, uniquely characterising electronic documents. The use of PGP is not yet well established though.
3. Stuart Multhrop (1997) has written perceptively on the second-level importance of disruption of computer-mediated communication.
4. Barthes uses Roman numerals, another suggestive device.

12

Tutors and Students without Faces or Places

NIGEL BLAKE

Online tuition is a practice—practised by this writer—in which students form tutorial relationships with a teacher, and in some models with each other, by the modes of email, Web-mediated file exchange and asynchronous computer conferencing (the construction of multiple threads of conversation and dialogue, as in Web chat rooms). It may centrally revolve around an exchange of assignments and comments. It is quite different from simply referring students to the information and activities on various Web-sites. Centrally, tuition is conducted here in personal interaction through the written word.

However, it is constantly compared and contrasted negatively with conventional education in at least one respect: that it is not 'face-to-face'. Teachers and students do not physically meet and are typically not even present in the same physical institutions (campuses, offices and so on). Obviously it has much to offer the 'distant' and perhaps even isolated student, in particular some kind of academic relationship with a tutor which might otherwise be impossible for them. In pure cases of distance education, such as the one this author practises, the student may well be (and in my own case, often is) in another continent and a different time zone. Insofar as physical interaction is lacking, online education is typically taken as second best. Even Burbules and Callister (n.d.), in 'Universities in Transition', arguing that academics are mistaken to disparage extensive use of IT in teaching, nonetheless have recourse to the standard Distance Education argument that, for many students who have little or no chance to attend an institution physically, this is not the second-best mode but the only alternative to nothing at all. So not even they consider the possibility that it may be in some ways as good as or even superior to face-to-face teaching.

Moreover, it is not the mere fact that online education is a mode of Distance Education that provokes these misgivings. In my own well-established distance teaching institution (the UK Open University), recent research[1] has revealed that even students who are well used to our pre-digital methods of tuition by post and telephone with occasional optional tutorials have deep worries about the imminent online future. And these worries are not merely technical. They share a widely held suspicion that Information and Communications Technology (ICT) is socially isolating and diminishes the quality of communication between tutors and students. They emphasise the belief that body language, as an aspect of communication, is an unqualified good. The problems that come with it go unmentioned. Spontaneity is also much valued, but its relevance to academic work, that least spontaneous of activities, is not questioned.

I have never come across an adequate defence of these fears and I want to question them severely. Nonetheless, my aim in this chapter is not to impugn the importance of face-to-face teaching, but first to get clearer as to just what might be important about it. My intention is to argue that when this is properly understood and acknowledged, the face-to-face model in turn will neither impugn the value of online education nor consign it to 'second best' status. On the contrary, I believe we will find that there is a proper 'ecological' relation between the two—that in certain circumstances online tuition can be at least as good or even better as a model for teaching, quite independently of any social or economic advantages which attend it, but that this is never likely to be achieved without the prior, and possibly even continuing, involvement of students with face-to-face tuition as well. I shall also suggest that it is more suited to higher education than to schooling.

PHYSICAL PRESENCE AND USES OF LANGUAGE

The idea that there is something special and important about the physical co-presence of teachers and students may be ill-articulated but it obviously has a plausible appeal. More generally, for most of us, the idea of doing without the physical company of other people for significant stretches of time is uncomfortable and even at worst distressing. Even those who enjoy solitude rarely wish for nothing but solitude.

To say why this is so is not obviously a matter for philosophers. There is something primitive about our need for physical company which commends the question rather to psychoanalysts and other theorists in psychology. Obviously, if one is going to spend most of one's day in educational activities, human drives and instincts dictate a preference for some face-to-face interaction. But even so, this does not show that face-to-face teaching is educationally superior. After all, this argument makes no reference to distinctively educational considerations. And arguably, education has always been thought of as including some occasions when human company has to be forgone. We typically think of study as a private activity, but one quite central to higher education. The student who cannot face the solitude of study and the concentration it involves is headed for failure. So we need some specifically educational reasons if we are to believe that the best teaching, unlike study, involves face-to-face interaction.

Distance education has rendered such reasons harder to find by conflating the occasions of study and 'teaching'. For the distant student, a live teacher is replaced by a 'teaching text'. This is not to say that the text actually 'does' some teaching. Rather, this approach better adapts the material to the needs of particular students. And instead of the text actually teaching, the student has to actively study the text, just as she might also study primary sources. Nonetheless, behind the text is a writer who is plausibly described as 'teaching at a distance'. So if we force the question what goes on, teaching or study, on such occasions, the question has really no point or interest. The answer is rather that a conventional link between teaching and physical presence is less fundamental than we often think and has been broken here. In this mode of education, we discover that the solitude of the student is as compatible with teaching as with study. And I want next to reinforce this doubt about the need for face-to-face interaction in teaching.

It might be suggested that little is written about the superiority of face-to-face encounters in tuition because their advantages are so obvious. On the one hand, the possibilities for vocal intonation, facial expression and body language certainly enhance the communicative repertoire of both teachers and students. On the other hand, there is a presumption in favour of rapid feedback which seemingly places distance teaching at a poor second best. I will return later to this second point, because the first is trickier. The problem is the implicit assumption that a communicative repertoire enlarged by body language is normatively neutral vis-à-vis higher education—that face-to-face tuition offers increased possibilities for communication, yet brings with it no inherent problems. This seems to me simply not so.

Consider those kinds of interaction for which their face-to-face character is arguably their defining characteristic. I do not mean, then, face-to-face interactions which have some defined institutional purpose more important than their face-to-face character—council debates, church ceremonies, business meetings and so on. Nor do I mean face-to-face interactions which happen to involve important physical actions determined by their subject or occasion—sporting activities, health care, music or other performance activities. I am thinking rather of banal cases of meeting people and sharing the ordinary activities of living with them—eating together in the cafeteria, passing in the corridor, chatting over the photocopier, gossiping with colleagues and so on.

And now consider the less obvious question about such interactions: what kinds of speech act are typically involved in them? We might mention greetings and pleasantries, obviously, also jokes and compliments, advice and warnings, offers of assistance, but sometimes, less happily, rebukes, evasions or even insults. Do these speech acts have anything much in common? I notice two things in particular. First, though they all have a cognitive content (even a greeting acknowledges a new presence as such), the cognitive content is not necessarily the most important aspect of speech here. Warnings, for instance, may have less to do with imparting information than with cordial mutual concern. Advice such as 'Watch that step!' or, jokingly, 'I'd avoid the fish course, if I were you' is often cognitively unnecessary, but socially, it 'oils the wheels'.

These kinds of speech act are examples of what J. L. Austin, in his first attempt to formalise the notion of a speech act (1962, Lecture 1), classified as 'performatives', in contradistinction to 'constatives', speech acts whose character as social actions is at least as important as their character of communicating information. As speech acts, as events at some particular time and place, performatives are highly sensitive to social and material context. By contrast, constatives, speech acts mainly concerned with the exchange of information or ideas, are not so context-bound. The main virtue or vice of constatives lies in their relation to truth—to be true or false, correct or incorrect, informative or misleading, and none of this depends on their social context of utterance (though understanding them might depend on their context in some discourse). Performatives, by contrast, are not evaluated this way. Performatives are not right or wrong so much as successful or unsuccessful in different ways—'misfires' and 'abuses' are Austin's words (*ibid.*, p. 16). Warnings can be helpful or unhelpful, compliments may be welcome or discomforting. And if performatives are not to misfire, the social background has to be right (and properly understood by both speaker and hearer). For instance, a greeting is likely to misfire if addressed to someone who is walking away from you. The advice about the fish course is not going to be a 'happy' speech act of advice if addressed to someone who resents familiarity or whose status renders casual advice impertinent. And if someone greets you with 'Good morning', it is a joke and a wilful misconstrual to treat it as a constative and reply 'No, I don't think so, actually'.

Austin's own paradigms of performatives end up being highly institutionalised utterances such as 'I name this ship the Titanic' or the bride and groom's 'I do' in a marriage ceremony. The kind we have to do with above are less institutionalised, less rigidly rule-governed but still sensitive to their social and material context. Plausibly, it is the nature of the social relationship between the speakers and how it is reinforced or transformed which is the important issue in these speech interactions.

A second point to note is that all of these speech acts are easily aligned with familiar kinds of intonation, body language and facial expression. In these cases of mundane face-to-face interaction, there seems a characteristic intertwining between the physical and the verbal. I do not mean to suggest that these speech acts are impossible in non-material contexts, such as that of online communication—they are not. For instance, the reprehensible online activity of 'flaming', vehemently insulting the recipient of one's email, for instance, can be dreadfully effective—deeply upsetting for the recipient, notwithstanding the 'virtuality' of the sender. Nonetheless, there is something patently *appropriate* about physical interaction in these banal contexts. Those with whom we cement relationships are embodied people, and their personal characteristics *as* embodied are often relevant to the nature of the relationship we have with them.

Moreover, the inherent actual or potential embodiedness of relationships—the inherent address of relationships to the Other *as* embodied—is betrayed by the fact that 'body language' and facial expressions are not in fact simply items of a kind of shared, intuitive physical 'vocabulary'. They also reveal aspects of ourselves to others quite unintentionally and often without our realising it, thus cementing or impeding relationships all the more effectively. So in this unconscious way too, bodies can and do intervene in the construction of relationships. And of course, intonations, expressions and body language are themselves also highly context-bound and context-sensitive. The wrong grimace in the wrong social situation can be highly embarrassing. (Conventional gestures, for instance, can have absolutely contrary meanings in different countries, and provide rich possibilities for social disaster.) Face-to-face interaction is of primary importance in 'rubbing along together' in the ordinary, day-to-day, social and physical world. It can also let us down badly.

So how much of this is apposite to higher education? Arguably it is problematic. And it is not just that face-to-face interaction isn't very important in higher education. Rather, there are some familiar reasons for seeing it as in some ways inappropriate in interpersonal interactions in teaching.

INTELLECTUAL DISINTEREST AND ACADEMIC DECORUM

In the preceding paragraphs, I defined pure face-to-face interaction in contradistinction to institutionalised interactions, as for instance one might contrast conversation between people queuing for drinks at the same bar with the swearing-in of jurors in a court. Some aspects of higher education at least share more of the latter formality than the former informality, if not necessarily the element of ritual. My purpose is to pin down any possible role of the face-to-face in typical academic interactions such as the exchange of information and ideas, by eliminating inappropriate roles. Is the function of face-to-face communication in academic teaching basically the same as in queuing at a bar, and its role a kind of happy 'add-on' to academic interactions? Or does its function change here? Does it have any role of importance at all? To address the question of appropriateness, we should consider some guiding values and attitudes in higher education. (Inevitably, then, much of what follows immediately will be platitudinous.)

One of the fundamental values governing any kind of intellectual work is that of disinterestedness. And correlatively, the most characteristic vices in academic life are such faults as bias, partiality, vested interest, prejudice and so on.[2] In higher education, our attention is expected to focus on the substance and complexities of the discipline and topic under discussion, not on our selves, our own interests or even on our personal reactions to the topic. Academic objectivity requires us to sift very carefully questions of true and false, right and wrong, valid or invalid, good and bad, insightful or obtuse from those of personal taste or distaste, political or religious commitment, fear or loathing, enthusiasm or delight. The pursuit of objectivity and the mistrust of the personal and the private is the Platonic moral heritage of all higher learning in the Western world.

And this, of course, has implications for teaching. If teaching in higher education is to aim at strengthening students' grasp of objective aspects of intellectual disciplines and discourses, then the personal, the subjective and the individual have to be somehow bracketed off and kept in their place, on both sides of the teaching interaction. This much surely is banally obvious. (It is one of many reasons for contemporary concerns about the dangers of emotional entanglements between tutors and students.) And as well as exercising academic self-discipline, one of the tasks of a teacher may often be to alert the student to her own lapses of objectivity, to the moments where her own personal values, emotions and limitations may be clouding or distorting her judgement. (This is as important in the social sciences as the humanities, and may even be relevant where the natural sciences can also get entangled with social, moral, economic or political life—environmental or biological questions, problems about commercial, government or military sponsorship, and so on.)

But surely, in cases where there is some reason to beware the personal, and thus personal relationships too, the kinds of speech act typical of 'pure face-to-face interaction' will not be at a premium, and face-to-face interaction itself will not be sought to support purely personal attitudes and relations, whether or not it might be sought for other reasons. This kind of speech act and this kind of accompanying intonation, facial expression and body language are generally understood to be breaches, perhaps minor but sometimes perhaps not so minor, of good academic practice. There is a presumption against them as inappropriate to interactions in teaching. We do not have to be excessively puritanical about them in practice, of course. Comic exaggeration or slips into the personal or even confessional can help a tutorial 'go with a swing', and etch some lesson in the student mind. But these are minor examples of 'living dangerously' in academic terms, and need to be understood as such by all concerned if they are not to cause difficulties. They should not be treated as normal.

The important point is that academic life has its own decorum, functional for the pursuit of its higher aims. The purpose of this decorum is precisely to bracket off, to tame or even sometimes to expunge the influence of non-academic personal relations, personal interests, emotions and commitments. It is an aspect of the sustenance of academic freedom. Academic freedom obviously goes beyond this decorum, involving most importantly the autonomy of academia vis-à-vis political, religious, commercial, military or sectional social interests. But academic decorum also plays its part at the level of personal impediments to disinterestedness.

Accordingly, the kinds of speech act which seem to typify (but of course are not exclusive to) pure face-to-face interaction seem marginal, where not actively inappropriate in teaching and learning. Recourse to them might seem to indicate some academic lapse. So does this show that face-to-face interaction is irrelevant or invidious even to academic teaching? It does not imply this immediately. There might be other kinds of reason for valuing face-to-face interaction in teaching. But the argument so far does indicate a range of face-to-face interactions which may be positively inappropriate to teaching. Inducting a student into a discipline is not a matter of cementing a personal relationship in the sense of involving them as part of one's local social or intimate network. And the fact that face-to-face interactions are impossible in online teaching seems in some sense at least in its favour. We have perhaps shifted the burden of proof in judging the relative value of the online and the face-to-face.

PRESENTATION OF SELF IN ONLINE INTERACTION

We have been exploring the truism that in teaching and learning, cognitive uses of language come first, in particular taking priority over the use of language to form or modify interpersonal relation-ships. But this is not to say that academic language, as constative (using Austin's original but abandoned term), involves no distinctive kinds of speech act. Of course academics 'do things with words' of many different sorts—urge, object, rebuke, welcome, express a fear, insist, a whole range of illocutionary acts, to use Austin's second, and more discriminating terminology. Austin came to recognise that all speech acts seem to have some cognitive core—that to understand a speech act is first and necessarily to understand its semantics, grammar and references (or denotations). But equally, all utterances can be described as also having some particular kind of pragmatic force, or character as speech acts. The pragmatics of any particular utterance are what Austin came to call its 'illocutionary force' (see Austin, 1962, pp. 99–131).

But the kinds of thing which academics 'do with words' are typically the kinds of speech act whose illocutionary force can be made evident not by some explicit social setting with concomitant conventions (such as the settings for taking marriage vows or for naming a ship), but by the use of conventional verbal formulae which can help to constitute the speech act as being of a particular illocutionary kind[3]—thus '*I welcome* Jones' reminder to us that . . .' or 'I *insist* that we cannot overlook such and such', or '*We must object* to any theory which ignores . . .' (The point is not that these formulae are used always or even typically, but that they can be used coherently to make the illocutionary force explicit.)[4] And to notice this is to suggest that typical academic speech acts are well-suited to the exclusively textual context[5] of online communication. Speech acts such as these do not need vivid social or material contexts in order to 'work' or be understood. Their textual or discourse context is typically adequate to make these things clear. Where they are not, then using the verbal formula is enough to clear things up.

So the academic online context need not be conceived as one where speech acts and interpersonal interactions are replaced by inactive tokens of text, shorn of reference to their author and addressed to nobody in particular, or devoid of a context relevant to their interpretation—text without interactive potential. On the contrary, this context fosters its own kind of linguistic pragmatics. But it is a context in which social and material aspects of context may be of little or no relevance at all for the decipherment of meaning and illocutionary force by the addressee. Yet arguably, this possibility of detachment from social context explains certain positive advantages of online interaction in academic life, advantages which are some-times noted in conversation on the topic.

For instance, it has been widely recognised, not without a salacious thrill, that online communication with strangers offers opportunities for disguising many features of one's identity and even, seemingly, to assume quite different ones. Gender, in particular, seems to be a favourite characteristic to play around with. The online community is a Masked Ball, apparently, rich in adventurous possibilities, not least for erotic play. But before we get carried away with the more extreme possibilities here, we should notice some more modest effects of this potential for clouding identity which are arguably functional for academic work.

In online communication, correspondents know nothing of each others' voice or appearance, unless they have taken steps to exchange photos or audio messages. And lacking this knowledge, a significant array of information is missing—age (and so too family status) may be unclear, as may race where the name is misleading or unrevealing, and sexual orientation need not be evident. Disabilities may be hidden, as too may be particular beauty or athletic prowess. Social background, attitudes and personality may all be clouded in some respects and to some degree. For instance, assumptions about political or religious alignments are more difficult to make than usual, unless a respondent chooses to hint at them or lets something inadvertently slip. (Just think how even modes of dress can suggest political conservatism or radicalism.)

Now for some people this seems a sorry state of affairs, a degree of anonymity quite inappropriate to concerned and serious teaching. But the positives should also be noted from a pedagogic point of view. The most scrupulous of teachers is only human, and as such as vulnerable as anyone to irrational likes and dislikes, sympathies and antipathies, commitments or failures of comprehension vis-à-vis other people, based on adventitious characteristics. And much of what is screened out or clouded in online education is precisely the kind of personal characteristic that can interfere irrationally in human interaction, and in education can distort, disrupt and at the extreme pervert the interaction of tutor and student. And students are no less vulnerable to the same possible irrationalities, either taking against a tutor as a kind of person they just 'don't get on with' or 'falling for them' as seductively attractive—and treating them with unjustified scepticism or perhaps undue deference.

Moreover, it is not just the actuality of such irrationality but its mere possibility that can cause problems. However fair and scrupulous the tutor may really be, nonetheless fear of looking foolish or out of place may still inhibit a student. What is more, her fears may be of her fellow students more than her tutor. So it is no surprise that there is an accumulation of folk wisdom and anecdotal evidence amongst online tutors that students are often much happier to contribute to online discussions, in bulletin board systems, computer conferences or on listservs, than in face-to-face tutorials.

This, if real, constitutes a major pedagogic gain, for the tutorial group no less than for the individual student, and an instance of academic advantage in avoiding the face-to-face and protecting oneself from inappropriate or irrelevant misperceptions by veiling one's identity. Yet we are still dealing with genuine interpersonal linguistic interaction here, not with isolated students pretending to 'interact' with inanimate multimedia displays, for instance.

This point relates to another familiar, and surely valid claim, that online communication, even though it places written language skills at a premium, nonetheless also throws a lifeline to students with poor language skills, or particular problems with spoken language. These kinds of online interaction are typically asynchronous; they do not take place in 'real time'. So every participant has a real opportunity for writing in a more considered way than she could speak in a tutorial. She can edit, correct, expand and revise her statements before electronically committing them to discussion. And as we all know, the emotional inhibitions and problems that can interfere in tutorial work can impact very negatively on a student trying to articulate novel, difficult or challenging ideas, perhaps in a social context which she may find uncongenial or unconvivial. Spontaneity can be as much a problem in academic interaction as a value, derailing the student and impairing her opportunities for thought and learning. And the tutor's opportunity for quick 'feedback' is not that much to value if it is a quick response to a confused contribution which misrepresents the student's best thinking.

Ironically, then, the distantiation inherent in online communication, which makes a degree of veiling of personal identity possible, may also foster and encourage a more vivid disclosure of what we might call the student's academic identity.

WRITER IDENTITIES AND ACADEMIC IDENTITY

However, it would be naïve to expect that this veiling of identity is ever likely to be completely successful. At the simplest, students often do choose to identify themselves in certain ways in academic discussion online, for instance in 'getting to know you' conversation threads at the start of a course, and moreover there are limits to what is possible to hide in an academic context. Students must be registered, and it is risky to register under a false name, even as a distant student. Names alone readily betray gender and often race or nationality. Postal addresses, when used, may also tell a tutor a lot.

But, more interestingly, the quality of the written word itself can disclose a lot about both students and tutors. Linguists have posited the concept of 'writer identities'.[6] A wide range of linguistic usages, tropes, idiosyncrasies and so on will suggest to the competent reader a particular social identity for the writer. This is possible inasmuch as they are typically associated with particular and distinct styles or modes of discourse. Roz Ivanic (1994) offers such an analysis of a brief paragraph from an essay (not online) by a student at her own university. The student identifies herself as a [British] black in her use of non-standard locutions (for British English) such as 'despite of' and 'telling it . . . like it is', and seems to identify herself with black activism by using a capital for the word 'Black'. She also suggests her gender not simply by the feminist use of 'herstories' (in contrast to histories), but wrapping inverted commas around the word and referring the usage to '[Collins: 1990]', who in the context of that essay is a feminist writer.

A significant point about writer identities is that they are attributed by the reader rather than given in the text. The reader's reception depends partly on her own experience and linguistic sensitivity. However, this being so, a writer can nonetheless attempt to assume an identity by playing on the expected reader's assumptions and insights (though in this she may also fail, of course). A writer identity can be consciously constructed; but it can also be unconsciously betrayed. Just as body language may give away more than we intend, so too can our written word (even when typed).

Moreover, we see here that writer identities can readily be multiple. Those points which tell us that this student (actually called Donna) is a woman are independent of those that position her as black. They construct two different, if compatible, identities. But most interestingly for us, a third writer identity also emerges in Donna's writing, that of the novice academic. Ivanic notes that she 'writes about people like herself in the third person as objects of discussion, as if they did not include her, referring to them as "Black women", "them", "their"; instead of "we", "us", "our"'. Similarly, she identifies in Donna's writing reference to abstract entities, the use of complex nominal groups, 'academic' conjunctives like 'thereby', the use of attributions in square brackets, latinisms such as '*et al.*', and an academic *lexis*, including 'challenged', 'construct' and 'asserting', all of which conspire to position her as a member of the academic community.

It is primarily (if not exclusively—see below) the academic 'voice' amongst other possibilities which university teachers are concerned with and to which they need to listen most carefully. (Let us recognise as valid but marginal those emancipatory courses which actually do address questions of identity explicitly.) The tutor's obligation is to listen to each of her students as proto-academics, rather than as gendered or as members of a specific ethnic group or sexual orientation, for instance.[7] And it is surely appropriate to value online tuition particularly for throwing this voice into relief, relatively (though only relatively) less encumbered by the irrational colourings and biases which too easily intrude in face-to-face tuition, however scrupulously fair and objective we may try to be. Obviously the exchange of written assignments has always had such effects. But the replacement of face-to-face conversation by email enhances the possibilities for defining more clearly the student's academic identity.

Yet the case of Donna arguably shows this to be no simple matter. As we see in her case, it is not just the academic voice that will probably come through in writing, even if identity is more narrowly focused here than face-to-face. (In face-to-face conversation with Donna, we might also come to position her more precisely in terms of class, political or religious commitment—does she wear a crucifix or dreadlocks?—or age group, with all that that may entail, and so on.) As Bakhtin and the post-structuralists insist, writing invariably betrays fractured identities and multiple voices. (For instance, it is arguable that the traditional protocols of the scientific paper always position the author as male, even when she is actually female.) So if online tuition is nonetheless worth defending here, the reason must be something other than the nature of the writer identities it fosters.

ACADEMIC IDENTITIES AND RELATIONS—THE NEED FOR TRANSFORMATION

Some readers will have begun to feel that an excessively dry and cognitivist picture of online tuition is emerging in this chapter. And certainly, that is what I have chosen to emphasise up to this point. But I do not want to argue that ideally the online student is stripped of all but her academic writer identity or that the ideal tutor should disregard all other writer identities but this one. In fact, of course, there are computer-assisted courses, typically of a behaviourist kind, which do indeed 'strip' the student, and also the tutor (or designer) in such a way. There is no interaction between tutor/designer and student. At most, the student responds to tests, as in old-fashioned programmed learning. But the perfect personal neutrality of such courses is bought at the cost of an unavoidable degree of rigidity and insensitivity toward the student's responses, which have to be predicted and over-crudely categorised for a suitable automatic response to be programmed.

And here lies the interesting problem. If online tuition is to be genuine teaching, then insightful interpretation of the student's written word is at a premium. The question is not 'What do these words mean?' but 'What does this student mean [by these words]?' And in addressing that particular problem, any indications the tutor can garner from the student's text may seem relevant and appropriate to the task. Moreover, we cannot assume any *a priori* limits as to what aspects of a student's life and experience will influence or inform her own attempts to make sense of academic material and ideas. Indeed, her status as someone still learning almost guarantees that she will need to fall back on much of that which makes her who she is, other than her purely academic identity, which *ex hypothesi* is probably not yet adequate to her needs. Nonetheless, against this, as I have argued above, some kinds of cues and clues are academically dangerous if not irrelevant, in particular those disclosed in face-to-face interaction. The ideal would seem to be that, on the one hand, the tutor should have more than the writer's academic writer identity to go on. But on the other, there needs to be some kind of filtering of this non-academic disclosure. The tutor needs to interpret the student as a proper person; but not to assume untrammelled access, or a right to such access to all and any areas of her life and personality whatsoever.

I very much doubt whether one could set out, again *a priori*, any specification of what kinds of identity ascription are either appropriate or inappropriate to the academic teaching relationship. But the typical restriction of the tutor in online teaching to the student's writer identities does seem to me to shift the ethical balance in the right direction. On the one hand, writer identities are to some degree within the power of conscious construction by the student. Up to a point, she can influence, if not control, the ways in which her tutor 'sees' her as a person beyond a purely academic ego. And if one accepts that student autonomy is a value in itself, this degree of power over self-disclosure is a virtue. Moreover, for those of us who believe that a principal goal of higher education is personal transformation[8]—that the idea is that the student should come out of the process not just 'better informed' or 'more skilful', but in some senses *a different person* to the one who began—then again intentional kinds of self-disclosure are a virtue, insofar as the student can try to disclose mainly or even only those aspects of herself relevant to the *academic* transformation which is in question here. After all, the transformations wrought by academic study are not intended to include all and any transformation whatsoever of the student, for instance, of her religious affiliation or sexual orientation or emotional stability. But in the transformation of a mature student of biology, for instance, any previous experience in bio-industry or farming or veterinary work would probably be relevant to disclose, even if not purely scientific. Similarly, a young student's interest in psychotherapies or the 'personal growth' movement might be relevant in connection with the self-transformation possible in the study of imaginative literature.

But we have also noted that writer identities can also flow from unintended and even unconscious disclosure. Does this not undermine any supposed ethical advantages here? We noted that in this respect writing is not that much different from body language or vocal expression. In face-to-face tuition, unplanned disclosure remains a possibility. But the case of online tuition seems at least no worse in this respect. I suggest, moreover, that the risks of unintended or unconscious disclosure are more acceptable in the latter case, even where the disclosure may be in some sense more dramatic. For while it is a *settled assumption* in the ethics of higher education that bodily characteristics are irrelevant to personal judgements on academic matters, the case is rather less clear where such disclosures are textual.

For instance, if non-academic traits, interests or relationships are mixed up with the academic, and there is the possibility of their interfering with the academic, then that itself is a matter of academic interest, particularly to a tutor. And the judgement whether there really is interference seems much better justified when the evidence is textual. Consider a hypothetical instance of possible academic bias. Imagine a British student writing on Anglo-Irish history, whose tutor rightly or wrongly thinks the piece is distorted. The face-to-face tutor who may happen to recognise an Irish accent and an 'Irish face' may be quick—possibly too quick—to allege that nationality has biased the student's judgement, even if no Irish identity is constructed in the text. On the other hand, the online tutor who may not know of this nationality is not simply working in ignorance. For her, the null assumption is probably the appropriate one—that, in the absence of other information, a student's errors are to be judged as nothing more than errors, not as personal bias. But if Irish affiliations are positively constructed as an identity in the text, then the case is altered. And it is not simply that bias becomes overtly available as an hypothesis. It is positively significant in such a case that the student either was unaware of subconsciously constructing such an identity, yet could not keep it out of the text where it was appropriate either to edit or censor it; or that he actively and intentionally coloured the work this way. Both possibilities are typical (though not, I emphasise, constitutive—see Blake, 1992) of bias. Either way, a judgement of bias seems much more justifiable.

My general claim, then, is not that tutor and student in an online relationship should forego any personal relationship. On the contrary, some such relationship seems functional for their mutual understanding. They deserve to see each other (for I think these considerations are symmetrical) in three dimensions rather than two. My claim is rather that the online modality makes it easier for both sides—positively encourages them—to construct a relationship appropriate to their shared academic context and endeavour.

But in conclusion, it is essential to notice how much of this kind of online tuition depends on imagination and prior experience of face-to-face work. In constructing and ascribing non-academic writer identities, student and tutor both draw on their wider social experience. They draw in particular on their experience of the use of language in face-to-face situations and notice its intrusions, echoes, modifications and distortions in the written word. Face-to-face interaction shows everyone just what kinds of use of language align with which different identities. It is speculation, but surely highly plausible, to suppose that the online tutor will often construct some kind of image of the real individual behind the words, emotional at least and quite possibly visual ('I could enjoy a casual drink with this guy' or 'This sounds like a very stylish lady')—and this, of course, is both natural and enriching to a degree, yet full of dangers too. Education is like that. However, part of the online teacher's technique may be to stimulate cues from the student to provide appropriate corrections or enhancements of his understanding of the student. Online, the student accordingly has some greater degree of control as to what he or she reveals. Both tutor and student can work to ensure that the kind of disclosure is appropriate to the academic transaction.

It is this kind of dependence which entails that online tuition could never replace all face-to-face work and is likely to be most successful with tutors and students who have significant experience of face-to-face work. So as a general rule, the less experienced or the younger the student, the less appropriate is online teaching. Clearly it would be a disaster for it to become the primary model for teaching children. Yet even here, this is not to say it has no role at all. At least at secondary level, skill in the presentation of the self in written words and deciphering of the styles of others are significant achievements in literacy. While one would hardly dare to conduct all school education in this mode,[9] it surely has place at that level as a technique to begin to learn.

Like cohabiting species, face-to-face work and online tuition complement each other in complex ways. We have not yet begun to explore their ecology.

NOTES

1. Henessy, S., Flude, M. and Tait, A. 'An investigation of students' and tutors' views on tutorial provision', School of Education, East Anglian and South Regions, Open University, UK, May 1999.
2. For an attempt to distinguish these problems, in the context of a discussion of the problem of bias, see Blake, 1992.
3. Austin (1962, Lectures X–XII). These formulae are neither necessary nor sufficient. On the one hand they may be merely implicit. On the other, the cognitive content of the speech act must also be appropriate. For instance, a warning must refer to something undesirable, not to some outcome we might enjoy.

4. Austin noted that these formulae are typically in the first person indicative active. Arguably 'we' here conforms in meaning if not in lexis to that formula.
5. We can allow here that 'text' may include graphic or auditory elements, as in multimedia.
6. This concept builds on the work of Fairclough (1992) which builds in turn on that of Halliday (1985).
7. I simplify here, of course. Some feminists will argue that one fails to hear women without bias, for instance, if one fails to read them as competent female writers rather than incompetent male writers. This may be true. But if so, it argues for gender sensitivity as a precondition of fairness rather than as an intrinsic aim of the tutorial relationship. Those who insist that it is actually an aim to 'celebrate' women students as women beg the question as to the academic propriety of the exercise.
8. For a discussion of transformation as a goal of higher education, Blake, Smith and Standish, 1998, Chapter 1.
9. The distance education of 'remote' children in Australia, New Zealand and Canada typically involves face-to-face work with parents. And in New Zealand occasional visits from the usually distant teacher are greatly valued.

Glossary

Bandwidth: A measure of the capacity of a communications channel to carry information.

Browser: Software that enables the user to access Internet servers.

Bulletin Board (BBS):   A kind of virtual notice-board that can be used for the posting of messages to be seen by other subscribers.

Chat-rooms: See IRC.

Chip: Colloquial term for an integrated circuit etched on to silicon to form a microprocessor.

Computer conferencing: The synchronous or asynchronous participation in a discussion via computer link, commonly in written text but also sometimes including spoken communication (with video).

Cyberspace: A word coined by William Gibson in his 1984 novel, *The Neuromancer*, to refer to a future computer network where users can travel through data in various forms and with various intensities of virtual experience.

Ejournal: Electronic journal.

Flaming: The sending of insults electronically.

HTML: Hypertext Mark-up Language so that browsers can display text in the way intended by the authors. For example, coloured words in a text on which the user can click have been written in HTML.

Hypertext: Generally, text that is designed not to be read in a linear and sequential way from beginning to end but rather to be browsed by exploring internal links. Sometimes, the term is used to refer to the structure of links itself.

Internet: The worldwide network of computer networks.

Intranet: A network of computers restricted to an institution or set of institutions.

IRC: (Internet Relay Chat) A system that enables Internet users to engage together in 'real-time' discussions in virtual chat rooms. While subscribers to a mailing list automatically receive all messages, participants in a chat room 'drop in' on conversations as and when they choose.

ICT: Information and Communications Technology.

Link (hyperlink):   A link on a Web page to another part of that page or to other pages (whether on the user's own hard disk or on the Web). The transition is made through clicking on the link.

Listserv: See Mailing Lists.

Mailing Lists: These take two forms—closed and open. Subscribers to the former simply receive whatever the host decides to send them. Subscribers to open lists both receive and send messages, and these are distributed to all members. Open lists include numerous academic discussion and newsgroups. Lists can be moderated, where messages are screened before distribution, or unmoderated. Listserv and MajorDomo are automated list systems that manage vast numbers of such lists.

Multimedia: Combinations of text, graphics, sound and video.

MOO: A kind of MUD that is Object-Oriented—that is, it is based on pointing and clicking on visual objects. In contrast to the strictly hierarchically organised, and sometimes quite violent, adventure MUDs, MOOs are generally well-suited to the construction of text-based adventure games, conferencing systems and other collaborative software. Their most common use is as a multi-participant, low-bandwidth virtual reality. Every participant receives programming rights from the start—that is, participants create rooms and objects in the medium of writing and independently contribute to the shaping of the text-based educational and game landscape.

MUD: A Multi-User Dungeon (or Domain) is a kind of virtual world giving the user the illusion of moving through physical space, typically providing adventure role-playing games and simulations. These tend to be hierarchically organised and to be used for games in which violence is prominent.

MUSH: a type of MUD, a role-playing game in which multiple users can connect and interact in real time.

Online: The connection of a computer to the Internet or to a sub-network.

Search engine: A special program that searches the Web for items specified by the user. Some search engines, such as AltaVista, are indexing systems, while directories, such as Yahoo!, use human reviewers to compile sites in different categories.

Surfing: Browsing the Web casually.

World Wide Web: A hypertext-based Internet service linking electronic text, graphics, sound and video on computers all over the world.

WYSIWYG: What You See Is What You Get.

Videoconferencing: The presence of different groups or individuals in separate locations but able to speak to and see one another by television link.

USENET: A system of specialist discussion groups using email to post messages.

URL: (Uniform Resource Locator) The address format for accessing sites on the Web. A URL usually begins: 'http:// . . .'.

Note

More information on the items in this glossary and on other Internet terminology can found online at: http://winfiles.cnet.com/connect/ glossary.html, and at http://www.msg.net/kadow/answers/

Notes on Contributors

Nigel Blake works in the Institute of Educational Technology at the Open University and is Chair of the Philosophy of Education Society of Great Britain. His principal interests are in the politics and economics of higher education, the politics of educational discourse and problems of modernity and postmodernity, with particular reference to the Critical Theory of Jürgen Habermas and Lyotard. He has published numerous articles and is joint author of *Thinking Again: Education after Postmodernism* (with Smeyers, Smith and Standish, 1998) and *The Universities We Need: higher education after Dearing* (with Smith and Standish, 1998).

Steve Bramall lectures in philosophy of education at the Institute of Education, University of London, where he teaches on the MA 'Values in Education'. In 1998 he completed a PhD with a thesis entitled 'Hermeneutic Understanding and the Liberal Aims of Education'. His current output includes papers on hermeneutics and education, open-mindedness, the place of mathematics in the curriculum and the National Curriculum review.

Bertram Bruce is Professor of Library and Information Science and a Senior Research Scientist at the National Center for Supercomputing Applications at the University of Illinois at Urbana-Champaign. His research focuses on information and communication technologies, including the development and implementation of technologies to support inquiry-based learning, situated studies of educational practices and critical analysis of information age changes in social relations. He is author of *Network-based classrooms: Promises and realities* (Bruce, Peyton and Batson, 1993) and *Electronic Quills: A situated evaluation of using computers for writing in classrooms* (Bruce and Rubin, 1993).

Barbara Duncan is a doctoral candidate in the Department of Educational Policy Studies at the University of Illinois at Urbana-Champaign. She is writing in the area of philosophy of education with an emphasis on media and cultural studies, feminism and technology (http://www.students.uiuc.edu/~b-duncan).

Penny Enslin is Professor of Education at the University of the Witwatersrand, Johannesburg, where she teaches philosophy of education. Her teaching and research interests are in the area of

221

democracy and citizenship education, particularly issues in feminism, citizenship and liberal democracy. Recent publications have dealt with cosmopolitan citizenship, the family as a private sphere and political liberalism.

Herbert Hrachovec teaches philosophy at the University of Vienna. His main interests are in philosophical aesthetics, analytical philosophy and media philosophy. His most recent book is on film theory: *Drehorte. Arbeiten zu Filmen.* In 1997 he was Guest Editor of *The Monist*'s special 'Interactive Issue'. Additional information and a selection of papers can be found online at: http://philo.at/~herbert.

Michele Knobel is an adjunct Associate Professor for Central Queensland University in Australia, and lives happily in Mexico. Her current research interests are school students' in-school and out-of-school literacy practices, technological literacies and Mexican history. Her recent books include *Everyday Literacies: Students, Discourse and Social Practice, Critical Literacies* (edited with Annah Healy) and *Ways of Knowing: Researching Literacy* (with Colin Lankshear).

David Kolb is currently the Charles A. Dana Professor of Philosophy at Bates College in Maine. He has written essays, hypertexts and books about new modes of writing, and about modernity and postmodernity, German and Greek philosophy and architecture. His books include *Socrates in the Labyrinth* (Eastgate Systems), *Postmodern Sophistications: Philosophy, Architecture and Tradition* (University of Chicago Press) and *The Critique of Pure Modernity: Hegel, Heidegger, and After* (University of Chicago Press). A selected list of his essays can be found online at: http://www.bates.edu/~dkolb. (He is not, however, the author of the works on learning styles by another David Kolb.)

Colin Lankshear, formerly a professor of education specialising in language and literacy education, is currently a Heritage Fellow of the Mexican Council for Science and Technology, an adjunct professor for Central Queensland University, a visiting researcher in the Center for University Studies at the National Autonomous University of Mexico and a freelance educational researcher and writer living between Mexico City and Coatepec (Mexico), and residing on the Web at: http://www.geocities.com/Athens/Academy/1160. His more recent books include *Changing Literacies, Ways of Knowing: researching literacy* (with Michele Knobel), *Teachers and Technoliteracies* (with Ilana Snyder) and *Curriculum in the Postmodern Condition* (with Alicia de Alba, Edgar Gonzalez Gaudiano and Michael Peters). His current circumstances reflect a trenchant abhorrence of and resistance to the cult(ure) of performativity.

Anthony Lelliott is Director of the Flexible Learning and Associate Colleges Unit and Assistant Dean in the Faculty of Education at the

University of the Witwatersrand, Johannesburg. His teaching and research interests include the uses of technology in open and distance learning. He is a member of a research team which has examined the effects of an in-service teacher education programme on classroom practice, and has led the development of flexible learning materials.

Jane McKie is a lecturer in the Department of Continuing Education, University of Warwick. She is particularly concerned with facilitating access to higher education and aiding colleagues with staff development and student support. With broad interests in teaching and philosophy, and previous degrees in psychology, anthropology and death and immortality studies, her current teaching and research are wide-ranging.

James Marshall is Professor of Education at Auckland University. His research interests are in philosophy of education, policy studies and French poststructuralist philosophy, especially Foucault. Recent books include *Philosophy of Education: accepting Wittgenstein's challenge* (edited with Paul Smeyers, Kluwer, 1995), *Michel Foucault: personal autonomy and education* (Kluwer, 1996), *Individualism and Community: education and social policy in the postmodern condition* (with Michael Peters, Falmer, 1996), *Wittgenstein: Philosophy, Postmodernism, Pedagogy* (with Michael Peters; Bergin & Garvey, 1999) and *Education Policy* (edited with Michael Peters; Edward Elgar, 1999).

Shirley Pendlebury is Professor of Education at the University of the Witwatersrand, Johannesburg. She has published articles and chapters on democracy and human rights education, wise practice in teaching and the transformation of teacher education in South Africa. She is currently working on an analysis of time and trust in teaching.

Michael Peters is Associate Professor in the School of Education, University of Auckland. His research interests are in the areas of philosophy, education and policy studies. He is the author of a number of books, including: *After the Disciplines: The Emergence of Cultural Studies* (ed.) (1999); *Wittgenstein: Philosophy, Postmodernism, Pedagogy* (with James Marshall, 1999) and; *Education and the Postmodern Condition*, with a Foreword by Jean-François Lyotard (ed.) (1995/97). He is currently Executive Editor of the journal *Educational Philosophy and Theory* and Co-editor of the online *Encyclopedia of Philosophy of Education* (http://www.educacao.pro.br/).

Mike Sandbothe is Assistant Professor in the Philosophy Department at Friedrich-Schiller-University, Jena. He has published in the fields of media philosophy, media ethics, philosophy of time, philosophy of science, pragmatism and aesthetics. Currently he is working on a book on the theme of pragmatic media philosophy in the age of the

Internet. In 1995 he was a visiting scholar at Stanford University, and in 1996/97 participated in a research project entitled 'Theatrical Aspects of Hypertextuality in the World Wide Web'. He is Co-editor of the book series *Edifying Spaces of Digital Worlds*. His homepage can be visited at http://www.uni-jena.de/ms/.

Paul Standish is Senior Lecturer in Education at the University of Dundee. His main research interest is in the relationship between analytical and Continental philosophy and its significance for education. His publications include *Beyond the Self: Wittgenstein, Heidegger, and the Limits of Language* (1992); *Teaching Right and Wrong: Moral Education in the Balance* (1997) (co-edited with Richard Smith); *Thinking Again: Education after Postmodernism* (co-authored with Blake, Smeyers, and Smith) (1998); and *The Universities We Need: higher education after Dearing* (co-authored with Blake and Smith) (1998). He is Assistant Editor of the *Journal of Philosophy of Education*.

Bibliography

Austin, J. L. (1962), *How to Do Things with Words*. (Oxford: Clarendon Press).

Barthes, R. (1970), *S/Z*. (Paris, Seuil).

Barber, B. (1984), *Strong Democracy: Participatory Politics for a New Age*. (Berkeley: University of California Press).

Bellafante, G. (1998), Feminism: it's all about me, *Time*, June 29, pp. 54–62.

Benedikt, M. (1987), *For an Architecture of Reality* (New York: Lumen).

Benjamin, W. (1973), *Charles Baudelaire: a Lyric Poet in the Era of High Capitalism*. (London: New Left Books).

Bergmann, G. (1954), Two types of linguistic philosophy, in: *The Metaphysics of Logical Positivism*. (New York and London, Longmans & Green), pp. 106–131.

Bigum, C. and Lankshear, C. (1998), Literacies and technologies in school settings: findings from the field. Keynote Address to 1998 ALEA/ATEA National Conference, Canberra, 7 July. http://www.schools.ash.org.au/litweb/bigum.html.

Blake, N. (1999), Allegations of bias; their logic and morality, *Studies in Higher Education*, Autumn, pp. 305–316.

Blake, N., Smith, R. and Standish, P. (1998), *The Universities We Need: higher education after Dearing*. (London: Kogan Page).

Blake, N. (1999), The machine stops: education and autonomy in a mature global economy, in: *Globalisierung: Perspectiven, Paradoxien, Verwerfungen, Jahrbuch fur Bildungs—une Erziehungsphilosophie*, 2.

Bohman, J. (1998), The globalisation of the public sphere: cosmopolitan publicity and the problem of cultural pluralism, *Philosophy and Social Criticism*, 24.2/3, pp. 199–216.

Bolter, J. D. (1991), *Writing Space: the computer, hypertext, and the history of writing*. (Hillsdale, NJ: Lawrence Erlbaum).

Borges, J. L. (1962), *Ficciones*, (ed. A. Kerrigan) (New York: Grove).

Borgmann, A. (1992), *Crossing the Postmodern Divide*. (Chicago and London: University of Chicago Press).

Boshier, R., Wilson, M. and Qayyum, A. (1999), Lifelong education and the World Wide Web: American hegemony or diverse utopia? *International Journal of Lifelong Education*, 18.4.

Boyer, M. Christine (1994), *The City of Collective Memory: Its Historical Imagery and Architectural Entertainments*. (Cambridge, MA: MIT Press).

Bramall, S. (1998), Hermeneutic Understanding and the Liberal Aims of Education (PhD thesis, University of London Institute of Education).

Brandom, R. (1994), *Making it Explicit. Reasoning, Representing, and Discursive Commitment*. (Cambridge, MA: Harvard University Press).

Bruce, B. C. (1999), Digital content: the Babel of cyberspace, *Journal of Adolescent and Adult Literacy*, 42.7 April, pp. 558–563.

Buck, M. (1997), The global demands for change, in: Field, J. (ed.) *Electronic Pathways* (Leicester: National Institute for Adult and Continuing Education).

Burbules, N. (1997), Rhetorics of the web: hyperreading and critical literacy, in: Snyder, E. (ed.) *Page to Screen: Taking Literacy Into the Electronic Era* (New South Wales: Allen & Unwin), pp. 102–122.

Burbules, N. (1998), Questions of content and questions of access to the Internet, *Access: Critical Perspectives on Cultural and Policy Studies In Education*, 17.1, pp. 79–89.

Burbules, N. and Callister, T. (1997), Who lives here? access to and credibility within cyberspace, in: C. Lankshear *et al.* (eds) *Digital Rhetorics: Literacies and Technologies in Education—Current Practices and Future Directions*. (Canberra: Department of Employment, Education, Training and Youth Affairs) 3.

Burbules, N. and Callister, T. (n.d.) *Universities in Transition*. Online at: http://www.ed.uiuc.edu/facstaff/burbules/NickB.html.

Carlson, P. A. (1994), Varieties of virtual: expanded metaphors for computer-mediated learning, in: E. Barrett (ed.), *Sociomedia*. (Cambridge, MA and London: MIT Press).

Casey, E. S. (1993), *Getting Back Into Place: Toward a Renewed Understanding of the Place-World*. (Bloomington: Indiana University Press).

Casey, E. S. (1997), *The Fate of Place: A Philosophical History*. (Berkeley: University of California Press).

Castells, M. (1998), *End of Millennium*. (Oxford: Blackwell).

Chapman, J. (1996), A new agenda for a new society, in: K Leithwood *et al.* (eds.), *International Handbook of Educational Leadership and Administration*. (Dordrecht: Kluwer).

Chernaik, W., Deegan, M. and Gibson, A. (1995), *Beyond the Book: Theory, Culture, and the Politics of Cyberspace*. (Oxford: Office for Humanities Communication Publications).

Chisholm, L., Makwati, G. J. T., Marope, P. T. M. and Dumba-Safuli, S. D. (1998), SADC Initiative in education policy development, planning and management: report of a needs assessment Study (UNESCO, SADC and The Netherlands Government).

Clarke, A. (1998), The path towards computer literacy, *Adults Learning*. (National Institute for Adult and Continuing Education) January, pp. 18–19.

Cline, A. (1998), *A Hut of One's Own: Life Outside the Circle of Architecture*. (Cambridge, MA: MIT Press).

Csikszentmihalyi, M. and Robinson, R. E. (1990), *The Art of Seeing: An Interpretation of the Aesthetic Encounter*. (Los Angeles, CA: The J. Paul Getty Museum).

Davidson, D. (1984), On the very idea of a conceptual scheme, in: *Inquiries into Truth and Interpretation*. (Oxford: Clarendon), pp. 183–198.

Davidson, D. (1996), A nice derangement of epitaphs, in: A. P. Matinech (ed.), *The Philosophy of Language*. (New York and Oxford: Oxford University Press), pp. 465–475.

Deleuze, G. and Guattari, F. (1986), *Nomadology* (a separately published excerpt from A Thousand Plateaus), (New York & Semiotext(e)).

Derrida, J. (1974), *Of Grammatology*, trans. G. Chakravorty Spivak (Baltimore: Johns Hopkins University Press).

Derrida, J. (1982), Différance, in: *Margins of Philosophy*, trans. A. Bass (New York: Harvester Wheatsheaf), pp. 1–27.

Derrida, J. (1989), *Of Spirit: Heidegger and the Question*, trans. Geoffrey Bennington and Rachel Bowlby. (Chicago and London: University of Chicago Press).

Derrida, J. (1994), *Specters of Marx: the state of the debt, the work of mourning, and the new international*, trans. Peggy Kamuf. (London: Routledge).

Derrida, J. (1998), *Of Grammatology*, trans. G. Chakravorty Spivak. Corrected Edition (Baltimore: Johns Hopkins University Press).

Dewey, J., and Bentley, A. F. (1949), *Knowing and the Known*. (Boston: Beacon).

Djamen, J-Y. (1995), Networking in Africa: an unavoidable evolution towards the internet, Technical Report 937, *Department Journal of Educational Studies*, XXXXIII.3, pp. 290–304.

Dreyfus, H. (1991), *Being-in-the World: A Commentary on Heidegger's Being and Time, Division I*. (London and Cambridge, MA: MIT Press).

Dryzek, J. (1999), Transitional democracy, *The Journal of Political Philosophy*, 7.1, pp. 30–51.

Fairclough, N. (1992), *Discourse and Social Change*. (Cambridge: Polity Press).

Feenberg, A. (1999a), *Questioning Technology*. (London and New York: Routledge).

Feenberg, A. (1999b), My adventures in distance learning. Online at: http://www-rohan.sdsu.edu/faculty/feenberg/TELE3.HTM.

Foucault, M. (1979), *Discipline and Punish: the birth of the prison*. (New York: Vintage).

Foucault, M. (1980), *The History of Sexuality Vol. I*. (New York: Vintage).

Foucault, M. (1983), Afterword: the subject and power, in: Dreyfus, H. and Rabinow, P., (eds), *Michel Foucault: Beyond Structuralism and Hermeneutics.* (Chicago: Chicago University Press), pp. 229–252.

Foucault, M. (1984), The ethics of the concern for the self as a practice of freedom, in: P. Rabinow (ed.), *Michel Foucault: ethics, subjectivity, truth.* (New York: The New Press), pp. 281–301.

Foucault, M. (1985), *The Use of Pleasure: the history of sexuality, Vol. II.* (New York: Vintage).

Foucault, M. (1990), *The Care of the Self: the history of sexuality, Vol. III.* (Harmondsworth: Penguin).

Fraser, N. (1993), Rethinking the public sphere: a contribution to the critique of actually existing democracy, in: Robbins, B. (ed.), *The Phantom Public Sphere.* (Minneapolis: University of Minnesota Press).

Gadamer, H.-G. (1976), *Philosophical Hermeneutics.* (Trans. and ed. D. E. Linge). (Berkeley: University of California Press).

Gadamer, H.-G. (1989), *Truth and Method.* (London: Sheed & Ward).

Gee, J. P., Hull, G. and Lankshear, C. (1997), *The New Work Order: Behind the Language of the New Capitalism.* (Boulder, CO: Westview Press).

Gilster, P. (1997), *Digital Literacy.* (New York: John Wiley & Sons, Inc).

Goldhaber, M. (1997), The attention economy and the net. Online at: http://firstmonday.dk/issues/issue2_4/goldhaber/.

Goldman, A. (1986), *Epistemology and Cognition.* (Cambridge, MA: Harvard University Press).

Goldman, A. I. (1992), *Liaisons: Philosophy Meets the Cognitive and Social Sciences.* (Cambridge, MA: MIT Press).

Graham, G. (1999), *The Internet: A Philosophical Inquiry.* (London: Routledge).

Green, K. and Taormino, T. (eds) (1997), *A Girl's Guide to Taking Over the World: Writings From the Girl Zine Revolution.* (New York: St. Martin's Press).

Grosz, E. (1995a), *Space, Time, and Perversion.* (New York and London: Routledge).

Grosz, E. (1995b), Women, chora, dwelling, in: Watson, S. and Gibson, K. (eds.), *Postmodern Cities and Spaces.* (Oxford: Blackwell).

Grusin, R. (1996), What is an electronic author? theory and the technological fallacy, in: Markley, R. (ed.) (1996), *Virtual Realities and their Discontent.* (Baltimore and London: Johns Hopkins), pp. 39–53.

Guernsey, L. (1999), Seek - but on the web, you might not find, *New York Times on the Web.* Online July 8 at: HYPERLINK http://www.nytimes.com __www.nytimes.com_.

Halliday, M. A. K. (1985), *An Introduction to Functional Grammar.* (London: Arnold).

Harries, K. (1997), *The Ethical Function of Architecture.* (Cambridge, MA: MIT Press).

Heidegger, M. (1962), *Die Technik und die Kehre.* (Pfullingen: Neske).

Heidegger, M. (1977), *The Question Concerning Technology and Other Essays,* trans. W. Lovett (New York: Harper & Row).

Heidegger, M. (1982), *Being and Time.* (Oxford: Blackwell).

Heidegger, M. (1988), *The Basic Principles of Phenomenology,* trans. A. Hofstadter. (Bloomington and Indianapolis: Indiana University Press).

Heidegger, M. (1991), *The Principle of Reason,* trans. J. Glenn Gray. (New York and London: Harper & Row).

Heim, M. (1993a), *The Metaphysics of Virtual Reality.* (New York: Oxford University Press).

Heim, M. (1993b), The erotic ontology of cyberspace, in: Benedikt, M. (ed.), *Cyberspace: First Steps.* (Cambridge, MA and London: MIT Press).

Heim, M. (1995), The design of virtual reality, in: Featherstone, M. and Burrows, R. (eds), *Cyberspace/Cyberbodies/Cyberpunk.* (London: Sage).

Heim, M. (1999), Transmogrification. Online at http://www.mheim.com/transmog/.

Hirst, P. (1974), *Knowledge and the Curriculum.* (London: Routledge & Kegan Paul).

Hughes, C. and Tight, M. (1995), The myth of the learning society, *British Journal of Educational Studies,* 43.3, pp. 290–304.

Hugo, V. (1967), *Notre-Dame de Paris, 1482.* (Paris: Garnier).

Ivanic, R. (1994), I is for interpersonal: discoursal construction of writer identities and the teaching of writing, *Linguistics and Education*, 6.1, pp. 3–15.

Jensen, M. (1999a), Access to the web and its use in Southern Africa. Rand Afrikaans University Conference on WWW Applications, 9–10 September, Johannesburg.

Jensen, M. (1999b), African internet status. Online at: http://www3.sn.apc.org/africa/afstat.htm.

Johnson, S. (1997), *Interface Culture: how new technology transforms the way we create and communicate.* (New York: HarperCollins).

Kaufmann, W. (1977), The art of reading, in: *The Future of the Humanities.* (New York: Thomas Y. Crowell), pp. 47–83.

Kelbaugh, D. (1997), *Common Place: Toward Neighborhood and Regional Design.* (Seattle: University of Washington Press).

Landow, G. (1992), *Hypertext. The Convergence of Contemporary Critical Theory and Technology.* (Baltimore and London: Johns Hopkins University Press) second edition 1997.

Lanham, R. A. (1993), *The Electronic Word.* (Chicago and London: University of Chicago Press).

Lanham, R. (1994), The economics of attention. Proceedings of 124th Annual Meeting, Association of Research Librarians. Austin, Texas. Online at: http://sunsite.berkeley.edu/ARL/ Proceedings/124/ps2econ.html.

Lankshear, C., Bigum, C. *et al.* (1997), *Digital Rhetorics: Literacies and Technologies in Classrooms—Current Practices and Future Directions.* (Canberra: Department of Employment, Education, Training and Youth Affairs).

Lankshear, C. and Snyder, I., with B. Green (2000), *Teachers and Technoliteracies.* (Sydney: Allen & Unwin).

Lawrence, S. and Giles, C. L. (1999), Accessibility of information on the web, *Nature*, 400. 8 July, pp. 107–109.

Levinson, P. (1997), *The Soft Edge: a natural history and future of the information revolution.* (London and New York: Routledge).

Lippard, L. R. (1997), *The Lure of the Local: Senses of Place in a Multicentered Society.* (New York: New Press).

Lyotard, J-F. (1984), *The Postmodern Condition: A Report on Knowledge*, trans. G. Bennington and B. Massumi, Foreword by F. Jameson. (Minneapolis: University of Minnesota Press).

Lyotard, J-F. (1993), A svelte appendix to the postmodern question, in: *Political Writings*, trans. B. Readings and K. P. Geiman. (Minneapolis: University of Minnesota Press).

Mansell, R. and Wehn, U. (eds), (1998), *Knowledge Societies: Information Technology for Sustainable Development.* (Oxford: Oxford University Press for The United Nations).

Margolis, M. and Resnick, D. (1999) Online at: http://firstmonday.dk/issues/issue4_10/margolis/index.htm.

Markley, R. (ed.) (1996), *Virtual Realities and their Discontents.* (Baltimore and London: Johns Hopkins).

Marshall, J. (1998a), Performativity: Lyotard, Foucault and Austin. Paper delivered to the American Educational Research Association's Annual Meeting. 11–17 April. San Diego.

Marshall, J. (1998b), Information on information: recent curriculum reform, *Studies in Philosophy and Education*, 17.4, pp. 313–321.

Marshall, J. D. (1999), Technology in the New Zealand curriculum, *New Zealand Journal of Educational Studies*, 34.2, pp. 167–175.

Marx, K. (1886), *Capital: a critical analysis of capitalist production.* (London: William Glaisher Limited).

McLuhan, M. (1996), *Understanding Media: The Extensions of Man.* (Cambridge, MA: MIT Press).

Members of the Clever Project (1999), Hypersearching the web, *Scientific American*, 280.6, pp. 54–60.

Metcalfe, B. (1995), From the Ether Metcalfe's Law: A network becomes more valuable as it reaches more users, *Infoworld*, 17.40, 2 October.

Mitchell, W. J. (1992), *The Reconfigured Eye. Visual Truth in the Post-Photographic Era.* (Cambridge, MA and London: MIT Press).

Moore, G. (1998), An update on Moore's Law. Intel Developer Forum Keynote, San Francisco, 30 September. Online at: developer.intel.com/design/idf/archive/sept97/.

Morrow, W. (1993/4), Entitlement and achievement in education, *Studies in Philosophy and Education*, 13.1, pp. 33–37.

Multhrop, S. (1997), Pushing back: living and writing in broken space, *Modern Fiction Studies*, 43.3.

Naughton, J. (1999), *A Brief History of the Future: the origins of the internet.* (London: Weidenfeld & Nicolson).

Nel, J. (1999), The worldwide web and the African (and South African) renaissance, Rand Afrikaans University Conference on WWW Applications, 9–10 September, Johannesburg.

Norbert-Schulz, C. (1984), *Genius Loci.* (New York: Rizzoli).

Norbert-Schulz, C. (1985), *The Concept of Dwelling.* (New York: Electra/Rizzoli).

Oakeshott, M. (1989), *The Voice of Liberal Learning: Michael Oakeshott on education.* Fuller, T. (ed.). (New Haven and London: Yale University Press).

Ochieng, R. and Radloff, J. (1998), Relevant and accessible electronic information networking in Africa, *Agenda: Empowering Women for Gender Equity*, 38, pp. 63–69.

O'Hagan, A. (1999), The magical history tour, *The Guardian*, 15 May.

Olsen, C.P. (1987), Who computes? in: D. Livingstone (ed.) *Critical Pedagogy and Cultural Power.* (South Hadley, MA: Bergin & Garvey), pp. 179–204.

Patron, E. (1998), Virtual Paradise: the cruise industry turns to total design in its quest for the ultimate destination, *Metropolis*, February/March 1998, p. 67ff.

Pendlebury, S. (1998) Transforming teacher education in South Africa: a space–time perspective, *Cambridge Journal of Education*, 28.5, pp. 333–349.

Peters, M. A. (ed.) (1995), *Education and the Postmodern Condition.* (Westport, CT and London: Bergin & Garvey).

Pinch, T. and Bijker, W. (1987) The social construction of facts and artefacts, in: Bijker, W., Hughes, T., and Pinch, T., (eds), *The Social Construction of Technological Systems.* (Cambridge, MA: MIT Press).

Plato (1977), *Timaeus* and *Critias* (Harmondsworth: Penguin).

Poster, M. (1990), *The Mode of Information: Poststructuralism and the Social Context.* (Cambridge and Oxford: Polity Press).

Poster, M. (1993), *The Mode of Information: Poststructuralism and the Social Context.* (Chicago: University of Chicago Press).

Poster, M. (1995), *The Second Media Age.* (Cambridge, MA: Polity Press).

Postman, N. (1993), *Technopoly: The Surrender of Culture to Technology.* (New York: Vintage Books).

Republic of South Africa, (1996), White Paper on Science and Technology: Preparing for the 21st Century, Department of Arts, Culture, Science and Technology Pretoria.

Reynolds, D. (1997a), *Times Educational Supplement*, 27 June, p. 21.

Reynolds, D. (1997b), School effectiveness: retrospect and prospect, *Scottish Educational Review*, 29.2, pp. 97–113.

Rheingold, H. (1993), *The Virtual Community: Homesteading on the Electronic Frontier.* (Reading, MA: Addison-Wesley).

Ricoeur, P. (1981), *Hermeneutics and the Human Sciences.* (Cambridge: Cambridge University Press).

Roland Martin, J. (1993), Curriculum and the mirror of knowledge, in: Barrow, R. and White, P. (eds), *Beyond Liberal Education: essays in honour of Paul H. Hirst.* (London and New York: Routledge).

Rorty, R. (ed.) (1967), *The Linguistic Turn. Essays in Philosophical Method.* (Chicago: University of Chicago Press).

Rorty, R. (1979), *Philosophy and the Mirror of Nature.* (Princeton, NJ: Princeton University Press).

Rorty, R. (1982), Introduction: pragmatism and philosophy, in: *Consequences of Pragmatism (Essays: 1972–1980)*. (Minneapolis: University of Minnesota Press), pp. xxxvii ff.

Rorty, R. (1989a), *Contingency, Irony, and Solidarity*. (Cambridge: Cambridge University Press).

Rorty, R. (1989b), Deconstruction, in: Brooks, P. (ed.), *The Cambridge History of Literary Criticism, vol. 8: From Formalism to Poststructuralism*. (Cambridge/New York: Cambridge University Press), pp. 166–196.

Rorty, R. (1991a), The priority of democracy to philosophy, in: *Objectivity, Relativism, and Truth: Philosophical Papers, vol. 1*. (Cambridge/New York: Cambridge University Press), pp. 175–196.

Rorty, R. (1991b), Deconstruction and circumvention, in: *Essays on Heidegger and Others: Philosophical Papers, vol. 2*. (Cambridge/New York: Cambridge University Press), pp. 85–106.

Rorty, R. (1993), Putnam and the relativist menace, *The Journal of Philosophy*, XC.9, September, pp. 443–461.

Rorty, R. (1994a), Sind Aussagen universelle Geltungsansprüche? *Deutsche Zeitschrift für Philosophie*, 42, pp. 975–988.

Rorty, R. (1994b), *Hoffnung statt Erkenntnis. Eine Einführung in die pragmatische Philosophie*. (Vienna: Passagen).

Rorty, R. (1998a), Pragmatism, in: Craig, E. (ed.), *Encyclopedia of Philosophy*. (London/New York: Routledge) vol. 7, pp. 633–640.

Rorty, R. (1998b), Human rights, rationality, and sentimentality, in: *Truth and Progress: Philosophical Papers, Vol. 3*. (Cambridge/New York: Cambridge University Press), pp. 167–185.

Sandbothe, M. (1996) Interaktive Netze in Schule und Universität—Philosophische und didaktische Aspekte, in: Bollmann, S. and Heibach, C. (eds), *Kursbuch Internet. Anschlüsse an Wirtschaft und Politik, Wissenschaft und Kultur*. (Mannheim, Bollmann), pp. 424–433.

Sandbothe, M. (1998a), Pragmatismus und philosophische Medientheorie, in: Dölling, E. (ed.) *Repräsentation und Interpretation*. (Berlin: Reihe: Arbeitspapiere zur Linguistik der TU Berlin), pp. 99–124.

Sandbothe, M. (1998b), Media temporalities in the internet: philosophy of time and media in Derrida and Rorty, *Journal of Computer-Mediated Communication*, 4.2, December, Annenberg School of Communication, University of Southern California. Online at: http://www.ascusc.org/jcmc/.

Sandbothe, M. (2000a), *Pragmatische Medienphilosophie. Grundlagen und Anwendungshorizonte im Zeitalter des Internet*. (Frankfurt a. M.: Suhrkamp).

Sandbothe, M. (2000b), Interactivity–hypertextuality–transversality: a media-philosophical analysis of the Internet, *Hermes: The Journal of Linguistics*, 24, February.

Sandbothe, M. (2000c), Media temporalities in the internet: philosophy of time and media in Derrida and Rorty, in: Ess, C. and Sudweeks, F. (eds), *Cultural Attitudes towards Technology and Communication*, a special issue of *AI & Society*, 14.1 (London: Springer).

Scheffler, I. (1965), *Conditions of Knowledge*. (Chicago: Scott, Foresman).

Schutz, A. (1972), *The Phenomenology of the Social World*. (London: Heinemann).

Sennett, R. (1990), *The Conscience of the Eye: The Design of the Social Life of Cities*. (New York: Knopf).

Shenk, D. (1998), *Data Smog: Surviving the Information Glut*. (New York: HarperCollins).

Shirk, H. N. (1994), Cognitive architecture in hypermedia instruction, in: Barrett, E. (ed.), *Sociomedia* (Cambridge, MA and London: MIT Press).

Slater, D. (1995), Photography and modern vision, in: Jenks, C. (ed.), *Visual Culture*. (London and New York: Routledge).

Smith, R. A. (1989), On the third realm—on observing a different society, *The Journal of Aesthetic Education*, 23.1, pp. 5–7.

Standish, P. (2000), Only connect: computer literacy from Heidegger to Cyberfeminism, *Educational Theory* (forthcoming).

Taylor, C. (1979) What's wrong with negative liberty? in: Ryan, A. (ed.), *The Idea of Freedom: Essays in Honour of Isaiah Berlin*. (Oxford: Oxford University Press), pp. 175–193.

Thagard, P. (1997), Internet epistemology: contributions of new information technologies to scientific research. Online at http://cogsci.uwaterloo.ca/Articles/Pages/Epistemplogy.html.

Thompson, J. (1990), *Ideology and Modern Culture*. (Stanford: Stanford University Press).

Thorngate, W. (1988), On paying attention, in: Baker, W., Mos, L., Van Rappard, H. and Stam, H. (eds.), *Recent Trends in Theoretical Psychology*. (New York: Springer-Verlag), pp. 247–164.

Thorngate, W. (1990), The economy of attention and the development of psychology, *Canadian Psychology*, 31, pp. 262–71.

Tschumi, B. (1994), *Architecture and Disjunction*. (Cambridge, MA: MIT Press).

Tunbridge, N. (1995), The cyberspace cowboy, *Australian Personal Computer*, September.

Turkle, S. (1995), *Life on the Screen: Identity in the Age of the Internet*. (New York: Simon & Schuster).

Turkle, S. (1996), *Life on the Screen: Identity in the Age of the Internet*. (London: Weidenfeld & Nicolson).

Ulmer, G. L. (1985a), *Applied Grammatology: Post(e) Pedagogy from Jacques Derrida to Joseph Beuys*. (Baltimore and London: Johns Hopkins University Press).

Ulmer, G. L. (1985b), The object of post-criticism, in: Foster, H. (ed.) *Postmodern Culture*, (London: Pluto Press), pp. 57–82.

Urry, J. (1990), *The Tourist Gaze*. (London: Sage).

Valdes, A. L. (1995), Ruminations of a feminist aerobics instructor, in: Findlen, B. (ed.), *Listen Up: Voices From the Next Feminist Generation*. (Seattle: Seal Press), p. 12.

Wearing, B. and Wearing, S. (1996), Refocussing the tourist experience: the 'flâneur' and the 'choraster', *Leisure Studies*, 15.4.

Weston, J. (1994), Old freedoms and new technologies: the evolution of community networking. Paper presented at the Free Speech and Privacy in the Information Age, University of Waterloo, Canada, 26 November.

Wittgenstein, L. (1953), *Philosophical Investigations*. (Oxford: Blackwell).

Wittgenstein, L. (1998), *Culture and Value*, ed. G. H. von Wright, trans. P. Winch (Oxford: Blackwell).

Index